CORE HANDBOOKS IN PEDIATRICS

FAMILY-FOCUSED BEHAVIORAL PEDIATRICS

William Lord Coleman, M.D.

Associate Professor of Pediatrics
Center for Development and Learning
Department of Pediatrics
University of North Carolina School of Medicine
Chapel Hill, North Carolina

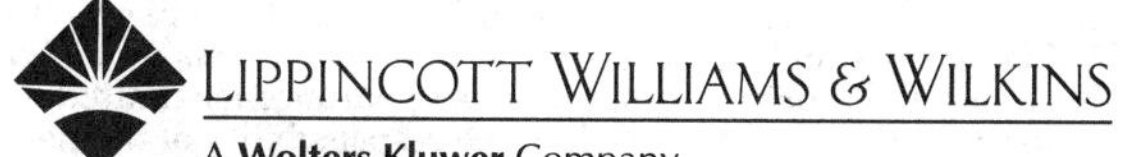

LIPPINCOTT WILLIAMS & WILKINS
A **Wolters Kluwer** Company
Philadelphia • Baltimore • New York • London
Buenos Aires • Hong Kong • Sydney • Tokyo

Acquisitions Editor: Timothy Y. Hiscock
Developmental Editor: Sonya L. Seigafuse
Production Editor: Christiana Sahl
Manufacturing Manager: Benjamin Rivera
Cover Designer: Jeane Norton
Compositor: Circle Graphics
Printer: R. R. Donelley/Crawfordsville

530 Walnut Street
Philadelphia, PA 19106 USA
LWW.com

Printed in the USA

Library of Congress Cataloging-in-Publication Data

Coleman, William L.
Family focused behavioral pediatrics / William Lord Coleman.
p. cm.—(Core handbooks in pediatrics)
Includes bibliographical references and index.
ISBN 0-7817-2857-6
1. Pediatrics—Psychological aspects—Handbooks, manuals, etc. 2. Family counseling—Handbooks, manuals, etc. I. Title. II. Series.

RJ47.5 .C65 2001
618.92'0001'9—dc21

00-067526

Care has been taken to confirm the accuracy of the information presented and to describe generally accepted practices. However, the author and publisher are not responsible for errors or omissions or for any consequences from application of the information in this book and make no warranty, expressed or implied, with respect to the currency, completeness, or accuracy of the contents of the publication. Application of this information in a particular situation remains the professional responsibility of the practitioner.

The author and publisher have exerted every effort to ensure that drug selection and dosage set forth in this text are in accordance with current recommendations and practice at the time of publication. However, in view of ongoing research, changes in government regulations, and the constant flow of information relating to drug therapy and drug reactions, the reader is urged to check the package insert for each drug for any change in indications and dosage and for added warnings and precautions. This is particularly important when the recommended agent is a new or infrequently employed drug.

Some drugs and medical devices presented in this publication have Food and Drug Administration (FDA) clearance for limited use in restricted research settings. It is the responsibility of the health care provider to ascertain the FDA status of each drug or device planned for use in their clinical practice.

10 9 8 7 6 5 4 3 2 1

Contents

Foreword

This remarkable, far-reaching book breaks new ground in pediatrics. It is especially useful for behavioral and interactional problems that persist or recur despite traditional child-centered interventions. Dr. Coleman's watchword of "your family is your greatest resource" comes alive on every page.

The reader can learn some of the following skills from this book:

- Identifying interactional problems;
- Making the shift from child-focused to family-focused intervention;
- Facilitating family meetings and family communication;
- Helping families rediscover love, respect, communication, and fair play;
- Helping families work together, find solutions, and become a team;
- Charging appropriately for these services.

This book also gives numerous examples of therapeutic strategies and family interviewing techniques as practical illustrations of the skill or skills that it has just taught.

Applying this book to clinical practice should bring the following results:

- An increased comfort level with family disagreements and parent problems;
- Rediscovery of the power of words;
- Increased creativity in interventions;
- Improved ability to help families find and utilize their strengths;
- Doubled therapeutic impact;
- Increased personal job satisfaction.

No matter what the reader's role in medicine or how much counseling he or she provides, this book helps the reader accomplish it more effectively. The family counseling model crosses many disciplines, giving this book immense value to all clinicians who work with children and adolescents, including general pediatricians, family medicine physicians, developmental-behavioral pediatricians, adolescent medicine specialists, physician assistants, nurse practitioners, physicians and nurses in training, clinical psychologists, social workers, and academic clinical faculty. This practical and timely book gives them methods for taking their skills to a higher level or for teaching those skills to others. This book is for the reader who loves behavioral pediatrics and who wants to learn more about the art and science behind it.

Barton D. Schmitt, M.D.
Professor of Pediatrics
University of Colorado School of Medicine and
The Children's Hospital, Denver, Colorado

Preface

There is no perfect child. There is no perfect parent. There is no perfect family. Every family needs help at some time. When they do, they often turn first to the clinician.

Helping children and adolescents with behavioral and interactional problems is one of the great joys and challenges for all clinicians who care for children. Although many of these problems can be solved with an approach that focuses on the child's symptoms, others prove more resistant. When those problems recur or intensify, the clinician should consider an approach that incorporates the family context. This approach, based on the biopsychosocial model, both assesses the child's problem and develops solutions within the family-social context. However, the family counseling skills needed to use this approach are either infrequently or inadequately taught in training programs or continuing education courses.

"Give a man a fish and he can feed himself for a day. Teach a man to fish and he can feed himself for a lifetime."

Chinese Proverb

Family counseling is effective and efficient because it supports the family, which is the child's greatest resource, and empowers the family to use its own strengths. In using this type of counseling, the clinician not only helps the family resolve the problem but also uses strategies that are more time-efficient and cost-effective. The clinician derives great satisfaction from knowing that the family has developed its own problem-solving techniques (with guidance from the clinician) that will help it not only now but also in the future. Finally, using a family context approach to child care provides the clinician with new intellectual challenges, stimulating him or her personally and revitalizing his or her career.

"Teach thy tongue to say, 'I don't know,' and thou shalt progress."

Maimonides

This manual is for clinicians and trainees who want to enhance their skills in working with children and adolescents within the context of their families. These clinicians include pediatricians, family practitioners, pediatric nurse practitioners, child psychologists, child psychiatrists, social workers, and school counselors. It is a beginner's guide intended for those just learning to use a family context approach to resolve behavioral and interactional problems. It is not a textbook on family therapy. This manual describes brief, practical, step-by-step methods for family counseling that the busy clinician can readily incorporate into primary care and can easily tailor for his or her own use. The methods and techniques are liberally illustrated with real-life case studies.

Clinicians work hard because of their deep commitment to improving children's health and well-being, but they must be paid for their effort and time. Therefore, methods for coding and documenting to insure adequate reimbursement are explained.

After reading this book, the clinician will know how to do the following:

- Identify problems suitable for family counseling.
- Plan family meetings in the office.
- Interview families using a family systems approach.
- Assess family interactions.
- Help families cooperate and develop adaptive behaviors.
- Support parents.
- Improve family communication.
- Deal with disappointments, failures, and difficult families.
- Code and document for reimbursement.
- Suggest strategies for specific problems.
- Make a mental health referral.

The family is the most central and enduring influence on every child. Thus, sometimes the best way to help a child is to help the parents. The family context is the domain of clinicians, who have been sanctioned by society to advocate for the child and the family. Family counseling both satisfies this obligation and also fulfills the clinician.

Acknowledgments

No one writes a book alone. It is a "family" effort because many people help make it happen. I thank those who have helped me:

The thousands of families with whom I have worked for over 20 years and who taught me much of what I know.

Colleagues and friends who have encouraged me over the years and/or provided specific advice about this book: Drs. James Blackman, Tom Boat, Douglass Carmichael, Wendy Chabot, Bill Cohen, Robert Coles, Paul Dworkin, Morris Green, Robert Greenberg, Robert Haggerty, Barbara Howard, Sam Katz, Desmond Kelly, Karen Miller, Julius Richmond, Edward Schor, Henry Shapiro, Marty Stein, Jack Sternbach, Lane Tanner, Stuart Teplin, Dominique Verut, Marc Wager, Lynn Wegner, Steve Wegner, Roberta Williams, Ms. Margot Jones, Ms. Nancy Aronie, and countless others.

Laura Martin, my assistant in Chapel Hill, for her invaluable secretarial support. Renee Hardin for her technical assistance. Cheryl Tucker, my editor in Chapel Hill. Sonya Seigafuse, Christiana Sahl, and Kathy Drasky, my editors at Lippincott Williams & Wilkins.

Tim Hiscock, acquisitions editor at Lippincott Williams & Wilkins, whose belief in families and in this book helped it become a reality.

Dr. Karen Wells (Duke University), Dr. Susan McDaniel (University of Rochester), and Ms. Insoo Kim Berg (Brief Family Therapy Center, Milwaukee, Wisconsin), for the training in family therapy that they gave me.

Dr. Edward Taylor (University of Illinois), for his friendship and family therapy mentoring.

Dr. Bart Schmitt, for his friendship and ongoing support of my professional work and this book.

Dr. Mel Levine, my "brother" and colleague in Chapel Hill, for 20 years of friendship, mentorship, and partnership.

My family especially, for its unending love, patience, support, and good humor—my wife Julie, my children Chandra and Justin, and my nephews Phil and Jeff.

I would also like to acknowledge the Administration on Developmental Disabilities (ADD) and the Maternal and Child Health Bureau in Washington, D.C. for their generous support of the Clinical Center for the Study of Development and Learning in Chapel Hill, North Carolina.

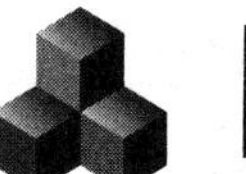

I

Shifting to a Family Focus

1 The Family-Oriented Approach: Why and How It Works

I. **Purpose**

The family-oriented approach is based on the biopsychosocial model and utilizes family systems principles. These principles guide the clinician as he or she shifts the focus from a view exclusively of the child's symptoms to one of the child within the family context.

The five levels of clinician involvement with families range from a minimal focus on the family to family therapy. Clinicians work at one of these "developmental" levels with every family encounter. Those beginning to utilize the family-oriented approach are at or near level 3.

This chapter describes (a) the clinician's qualifications to use a family-oriented approach; (b) family systems principles; (c) the family as a system; and (d) the five levels of clinician involvement with the family. This information helps the clinician understand the need for shifting from the biomedical approach to a family orientation.

II. **The Clinician's Qualifications for Using a Family-Oriented Approach**

The clinician is qualified to use a family approach because of his or her special long-standing relationship with the family. This relationship is based on knowledge, understanding, and trust. The clinician knows and understands the family and also trusts them to work together and to follow the clinician's recommendations. The family knows that the clinician understands them and cares about them, believes that he or she is knowledgeable, and therefore trusts the clinician to help them. This special relationship allows the clinician to treat a child's problem (e.g., depression) within a family context (e.g., divorce) and to "join" together with them as part of the treatment plan (i.e., the clinician facilitates the family's efforts to change their behaviors). Some qualifications of pediatric clinicians (specifically, the pediatrician, family physician, or pediatric nurse practitioner) are listed below.

A. **In the first few years of a child's life, the pediatric clinician is usually the first and only clinician to see a child.**

B. **Clinicians are therefore positioned to detect a "predictable" family problem (e.g., the stress of adapting to the new parental roles) as soon as it arises.**

C. **Pediatric clinicians are usually the first clinicians to see the child when the family presents with the child, who is the "identified patient" or the "symptomatic patient" of a disturbed family** (e.g., the child with recurrent somatic complaints whose parents are experiencing marital conflict).

D. **Pediatric clinicians are frequently the only clinicians that have continuing contact with children and their families.** Hence they can observe changes as they develop over time.

E. **This longitudinal experience allows clinicians to form a trusting and confidential relationship with the family.**

F. **By detecting and preventing behavioral, emotional, and developmental problems, clinicians contribute to parents' understanding of child behavior and child–parent relationships and also help family communication improve.**

Does the Clinician Always Know the Family?

The clinician knows a lot about the child, but he or she may not know a lot about the family.

G. **Clinicians can readily employ a family perspective to understand its problems, often an admixture of developmental variation/dysfunction, temperamental differences, behavioral and emotional problems, parental problems, and perturbed family dynamics.**

H. **With their knowledge of the family's social context, strengths, and weaknesses, clinicians appreciate the need for and benefit of shifting to a family perspective.**

I. **By using a family perspective, clinicians can more ably provide anticipatory guidance, screening for behavioral and family psychosocial problems, primary care treatment, and referral.**

J. **Some families do not feel comfortable (at least initially) seeing a mental health professional.** Because some clinicians (e.g., the physician and nurse practitioner) are not perceived as such, the family is more comfortable seeing these clinicians first.

K. **Some families refuse to see a mental health professional, making their clinicians the only professionals who are aware of the family's stresses and who are in a position to help.**

L. **Clinicians are sanctioned by society to advocate for children and families.** Courts, schools, police, social agencies, religious institutions, and community organizations expect clinicians to help families and look to them for guidance.

M. **Community resources, especially mental health professionals, may be otherwise unavailable or inaccessible to the family.** Barriers include long travel distances to resources, long waiting lists, lack of family financial resources, and lack of mental health providers with a family systems perspective.

N. **Teamwork between primary clinicians and other professionals (e.g., social workers, child psychiatrists) improves the effectiveness of support for children and families.**

O. **Because managed care restricts referrals to other specialists, clinicians may be the only ones available to provide the initial assessment and management**. However, "mental health carve outs" may also make it difficult, or even impossible, for the clinician to see the child and family.

The Family System

Clinicians are familiar with the organ systems perspective of health and illness. Because illness in one organ affects the whole system, the treatment of a specific organ must take into account its impact on other organs in the system. The clinician must view families with a similar systems perspective: a problem for any member affects every member of the family system.

III. Family Systems Principles

A. **Utilizing family systems principles helps the clinician maintain a family-oriented approach.** This approach, a component of the biopsychosocial model, places the child's or adolescent's problem within a large framework of multiple systems. To understand the presenting problem, the clinician must assess it at the following three levels:

1. *The child* (development, behavior, and physical and mental health).
2. *The family* (parents' physical and mental health, marriage/partnership, and parenting style).
3. *The larger social context* (housing, finances, friends/relatives, and community resources).

A change in one level affects the others. The interrelationship among these levels creates constant reciprocal feedback. The clinician must also realize and appreciate the nature and impact of the child–parent–clinician relationship.

B. **The family context is the major focus, but equal attention is placed on the child and the family.** Clinicians may shift back and forth between a child focus and a family focus as a way to better understand the problem, but the ultimate focus is the child within the family. The clinician may focus first on the biomedical aspects of the child's problem (level 1 of clinician involvement with the family), which may include measures such as prescribing medication for a child with attention-deficit/hyperactivity disorder (ADHD). The clinician then addresses family issues that are affecting the problem (level 3 of family involvement), including conflicting parenting practices, differing perceptions of the problem, or stressful career demands on the parent(s).

C. **The family is the primary source of many health beliefs and behaviors that affect the child and family.** The family's cultural background, traditions, expectations, and past experiences influence parenting practices.

D. **The clinician cannot fully understand the child–parent relationship by knowing them only as two separate individuals.** Clinicians usually focus on individual patients. However, because behavior takes place within a relationship, according to the family oriented approach, they must know the child–parent relationship and gauge the ways in which a change or stress in one affects the other, and indeed, the entire family.

E. **Presenting complaints (physical, psychosocial) often serve an adaptive function and thus are maintained by the family.** The child's problem may serve a parent's or the family's need. For instance, a parent who is depressed may focus on a child's problem and maintain it in order to avoid confronting his or her own depression. The child's problem is also the family's problem, because the family is the social group most immediately affected by the child's problem and the treatment.

Conversely, when the child has a problem, the family is in pain. For example, the stress that a child and family feel when going through developmental transitions (either of the child or family) can manifest as somatic, behavioral, and emotional symptoms. These symptoms serve an adaptive function within the family, which then maintains them by its patterns of interaction.

The Family's Balance is Maintained by Perpetuating the Child's Symptom

Families sometime keep their balance or homeostasis by maintaining the very symptom that brought them to the clinician. For example, a child has recurrent abdominal pain; maintaining the symptom fulfills a parent's emotional need, role, and place in the family and thus maintains the family balance, so the family perpetuates it with its behavior.

F. **Change is inevitable, and the family must adapt to it.** Predictable changes include the birth of a child, the need to balance the marital and parental roles, and meeting the developmental needs of an adolescent. Some unpredictable changes are divorce, illness in any member, or the diagnosis of a developmental disability in a child. Families with children must accommodate to their rapidly changing physical, social, and emotional needs.

G. **The well being of the child is powerfully influenced by the well being of his or her parents.** When a child has a problem, the developmental tasks of the family are complicated and stressed by the extra attention that the child needs. Therefore, families become a valuable resource for support in managing these problems. Involving the family in the assessment and treatment phases ensures its rightful place in the process as well as a better outcome for everyone.

H. **Every member plays a role in the family dynamics that tend to maintain problems.** Blaming each other for the family's problems worsens those problems. If the clinician implies blame, he or she will lose the trust of the family. For instance, if a child with asthma learns that she can get her way by having a tantrum and inducing an asthmatic attack, who is to blame? The child who wheezes? The parent who "rewards" her when she has an attack? Neither is to blame.

I. **The behavior of families is governed by repeating interactive patterns.** In the above case, the parents naturally become very sensitive and reactive to their daughter's tantrums, but they may have different approaches. The father may want to indulge her, but the mother may want a firmer approach. While they disagree, argue, and blame each other for the problems, the girl continues to have tantrums and asthmatic attacks. The family perpetuates the problem through its continued interaction patterns, yet no one is to blame. A family systems approach addresses the interactive influences of the girl's learned manipulative behavior, her asthma, and the parents' differing perceptions and responses.

J. **The clinician "joins" with the family and forms a therapeutic alliance.** He or she is seen as "a part of" rather than "apart from" the treatment plan. The family's presence and openness are acknowledgements that they need help. The members invite the clinician to enter their family system to help them change a situation that is causing them pain.

Benefits of the Family Systems Approach

Involving the family in the care of a child provides the clinician with:

- Information not available from the index patient. Every family member has valuable information, perceptions,

continued on top of page

continued from bottom

and insights that enhance the clinician's understanding of the child and the presenting problem.
- The opportunity to observe family interactions. Understanding how family members communicate and interact is key to understanding the child and the family.
- The opportunity to involve the family in the treatment. Helping family members cooperate and develop their solutions (drawing on their own resources, seeking individual and family help, and using social supports) is best accomplished, at least initially, in the family meetings.
- If the family members can't or won't cooperate in the meeting, they won't do it at home.

IV. **The Family as a System**

The family system is characterized by its structure and function, both of which define relationships. The family structure includes the composition and organization of the family, the hierarchy (power structure), the subunits (e.g., parent dyad, siblings), and the family membership (all who live in the home). Each member has a position in the family structure. Family function is how the members and the subsystems interact, how they perceive each other, and how they designate roles. The family system maintains the family balance or stability and helps them adapt to change and stress.

A. **The family: a definition.** A family is a group of individuals who live together and who are related biologically, legally, or socially (e.g., an unmarried partner of a parent). A family, however, is more than just a group; it is a unit with its own image, including the attendant goals, problems, values, strengths, and attributes. All families have several roles in common. Together they attempt to carry out the multiple responsibilities of family life, such as providing food, clothing, shelter, education, moral values, love, and nurturing. Families share their lives emotionally as they meet the needs of each individual as well as the whole.

B. **Assessing structure and function: questions for the clinician.** As the clinician deals with each family situation, he or she needs to think through the following areas in order to get a picture of the family as a whole and to create a strategy for helping the family adapt, cooperate, and solve the problem.

1. *Family membership.* Who are the members of the family? Do they live in the same house? Who do members turn to for support?
2. *Family balance or stability.* How does the family maintain emotional and functional stability? What are the interpersonal processes that allow the family to function in

a healthy way? What are the actions and interactions of the family members? How does the family cope with sudden change or stress?

3. *Family adaptability.* How does the family adapt and cope with sudden change, loss, or stress? How do members interact in the face of change? Do they shift their positions and roles, change their expectations and behavior, or adapt to changing family relationships?

4. *The symptom(s) in a family–relationship context.* Because the child's symptom is influenced by the family–psychosocial context, the physician must examine it by asking questions, such as those that follow. What is the significance of the symptom to the family? What purpose does it serve? How does the family affect the child's symptom? How does the child's symptom affect the family? Understanding the relationship between the symptom and the family context reveals important diagnostic and therapeutic information. For example, a child's recurrent headaches may have begun when his father suffered a severe stroke.

5. *Hierarchy.* Hierarchy is the power structure that defines leadership and authority. Who is in charge (e.g., the parents, the child, a grandparent)? How does he or she assert authority or get his or her own way? Families are not democracies. Parents normally are in charge, but sometimes, inappropriate hierarchies exist so that the children control parents. Other determinants of authority include age (e.g., an older sibling is in charge of younger ones) and gender. Mothers tend to be in charge of family function, emotional well being, and day-to-day parenting responsibilities. Fathers tend to be major providers and ultimate authority figures and may take some responsibility for daily family–parenting roles. However, these traditional roles are changing.

6. *Subsystems.* Within the family system, subsystems comprised of one, two, three, or more persons exist. The major subsystems, which are the marital/partner, parental, and sibling groups, all affect each other. Therefore, when a clinician encounters a parent–child problem, he or she should also inquire about other subsystems that influence the problem and/or that are influenced by the problem (e.g., the marital subsystem). Roles are often "assigned" to subsystems to carry out the family's tasks. For example, nurturing and socialization are the roles of the parental subsystem.

7. *Boundaries.* Boundaries are two-way streets of interaction and emotional closeness. They specify who enters or stays outside of a subsystem and determine how members should interact. They provide guidelines for privacy, intimacy, and communication as well as rules for how family members interact with and relate to one another. Boundaries provide the rules and expectations that protect subsystems. They must be clear to all family members and yet

flexible enough to allow contact between subsystems. For instance, the spousal and parental subsystems are "protected" from the sibling subsystem by a clear boundary. Most importantly, boundaries define emotional relationships (e.g., appropriate, too close, or too distant). The spectrum of boundary clarity ranges from enmeshed (overly close and too engaged) to disengaged (distant, estranged); clear and appropriate boundaries exist in the middle of that continuum. However, all families at different stages of the family life cycle experience these two extremes temporarily (e.g., a parent may be enmeshed with an ill child or a teenager may be disengaged from the family). In families with behavioral and interaction problems, the clinician finds that boundaries are often blurred, confusing, and problematic. Three types of boundaries and relationships are described below.

a. ***Diffuse boundaries.*** Diffuse boundaries appear unclear, limit individual autonomy, and provide little private space. They result in enmeshment where family members become over-involved in each other's activities and personal lives. Anyone can enter another's subsystem (e.g., the parents—marital/partner subsystem—have no privacy or time for intimacy; a child continuously interrupts his parents' conversation or telephone calls). A mother and son are enmeshed when the mother answers all questions for her son at any age or wishes to be present when the clinician performs a physical examination on a teenager. When enmeshment occurs, family members rarely act independently. The family is too emotionally reactive; thus, any level of stress causes an immediate family response.

b. ***Rigid boundaries.*** Rigid boundaries, those that are unyielding and inflexible, allow very little contact or interaction between subsystems. The family system is characterized by disengagement, and the members are emotionally distant, withdrawn, and unresponsive to each other (e.g., a father rules by firm, authoritarian means and appears unapproachable; a child is experiencing emotional stress at school but does not tell her parents). The family resists change. These disengaged families lack family cohesion and mutual support, and children receive little individualized attention and guidance. When rigid boundaries exist, families require a high level of stress to activate a supportive family response.

c. ***Clear boundaries.*** Clear boundaries are plain, apparent boundaries between subsystems that are appropriate (e.g., the marital subsystem and the children). Each subsystem remains functional and healthy and maintains contact with other subsystems. Relationships allow communication and cooperation within the appropriate hierarchy—the parents are in charge.

C. **The mobile as a metaphor of the family system.** Another way to understand family systems is to envision a mobile (Fig. 1.1). Every member can be positioned and connected in a way that illustrates the structure, hierarchy, relationships, and function of their family system. In this particular mobile (family), the mother is at the top of the hierarchy, and the father is just below her but is slightly above (or at the same level of) his eldest daughter. A second daughter is just below the eldest daughter. Below them, illustrating descending power, are two more daughters and a son.

Figure 1.1. The mobile as a metaphor for the family. (Courtesy of John DeNapoli/PhotoDisc.)

Each member has a particular relationship with every other member (i.e., emotional and physical distance and closeness). The interpersonal relationships are created and maintained by each member's behaviors, roles, expectations, self-image, position in the hierarchy, boundaries, and perceptions of others. Like the mobile, the family is in constant motion. Each member's movement contributes to the family movement. Some members move more than others; some are more affected by the movement more than others; but all are affected. The whole family works together to balance the system, maintain homeostasis, and keep the members' particular roles and relationships.

The Ripple Effect

Everything that happens to a child occurs, at some level, within the family and always affects the family. Everything that affects the family affects the child, like the ripple effect of a pebble dropped in a pond.

Now, blow on the mobile—imagine that this is a breeze (i.e., a stress, demand, change) suddenly striking it, causing the mobile to move about and temporarily to lose its balance. As the breeze subsides, the mobile quiets and regains its balance. The breeze is a metaphor for the normal transitions and problems that all families encounter. For example, all families face normal developmental transitions (e.g., marriage, birth of first child, onset of adolescence, children leaving home, parents at midlife, retirement, and growing older). Any acute psychosocial stress on the family affects the physical, emotional, and social health of each family member. This stress may be temporary and self-resolving; or with the guidance of its clinician, the family resolves the problem. The clinician may also provide directives and interventions (e.g., advice, medication, and/or referral).

Now attach a paper clip to one of the figures on the mobile, and imagine it as a significant stress or burden on that family member (e.g., the diagnosis of a serious medical illness, a changed relationship, or the loss of a parent's job). Notice the change in structure and relationships: some members are grouped closer to the affected member; others become more distant. The hierarchy itself is different. If the problem is resolved, the family mobile regains its balance and resumes its original configuration. However, if the problem is not resolved or if it is only partially alleviated, the family needs to adapt in order to cope with its new reality, represented by the new configuration of the mobile, which is the family's new structure and function.

V. Five Levels of Clinician Involvement with the Family

Five levels of clinician involvement with families are found in clinical practice, ranging from minimal involvement with the family (level 1) to family therapy (level 5). Clinicians beginning to use a family systems approach are at level 3. Clinicians often move from one level to another depending on the situation, (e.g., working at level 1 when faced with a minor acute illness and at level 2 or 3 when dealing with a child's behavioral problem, serious illness, or parenting stress). Clinicians can assess their own level of involvement with the family and then can determine what they need to do to improve their clinical skills or to move to the next level. The five-level model described by Doherty and Baird is explained below.

> **The Clinician at Level 3**
>
> A major goal of this handbook is to help the clinician move from levels 1 and 2 to level 3 (feelings and support). To move to levels 4 and 5, the clinician will need additional experience and supervised training. See Chapter 15, "Getting More Training," for more information.

A. **Level 1. Biomedical care with minimal emphasis on the family.** This level is the most basic of biomedical care. In this level, "biomedical issues are the sole focus of patient care," and families are considered "only as necessary for practical and medical–legal reasons."

1. *Example 1.* If a child presents with symptoms of inattention, distractibility, and "lack of motivation," the clinician might take a detailed history of the symptoms; review the child's development; perform a physical examination, including vision and hearing; and obtain teacher and parent rating scales of attention and activity. A probable diagnosis would be attention-deficit/hyperactivity disorder (ADHD), and the clinician would probably suggest a trial of stimulant medication and the use of behavior management strategies. However, other issues could possibly be causing or contributing to the symptoms (e.g., family chaos or depression in a parent or the child).
2. *Example 2.* The clinician focuses only on the child's immunizations, growth, and development during well-child visits, does not inquire about social or behavioral problems, and/or ignores signs of maternal depression.

B. **Level 2. Initial focus on the family: family conference about medical conditions.** In this level, although the focus is still mainly biomedical, communication with the family about medical issues does occur. The clinician appreciates the role of the family in facilitating care, understands family situations that interfere with medical care, and feels comfortable making referrals. The clinician "develops competency in conducting family conferences to discuss the patient's medical problems and treatment." For example, a child is diagnosed with a chronic illness or a developmental delay, so the level 2 clinician educates the family about the problem, allows them to share their feelings, and helps them find supports (e.g., Cystic Fibrosis Foundation, school accommodations, and parent support groups). He or she makes referrals for the child (e.g., mental health, learning evaluation). Most clinicians are competent in levels 1 and 2 of involvement with the child and family.

C. **Level 3. Feelings and support: family meetings about medical problems and family communication/interaction.** At this level, which marks the beginning of family counseling, the clinician is "comfortable in switching back and forth between medical data and family feelings and concerns." The clinician adopts a biopsychosocial perspective and actively elicits information about the family's concerns, stressors, and strengths. The therapeutic approach centers on building successful problem-solving skills for the child and his problems and on individualizing them to the needs and abilities of the family.

For example, when the level 3 clinician encounters a child who has been diagnosed with a chronic medical illness or who presents with a new onset behavioral problem, he or she will, in addition to offering services from level 2, also actively inquire about the impact of the illness/problem on the family with regard to the following:

- the emotional status of the child and parents,
- parenting abilities,
- maintaining roles and routines,
- financial and job pressures,
- sibling relationships,
- attention to other children, and
- the marriage.

This clinician should also inquire about the family's strengths and supports, such as organizations, religious beliefs and practices, friends, and relatives. He or she would schedule meetings either with the whole family or with just the most involved members to help them work together on problem solving, including adjusting roles and expectations, communicating more effectively, and sharing feelings with each other. The clinician generally focuses on the child but is comfortable exploring the family context that seems relevant to the child's problem. This clinician is beginning to feel comfortable with and adept at making referrals for family and/or parent problems. The clinician and another professional might work together to help the family solve these problems. This handbook is aimed at clinicians who want to move to level 3.

D. **Level 4. Systematic family assessment and planned intervention.** At this level the clinician has had some teaching and training in family systems theory and practice and can apply these skills to the assessment of the child and family. The clinician specifically helps the family work together and function in more satisfying ways. "These skills would tend to be effective with basically well-functioning families who are becoming disabled because of a medical or other situational crisis." Clinicians at level 1, 2, or 3 may refer a patient/family to a level 4 clinician.

For example, when a child presents with an acute or chronic pain complaint, the clinician at level 4 is skilled at approaching the problem from a biopsychosocial perspective and at giving special attention to the family and the social context in which the problem arises. This includes, in addition to evaluating the child and the specific complaint, exploring the following:

- parents' backgrounds (e.g., family history, social history),
- parenting styles,
- family patterns of behavior in response to the problem,
- family communication style,
- recent stresses associated with the child's problem,
- the parents' beliefs and interpretations about the problem,
- the parents' expectations for the child,
- and the impact of the problem on their marital/partner relationship.

This clinician is skilled at making referrals for child, parent, or family problems. When making referrals, these clinicians might collaborate with another professional (e.g., the clinician works with the child on a specific issue and with the family on family interaction problems, and a marriage counselor works with the couple).

E. **Level 5. Family therapy.** At this level, the clinician's training allows him or her to interview families with chronic interactional problems independently. The implication for a clinician at level 5 is that he or she has evolved "beyond the primary care domain into specialized family treatment." For example, the clinician at this level sees patients/families with chronic, moderate to severe problems (e.g., marital discord, substance abuse, domestic violence, psychiatric illness, abusive parenting styles, parent–child conflict, and difficulty coping with loss or stress) using his or her training in family therapy. These clinicians usually specialize in specific types of family problems (e.g., marital counseling or parent–adolescent conflict). This clinician/family therapist also works with other specialists and represents a resource to whom other clinicians can refer families in need.

VI. Summary

Family systems principles are the basis for a family-oriented approach to behavioral and interaction problems. Making the shift from a focus on the child and the symptoms to a focus on the child within the family context requires knowledge and understanding of family systems principles, including the following:

- The primary focus of care is the child within the context of the family.
- The family is the primary source of many health beliefs and practices.
- Presenting complaints often serve an adaptive function and are maintained by the family.
- The well being of the child is powerfully influenced by the well being of his or her parents.

The family is a system. Its structure and function are determined by the following components:

- family membership,
- hierarchy,
- subsystems, and
- boundaries.

The family may be visualized as a mobile in which all members have a place in the hierarchy. Their roles and interactive patterns maintain the family's balance.

Finally, all clinicians work at various levels of involvement with the family. Clinicians who want to shift to a family systems approach should aim for level 3 where they are "comfortable in switching back and forth between medical data and family feelings and concerns."

Many behavioral–interaction problems don't require family therapy. Primary care family counseling will often suffice. This combines basic family systems techniques (helping the family change behaviors) and traditional advice and directives from the clinician.

ADDITIONAL READING

Allmond BW, Tanner JL. *The family is the patient,* 2nd ed. Baltimore: Williams & Wilkins, 1999.

Barnes J, Stein A, Rosenberg W. Evidence-based medicine and evaluation of mental health services: methodological issues and future directions. *Archives of Diseases in Childhood* 1999;80:280–285.

Beavers WR, Hampson RB. *Successful families.* New York: Norton, 1990.

Cohen WI. Family-oriented pediatric care: taking the next step. In: Coleman WL, Taylor EH, eds. *Family focused pediatrics. Pediatr Clin N Am* 1995;42:11–20.

Doherty WJ, Baird MA. *Family therapy and family medicine.* New York: Guilford Press, 1983.

Doherty WJ, Baird MA. Developmental levels in family-centered medical care. *Fam Med* 1986;18:153, 155.

Engel GL. The need for a new medical model: a challenge for biomedicine. *Science* 1977;196:129–136.

Fiese BJ, Sameroff AJ. Family context in pediatric psychology: a transactional perspective. *J Pediatr Psychol* 1989;14(2):293–314.

Hansen J, Bobula J, Meyer D, et al. Treat or refer? Patient's interest in family clinician involvement in their psychosocial problems. *J Fam Pract* 1987;24:499–503.
Jackson D. The question of family homeostasis. *Psychiatr Q* 1957;31 [Suppl]:79.
Litman TJ. The family as a basic unit in health and medical care: a social-behavioral overview. *Soc Sci Med* 1974;8:495–519.
McDaniel S, Campbell TL, Seaburn DS. *Family-oriented medical care: a manual for medical providers.* New York: Springer-Verlag, 1990.
Minuchin S. *Families and family therapy.* Cambridge, MA: Harvard University Press, 1974.
Napier AY, Whitaker CA. *The family crucible.* New York: Harper & Row, 1978.
Richmond J. Child development: a basic science for pediatrics. *Pediatrics* 1967;39:645–647.
Richmond J. Ripeness is all: the coming of age of behavioral pediatrics. In: Levine MD, Carey WB, Crocker AC, eds. *Developmental-behavioral pediatrics.* Philadelphia: WB Saunders, 1983.
Schor E, Menaghan E. Family pathways to child health. In Amick B, Levine S, Tarlov A, et al., eds. *Society and health.* New York: Oxford University Press, 1995.
Surgeon General's Conference on Children's Mental Health. The National Institute of Mental Health. Bethesda, MD, 2000. (Website: http://www.surgeongeneral.gov/cmh/childreport.htm)
Waters DB, Lawrence EC. *Competence, courage and change: an approach to family therapy.* New York: WW Norton, 1993.
Whitaker CA, Bumberry WM. *Dancing with the family.* New York: Brunner/Mazel, 1988.

2 Determining Which Problems Are Suitable for Family Counseling

I. **Purpose**

How does the clinician determine which problems are suitable for family counseling? Although apparently mild, initial presentations may belie serious issues, problems are generally classified into three levels by their presenting complexity and the kind of approach (assessment/intervention) required. These levels are listed below:

- Level 1: Child-centered approach
- Level 2: Family counseling approach
- Level 3: Referral

This chapter describes the three levels of problems, focusing on those requiring a family-oriented approach.

II. **Three Levels of Problems**

Clinicians encounter all three levels of problems described above. The challenge lies in correctly identifying the level of each problem. Because behavior and interaction problems do not always fit neatly into one of the three levels, categorizing a problem can sometimes be difficult. For instance, clinicians frequently encounter problems that fall between levels 1 and 2 (or that combine aspects of both), thus requiring both a child-centered approach and family counseling. These problems can be differentiated only by their degrees of complexity and severity. Mild, normal toilet training problems are classified as level 1, but severe, chronic disagreement between parents better fits in level 2.

A. **Level 1—child-centered approach.** Level 1 problems are those that the clinician can usually manage with a child/symptom-centered approach. These problems generally do not require a family-oriented approach, even though ideally, clinicians should carry out a minimal family assessment (e.g., family and social histories) for all behavioral problems. The family with level 1 problems usually responds appropriately to the clinician's directives. The family is, in general, functionally intact and is capable of problem solving and communicating. It is characterized by understanding, love, and empathy for each other and by resiliency. The parents have no trouble directing the children because boundaries are clear and the hierarchy is appropriate. Level 1 problems can be characterized as follows:

- Generally predictable, mild, and situational.
- Often normal, developmental variations (e.g., sleep problems).
- Possibly transitory (less than 3 months in duration).
- Perhaps chronic (e.g., attention problems).
- Little chance of significant or long-lasting developmental or functional problems.

Table 2.1 lists examples of problems that often qualify as level 1 problems.

Table 2.1. Examples of level 1 problems[a]

Developmental variations: tantrums, sleep disorders, colic, feeding problems, toilet training, enuresis, encopresis
Developmental transitions: toddlerhood, entering school, entering adolescence
Mild, predictable behavior and parenting problems: noncompliance of child, sibling rivalry, parental disagreement, parental difficulty with imposing limits
Mild emotional and temperament problems: situational/reactive sadness, shyness, difficult child
Attention and learning problems: those that have mild emotional and behavioral complications
Peer interaction problems: child has no friends, teases, is bossy, bullies or is bullied
Family life cycle events: birth of a baby, death of a grandparent, parent "midlife crisis"

[a] Any level 1 problem may be symptomatic of more severe individual and/or family problems.

Problems Suitable for the Use of a Child-Centered Approach

Level 1 child-centered problems occur in families that are competent, caring, and capable of problem solving. Level 1 problems affect the family even though relationships are healthy and the family is coping. Level 1 problems require a minimal family assessment.

To resolve level 1 problems, the clinician uses good interviewing skills, knowledge of basic child development and behavior, and familiarity with an array of parenting techniques. The assessment and management focus on the child and his or her symptoms. The clinician generally uses traditional interventions, which can be summarized with five R's as follows: reassurance, readings, recipes, resources, and Rxs (i.e., various psychotropic medications) (Table 2.2).

Level 1 Problems—Symptomatic of a More Serious Problem?

Level 1 problems may actually be the initial presentation of a level 2 or level 3 problem. If they intensify or recur despite the clinician's interventions, the clinician should explore the family context.

Table 2.2. Five traditional interventions (the five R's)[a]

Reassurance: emotional support
Readings: educational material, demystification
Recipes: behavioral management advice, conventional wisdom
Resources: parent support groups, friends, relatives, community services
Rxs: medications

[a] These interventions are not exclusive to level 1 problems; they are also used in level 2 and level 3 problems.

B. **Level 2—family counseling approach.** Level 2 problems, which are psychosocial in nature, are characterized by relationship–interactive disturbances and thus require a family-oriented approach (i.e., family counseling, often combined with one or more of the five R's of the child-centered interventions). Level 2 problems are characterized by the indicators listed below:

- Maladaptive behavioral and communications patterns.
- Inadequate family adaptability.
- Chronic distress (longer than 3 months).
- Internal stresses (e.g., parental depression, marital/relationship stress, or parenting disagreement).
- External stresses (e.g., career demands, aging or dying relatives, financial problems).
- Changes in family structure and function and disturbances in the family system.

A problem is classified as level 2 when parents lack control (e.g., difficulty in establishing or enforcing rules, rewarding good behavior, or extinguishing inappropriate behavior). Furthermore, communication breakdowns occur; the resulting strain in family interactions leads to increasing behavioral and emotional problems that further disrupt the family.

These disturbances affect one or two domains of the child's functioning, such as physical health, school performance, peer interactions, family relationships, emotional well being, and feelings of security and self-esteem.

Family Counseling Does Not Imply Family Dysfunction

Although families experiencing level 2 problems are stressed, they are not dysfunctional. Therefore, they are very responsive to family counseling.

Table 2.3. Examples of level 2 problems[a]

Relationship problems: difficult interactions, "not getting along"
Social and emotional complications of attention-deficit/hyperactivity disorder (ADHD) and school learning problems
Family communication problems that discourage expressions of affection, acceptance, and approval and diminish self-esteem
Parenting difficulties: parent–child conflict and a poor fit between child and parent temperaments
Emotional problems: child is experiencing depression, anger, anxiety, grieving
Poor compliance with medical regimens
Vulnerable child syndrome
School refusal/separation anxiety
Chronic somatic complaints
Family life cycle events that cause significant stress
Behavior problems: defiant, aggressive behavior
Issues for gay and lesbian families in a heterosexual world
Issues for step, foster, and adopted children and their families
Issues for single parents and their children
The impact of divorce on children and families
Challenges for culturally and ethnically diverse families

[a] Level 2 problems may be symptomatic of more severe individual and/or family problems.

1. *Examples of level 2 problems.* Level 2 problems vary in range of severity and in description of the problem. Many are initially mistaken for level 1 problems and are treated as such; but when they recur or intensify, they are identified as level 2 or 3. Clinicians that frequently encounter problems that are a combination of levels 1 and 2 should respond with both child-centered interventions and family counseling. Examples of level 2 problems include significant social and emotional complications of attention-deficit/hyperactivity disorder (ADHD), family communication problems (e.g., patterns that lack affection and instead are characterized by anger and/or criticism), parent–child conflict, persistent and intense parental disagreement over rewarding and/or puni-

Clues Indicating the Need for Using a Family Systems Approach

- The clinician, working exclusively at the biomedical level, ignores the family context (e.g., parenting practices, parental depression).

continued on top of page

continued from bottom

- The clinician works too hard, repeats instructions, and experiences frustration and failure.
- The problems recur or intensify despite the clinician's interventions. The family is working too hard, is having difficulty communicating, and/or is disappointed and tired.
- The family is wrongly perceived as "dysfunctional," "noncompliant," or "resistant."

ishing the child, and mild to moderate mood disorders. Other types of level 2 problems appear in Table 2.3.

2. *Six manifestations of level 2 problems.* Level 2 problems manifest in several ways, some of which are listed below:

- A Level 1 problem recurs or intensifies despite the implementation of any or all of the five R's (see Case 1).
- The parent ignores the clinician's advice (see Case 2).
- The child presents as the "symptomatic patient" or the "identified patient" of a disturbed or stressed family system (See Case 3).
- Relationship and interaction problems become more apparent ("We don't get along; we need help.").
- The family is unable to resolve the problem and move forward; it feels "stuck" ("We've tried everything.").
- The clinician is unable to resolve the problem; the clinician feels "stuck" ("I've tried everything") and needs more information.

CASE 1: A 6-YEAR-OLD BOY WITH ENURESIS

A Level 1 Problem Recurs or Intensifies despite Multiple Symptom-centered Interventions

A mother brings her boy in for "bed wetting." The clinician performs a physical examination, orders a urinalysis, and suggests several interventions (medication and bladder-stretching exercises). At the next meeting, the mother reports that she and her husband haven't complied with the suggestions because they disagree with each other about them, especially the usage of medication. The clinician then suggests that the parents try withholding fluid after 6 P.M. and waking the boy to use the bathroom before they go to bed. The clinician asks that both parents come to the next meeting.

Both parents come in 2 weeks but state that they find that agreeing to carry out this second set of instructions is *"difficult"* for them. The clinician suggests an enuresis and tells the parents to *"put your differences aside for the boy's sake."* At the subsequent visit, the parents reveal that they are still *"at odds"* about treatment and state that *"the wetting is causing a lot of family tension."*

The boy, who is being teased at school, now refuses to attend. The mother and father take turns staying at home, convincing the boy to go, and then driving him to school when he agrees to go. The boy is sad and tearful, and the parents have become even more upset with him and with each other.

At this point, the clinician decides to adopt a family systems perspective and to explore the family context so that he can help them resolve the parental disagreements and the boy's enuresis. After explaining the purpose for using the family meeting approach, he asks the parents about their beliefs about enuresis, their family health histories, and their own experiences growing up with their parents ("parenting histories"). (For further discussion of this technique and its implementation, see Chapter 7, "Assessing Family Functioning: Additional Methods.")

The father reveals that he suffered from enuresis as a child and states that his parents *"beat it out of me."* He didn't like it, but *"it worked for me."* He feels his son *"should learn to control it like I did."* He doesn't spank his son, but he readily shows his displeasure.

The mother reports that her parents, who were indulgent, raised her by reasoning with her and showing affection and that they never spanked her. She tends to *"make excuses"* for her son and even hides his wet underpants from the father, only adding to the family tension. Although the mother wants to try the interventions, her husband refuses. The clinician closes by carrying out several level 1 tasks (child-centered) and helps the parents cooperate and develop more effective strategies—level 2 (family-centered) tasks.

The clinician explains the following:

- The influence of the parents' backgrounds on their differing beliefs and parenting styles;
- The effects of their conflict, which is prolonging the enuresis and affecting the boy's self-esteem and school life, on their son;
- The effects of the conflict, which is causing family tension and affecting their relationship with each other, on the family;
- Enuresis in a way that removes blame from the boy and that shows that his symptom is still within normal variation;
- Ways to change their behaviors.

The parents respond in the ways listed below:

- The father agrees not to show his anger;
- The father agrees to try the interventions for one month;
- The mother agrees not to "protect" the boy by hiding the underpants;
- They agree to contact their son's teacher who promises to try to stop the teasing;
- They insist that their son return to school;

The enuresis gradually resolves, even though the boy has occasional brief relapses. The parents still disagree on some aspects of parenting but do agree more often. Their arguments occur less frequently; when they do occur, they are less intense.

CASE 2: A 4-YEAR-OLD GIRL WITH TANTRUMS

The Parent Ignores the Clinician's Advice

A divorced father reports that his daughter's tantrums, which occur both at home and in public, are extremely *"embarrassing, because people think I'm abusing her."* She always asks for toys and candy; when her father refuses, she has a *"meltdown."* The clinician suggests that the father use *"extinction"* techniques and says, *"Just don't pay any attention. Let her scream all she wants. When she realizes that she's not getting your attention or the goodies, the tantrums will subside. You can praise her when she shows improvement of any kind."* During the visit, the girl plays with toys and draws pictures. She is well behaved.

At the follow-up visit, the father reports that the *"meltdowns are the same."* When asked about his attempts to use the technique, he states that he stopped after two attempts because *"people still think I'm abusing her."* He appears downcast and helpless. The clinician decides to shift to a family–social context to understand the problem better and the father's sadness. She explaines the purpose of a family meeting and the involvement of the family context of the problem, not just the child's symptom.

The clinician then inquires about the father's ex-wife and about their relationship. He reports that his former wife had moved to another city and that the girl visits her mother only one weekend a month. The relationship between the father and mother is *"cold."* The father then falls silent. After about 20 seconds of silence, the clinician reflects, *"You seem pretty sad and discouraged."* The father nods without making eye contact. She then asks, *"Have you been under any other stresses recently?"* The father states that his career involves long hours and frequent travel. He feels guilty about the divorce and the separation from his daughter.

He wants to be a *"good father"* when he is with his daughter. He fears that saying *"No"* or ignoring her demands will harm her self-esteem or that *"maybe she won't love me."* He also admits that, at the same time, he is becoming increasingly resentful toward her because *"every outing is spoiled."* This attitude leads to feeling even guiltier because of his resentment. He says, *"I'm really a bad father."*

During this visit, the girl plays quietly for a while. Later however, she begins pestering her father and interrupts him frequently. He pauses to respond to each interruption and tries to reason with her or to promise her ice cream if she behaves, all to no avail.

The clinician assures the father that he is not a bad parent and tells him very emphatically that he is a very devoted father and that he is doing a very good job as a single, hardworking dad. However, she explains, his guilt makes it difficult for him to respond appropriately to his daughter's tantrums. The clinician points out that tantrums are normal behavior for children of this age, but that his daughter's have intensified to a severe level, which is straining the parent–child relationship.

The clinician is directive. She encourages the father to say *"No"* without feeling guilty and to set limits. She gives him suggestions for what he can do when the girl acts up again.

The clinician encourages the father to develop his own solutions as well. She adds that setting limits will not cause the father to lose his daughter's love or to diminish her self-esteem. She also addresses the father's social context and asks him to consider ways in which to revive his social life.

At the next visit, the father reports that things are a bit better. He has called his ex-wife and explained the situation. They have agreed to change the visitation schedule so that he has more time to himself. Because the girl's mother wants to see her daughter more often, this gesture alone has improved the parents' relationship. This improvement in parental communication appears to exert a good influence on the girl. Both parents use the same approach to respond to the tantrums. Her tantrums occur less frequently, and she is not as whiny or irritable. The father is able to enjoy time with his daughter more than before. Over the next few visits, the situation remains stable.

CASE 3: A 9-YEAR-OLD GIRL WITH CHRONIC ABDOMINAL PAIN

Child Presents as the "Symptomatic Patient" or the "Identified Patient" of a Disturbed Family System

A mother makes an appointment for her daughter who suffers from chronic abdominal pain. The clinician takes a detailed history of the complaint and performs a physical examination. He finds no cause, so he refers the girl to a gastroenterologist who, after carrying out various tests and procedures, finds no organic etiology. The clinician prescribes an over-the-counter antacid medication.

The mother calls again, saying that the pain is still present and that *"the girl's grandmother is very worried."* This statement prompts the clinician to suggest a family meeting that includes the child's grandmother. When mother, father, daughter, and grandmother arrive, the clinician explains the purpose of the meeting. (See Chapter 3, "Getting Ready for a Family Meeting.") After asking about recent family changes, he finds that the pain began shortly after the grandmother moved in with the family.

The clinician takes a family history. The parents are in good physical and mental health, but the grandmother has ulcers, which are a daily topic of conversation. The grandmother complains about her ulcers and dietary restrictions, so the mother feels obligated to give her a lot of attention, including rides to the doctor's office and to the drugstore. In her free time, she works at her part-time job. She constantly feels tired and takes naps whenever she can.

The father has increased his work hours to help pay for the care and living expenses of the grandmother. Often he leaves the house at 6 A.M. and does not return until after dinner, leaving him with no time to spend with his daughter. Because the family routines and relationships are disrupted, the girl almost seems to be ignored by her parents. When she is alone with her grandmother, she is expected to keep her company and to take care of her. The grandmother, alarmed when the girl experienced abdominal pain because *"ulcers run in the family,"* had suggested to the parents the idea for the extensive medical evaluations.

The clinician is able to identify the dynamics influencing the daughter's abdominal pain. He explains how the family's changes have affected the relationships and how these changes are *"most likely"* contributing to the girl's symptoms. The family responds appreciatively to this explanation, and the clinician encourages them to develop a new interactional plan at home.

At the next meeting, the family shares its plan. The grandmother discusses her ulcers less frequently and does not mention them at all with her granddaughter; the mother enrolls the grandmother in the senior center 3 days a week. During that time, the mother and daughter spend time together talking, doing errands, cooking, or walking the dog. The parents make all decisions about their daughter's health care. When the girl is alone with her grandmother, they participate in activities that they both enjoy, such as reading, baking, or watching TV. However, the girl's pain continues. The clinician urges them to be patient and to *"keep doing the same things."*

By the subsequent visit, the girl's pain has decreased in frequency and intensity. The family, who is still adjusting to the grandmother living with them, finds that the plans do *"not always work."* Still, the family members feel that they are doing better. *"We can live with things now,"* they say.

C. **Level 3—problems for referral.**

Level 3 problems are identified by their tendency towards multiple, severe, chronic family psychosocial occurrences (e.g., domestic violence, significant spousal conflict, alcohol/substance abuse, child and/or parent psychopathology, child abuse, and family disintegration). These problems are detectable using a family interview and/or screening tests (see Chapter 7, "Assessing Family Functioning: Additional Methods"). These problems affect several functional domains because the level of parental worry and the burden of suffering on the family are significant. These families can be fearful of, resistant to, and distrustful towards medical and mental health professionals (Table 2.4). Therefore, they are often unfairly or inappropriately labeled "resistant" or "noncompliant."

Families with level 3 problems should be referred to mental health professionals, family therapists, and/or appropriate agencies. The family's many problems require long-term, specialized help. Initially the physician may believe that a level 3 problem is actually level 1 or 2. The clinician will not be able to identify the problem's extent until he or she has one or two family meetings to gain the family's trust, understand the problem and the family, and determine its

Table 2.4. Examples of level 3 problems

Domestic violence
Parent or child alcohol and substance abuse
Child/parental criminal behavior
Parental psychiatric problems; severe mood disorders in children
Physical and sexual abuse
Marital conflict and divorce
Any level 1 or level 2 problems that do not respond to the clinician's interventions and that exceed the clinician's abilities

needs. These are the first three steps in the referral process. See Chapter 14, "Making a Mental Health Referral," for further discussion.

III. **Summary**

Clinical problems can be classified into one of three categories or levels. Level 1 problems are mild to moderate problems occurring within a family that is competent in problem solving. These are generally resolved with the traditional child-centered interventions, known as the 5 R's: reassurance, readings, recipes, resources, and Rxs (various psychotropic medications). Level 2 problems are relationship problems, unresolved level 1 problems, somatic complaints, parent–child conflict, child mood disorders, aggressive behavior, and school refusal. They are best resolved with a family systems approach, often used in conjunction with the 5 R's, an approach known as family counseling. Level 3 problems are complex, severe, and chronic; and thus they require referral to mental health professionals and appropriate agencies. This chapter focused on helping the clinician identify level 2 problems.

ADDITIONAL READING

Allmond BW, Tanner JL. *The family is the patient*, 2nd ed. Baltimore: Williams & Wilkins, 1999.

American Academy of Pediatrics: Committee on Psychosocial Aspects of Child and Family Health. The pediatrician and the "new morbidity." *Pediatrics* 1993;92:731.

Black MM, Krishnakumar A. Children in low-income, urban settings: intervention to promote mental health and well-being. *Am Psychol* 1998;53(6):635–646.

Brazelton TB. Working with families. In: Coleman WL, Taylor EH, eds. *Family focused pediatrics. Pediatr Clin N Am* 1995(February); 42:1–10.

Cohen WI, Milberg L. The behavioral pediatrics consultation: teaching residents to think systemically in managing behavioral pediatrics problems. *Fam Systems Med* 1992;10:169–179.

Coleman WL, Taylor EH. Staging levels of family–parental stress and dysfunction. *Developmental and behavioral news* (newsletter of the Section for Developmental and Behavioral Pediatrics, American Academy of Pediatrics) 1993;2:6–8.

Combrinck-Graham L. *Children in family contexts.* New York: Guilford Press, 1989.

Dubowitz H, King H. Family violence: a child-centered, family-focused approach. In: Coleman WL, Taylor EH, eds. *Family focused pediatrics. Pediatr Clin N Am.* 1995(February);42:153–166.

Dworkin PH. Detection of behavioral, developmental and psychosocial problems in primary care practice. *Curr Opin Pediatr* 1993; 5:531–536.

Finney JW, Brophy CJ, Friman PC, et al. Promoting parent-provider interaction during young children's health-supervision visits. *Journal of Applied Behavioral Analysis* 1990;23:207–213.

Green M. *Bright futures: guidelines for health supervision of infants, children and adolescents.* Arlington, VA: National Center for Education in Maternal and Child Health, 1994.

Hickson GB, Altemier WA, O'Connor S. Concerns of mothers seeking care in private pediatric offices: opportunities for expanding services. *Pediatrics* 1983;72:619–624.

Horowitz SM, Leaf PJ, Leventhal JM, et al. Identification and management of psychosocial and developmental problems in community-based primary care pediatric practices. *Pediatrics* 1992;89:480–485.

Lavigne JV. Behavioral and emotional problems among preschool children in pediatric primary care: prevalence and pediatricians' recognition. *Pediatrics* 1993;91(3):649–655.

Ludwig S, Rostain A. Family function and dysfunction. In: Levine MD, Carey WB, Crocker AC, eds. *Developmental–behavioral pediatrics*, 3rd ed. Philadelphia: WB Saunders, 1999.

Minichun S, Rosman B, Baker L. *Psychosomatic families: anorexia nervosa in context.* Cambridge, MA: Harvard University Press, 1976.

Parker S, Zuckerman B: *Behavioral and developmental pediatrics.* Boston: Little, Brown and Company, 1995.

Young KT, Davis K, Schoen C, et al. Listening to parents: a national survey of parents with young children. *Arch Pediatr Adolesc Med* 1998;152:255–262.

3 Getting Ready for a Family Meeting

I. Purpose

A family meeting seldom occurs spontaneously. The clinician must carefully prepare by completing a series of tasks prior to the meeting. First, the clinician must detect a problem that requires a family-oriented approach (see Chapter 2, "Determining Which Problems Are Suitable for Family Counseling"). Then, he or she must suggest a family meeting in a way that is acceptable to the family. The clinician must also carry out other tasks, such as arranging the office, to prepare for the meeting. Getting ready entails the following five tasks:

- Detecting the problem;
- Suggesting the meeting;
- Arranging the office;
- Planning the meeting;
- Reviewing the elements of the family meeting.

The chances of a successful and satisfying family meeting (for both the family and the clinician) increase if the clinician has prepared for the meeting. This chapter describes the tasks involved in getting ready, including the individual components, and then uses case studies to illustrate the techniques.

II. Detecting the Problem: Three Clinical Settings

In daily, routine patient encounters, the clinician often detects the problems that may require a family meeting. The idea for a family meeting arises from three common settings: the well-child visit/doorknob question, a visit scheduled because of a behavioral problem, and a telephone call received from a family member about a behavioral problem. For additional clues that may prompt the clinician to consider a family meeting, see Chapter 2, "Determining Which Problems Are Suitable for Family Counseling."

A. **The well-child visit/doorknob question.** Imagine that, at the end of a well-child visit, a father spontaneously asks about a family-centered problem that is seemingly unrelated to the purpose of the visit (e.g., *"My kids are fighting so much my wife doesn't want to come home until they are in bed. What should we do?"*). This concern, the "doorknob question," is actually a call for help. It may be a "hidden agenda" or the "real reason for coming" (RRC). In this example, the parent shows his trust in the clinician by revealing sensitive and important information. The clinician must take advantage of this moment; if ignored, the parent may not ask again, and the problem will certainly intensify.

1. *The clinician should sit down with the father, obtain a quick overview of the problem, and acknowledge his concern.* For the clinician to say, *"I want to hear what's on your mind. We only have a few minutes now, so we can't address your concerns in depth; but we can arrange a visit as soon as possible,"* and for the father to reply briefly with an explanation only takes 3 to 5 minutes.

2. *After the brief discussion, the clinician shows support and interest by:*

a. ***Personally scheduling the next visit as soon as possible.*** The clinician can call the receptionist from the office in the presence of the parent and ask for the next available appointment time, or he or she can accompany the parent to the reception area to ensure that an appointment is made as soon as possible.

b. ***Checking his or her present schedule.*** If the next patient is running late or has cancelled, he or she can spend more time with the parent.

c. ***Suggesting to the parent that they follow-up by phone in the next day or two.*** The clinician can then schedule an appointment with the appropriate members.

d. ***Considering a referral if he or she feels that the problem is serious even though it would be based on little information.*** The parent must be open to that suggestion for this approach to succeed. See Chapter 14, "Making a Mental Health Referral."

B. **The scheduled visit for a "behavior problem."** If, after using several level 1 child/symptom-centered interventions (e.g., time out, medication), the behavior problem remains unresolved, the parent may make a comment, such as *"I try so hard, but I just can't go on like this,"* that suggests to the clinician the need for a family meeting. He or she can respond by saying, *"You have tried many interventions and worked hard, but things aren't getting better. You have a right to feel discouraged. When parents face this situation, scheduling a family meeting often helps them gain more understanding, support, and information."*

Parents may even make overt pleas for help, such as *"My mother-in-law and I are having very serious disagreements about how to raise my son. My husband takes her side, making me feel very frustrated and ineffective."* The clinician in this situation must avoid the appearance of taking sides with either the mother or the mother-in-law and father. Saying something like, *"It sounds like the family has different opinions. That makes it very hard for everyone. If we had a family meeting, we could try and understand the problems better to help the family work together. It would be very helpful to include your mother-in-law."*

C. **The telephone call about a behavioral problem.** Clinicians frequently receive calls from parents that indicate the need for a family meeting. In one example of such a call, a mother might say, *"My husband and I think that our son Robbie is smoking marijuana. His dad confronts him often, and they end up in a shouting match, which I have to break up. I'd like you to see Robbie."* The clinician should avoid either assuming the parent role or offering advice on the phone. An appropriate response might be, *"It sounds like everyone is pretty tense. In this kind of situation, meeting with* *the whole family to understand all the issues is the most helpful. Meeting with Robbie alone or with Robbie and just one parent wouldn't be enough. The whole family has a lot to offer, so I need all of you here."*

Responding to a Telephone Call

Phone calls are time consuming and are inadequate for a proper preliminary assessment. They also are not reimbursable. Keeping phone calls brief helps the clinician avoid the appearance of taking sides and prevents him or her from giving hasty and ill-informed advice (based on information from one member speaking privately to the clinician).

III. Six Ways to Suggest a Family Meeting

The clinician often wonders how to actually state the suggestion for a family meeting so that he or she does not appear intrusive, misguided, or dismissive of the parent's stated complaint. Therefore, when the clinician proposes the meeting, he or she must clearly communicate the shift to a family perspective, while emphasizing the importance of the family as a resource for resolving the problem. To do this, he or she might say, *"A family meeting would be very helpful because its purpose is not to focus on any one person or imply blame. Instead we need to understand the problem better by getting everyone's input. Your family is the best resource for that—everyone has something to offer. We will need everyone's perspectives and cooperation."*

Six ways to suggest a family meeting are described below.

A. **If the parents' initial complaint is centered on interaction and relationship issues,** the parent might say, *"My son and I are always arguing. We just can't get along; my husband is irritated with us both."* The **clinician** would respond by saying, *"The family has the best understanding of the issues. When someone has a problem like this, I find that getting information from other family members helps. You all have a lot to offer. The family meeting is the only way to do this."*

B. **If Level 1 child-centered interventions fail and the parents return for more advice, the clinician should review the situation with them.** Did they truly understand the problem and accept the suggestions? Did the parents agree with one another? Did they carry out the suggestions? The mother indicates that compliance has been difficult by saying, *"We did agree with your ideas, but we just couldn't seem to do them."* The clinician, acknowledging the family's efforts and frustration, says, *"Ms. Jones, I appreciate all you have done. You have worked very hard, and yet the problem is getting* *worse. I share your sense of frustration, and I feel that I don't have enough information. A family meeting is the best way to get a better understanding. It's time for to us to stop focusing on Josh alone. It's not enough and it's not working."*

C. **If the parents openly state a relationship problem, the clinician should view this as a direct plea for help.** In the course of assessing a problem, especially when parents know and trust the clinician, they often reveal a problem in their relationship. One of the parents might say, *"We never talk to each other."* The clinician could respond with, *"From what you say, everyone seems to be affected. That you have tried is apparent, but now things are getting worse because you don't talk to each other. A family meeting allows us to take a broader look at the family to understand the problem. From my experience, when things get to this point, a family meeting is helpful."*

Keep Realistic Expectations

Keep expectations for the meeting realistic for the family (and for the clinician). For example, the clinician should say, *"I'm going to help you improve the tantrum situation a bit, but it will take some time and work and several visits."*

D. **If parents make spontaneous "trigger" statements that hint at personal or relationship problems,** these statements often are indirect pleas for help for the family that should "trigger" a response from the clinician. For instance, a mother might imply that she doesn't feel supported by saying, *"My husband works longer hours and then stops at the sports bar for a few drinks with the boys."* The clinician can reply with, *"That must be difficult. I feel I am missing something that would help us all understand the issues. I need to hear what you and the others in the family think. A family meeting would be the best way to start."*

E. **If parents become upset (angry, tearful, frustrated) with each other or with their children in the office,** the clinician should explore the situation. He or she must first reflect their feelings (Always Acknowledge Affect—AAA). These supportive statements also serve as invitations for the parent to share information about the family situation. The clinician might say, *"I can see this is very upsetting to you."* After letting the family respond, the clinician might ask, *"Does this happen at home?"* If the family's answer suggests that it does, the clinician can ask what, if anything, the family has tried and can suggest the family meeting in the following way, *"From what I hear, everyone is feeling pretty upset, and you would like to see things get better. When I see a* *family issue like this, the best thing to do is to have a family meeting. That way no one is singled out. Everyone will share his or her feelings and thoughts, giving us a much better idea of what's going on. Then you can begin to work together."*

F. **If the clinician feels that he or she does not have enough information and needs to explore the family context,** the clinician should admit that he or she is confused and wants more information. He or she could say, *"I don't have enough information. I need to understand the family and how it is responding. A family meeting gives me information not available from an exclusive focus on one member; it also offers more interventions. I would like to schedule a family meeting."*

Suggesting a Family Meeting

The clinician suggests a family meeting in a way that does not convey blame or incompetence but that does communicate support, understanding, and hope. The clinician respectfully and clearly states that the family is affected by the problem, that the family is an important resource, and that the whole family will benefit from a meeting.

G. **If the clinician encounters other situations, additional practical tips for suggesting a family meeting and DOs and DON'Ts are available.** In addition to the techniques described above, the clinician should keep in mind several other practical tips to help the family understand and accept his or her suggestion. These tips (DOs and DON'Ts) are listed in Table 3.1.

IV. **Orchestrating the Family Meeting**

A. **Suggesting the meeting: A case study**

CASE 1: MARITAL DISCORD AND A 7-YEAR-OLD DAUGHTER WITH STOMACHACHES

Kate, a 7-year-old girl whom the clinician has followed for 5 years, recently has experienced recurrent abdominal pain. Several physical examinations and various tests during the last month were negative. Kate has stopped participating in after-school sports. Her mother, very worried, keeps asking if "another test" exists that might reveal the cause of the pain. At the latest visit, after another normal physical examination and careful review of all the tests, the clinician feels that she needs to know more of the family context. First, she decides to speak privately with the mother.

Clinician (to mother): *I'd like to speak alone with you for a few minutes.* (When Kate looks alarmed, the clinician reassures her by continuing with the following.) *Kate, all of the examinations and tests have been normal. You are a healthy girl. I just*

Table 3.1. DOs and DON'Ts: Practical tips for suggesting a family meeting

DOs

Do call the gathering a family meeting, family session, or family visit.
Do state clearly that the purpose of the family meeting is to gather more information and to help the family work together to solve the problem.
Do be direct, positive, and confident about the need and benefit for a family meeting.
Do make sure the purpose of the meeting is clear to the person who will inform the rest of the family of the meeting.
Do emphasize the importance of the whole family attending the meeting, ideally at the first meeting.
Do state that all families need help from time to time.
Do offer to meet with most of the family when others can't or won't attend.
Do provide time for questions after requesting a family meeting.
Do identify the family hierarchy and form an alliance with family leader.

DON'Ts

Don't call the meeting "family therapy."
Don't wait for a crisis to suggest a family meeting, if possible.
Don't imply that the meeting is to explore all aspects of the family life.
Don't imply that the meeting is to reconstitute the family or to challenge its values.
Don't say that the family meeting is to determine how family dynamics or problems affect the child's problem. Relevant issues will reveal themselves in the meeting.
Don't imply that the family is dysfunctional or incompetent.
Don't accept a family's initial hesitation or reluctance to agree to a meeting.
Don't be unclear, hesitant, or uncertain about the need for a family meeting.
Don't imply that anyone is to blame or is at fault.
Don't imply that you have the answer to the problem and that you plan to give advice.
Don't state or imply you are going to refer the family to a mental health professional. That issue, if necessary, will reveal itself in the first few sessions and should be addressed when appropriate.

need to speak with your mom alone. After Kate leaves for the waiting room, the clinician continues by saying, *Ms. Martin, I've known Kate for 5 years. As you know, all of the examinations and tests have been normal; it doesn't seem like there is a physical cause for her pain.*

Mother: *Why do you think she has these pains? Is she faking them to get out of sports?*

Clinician (demystifying the phenomenon): *No, I am sure she is not. I feel I know her very well. She has always enjoyed sports and done well. As a clinician, I can tell you that the body and mind are not separate. Each affects the other. This holds true for children and adults. For example, if we are worried about something either inside the family or outside but can't or don't want to talk about it, we may have a headache or muscle tension. Kate might be doing the same with her stomachaches.*

In saying this, the clinician has taken time to educate the parent about the connection between emotional/mental distress and somatic pain, has expanded the inquiry, and has created a family–social context for further questioning about nonmedical issues. She has discussed these issues in a calm, reassuring, gently probing manner.

Mother (somewhat doubtful): *I'm not sure what you mean.*

Clinician (exploring the family context): *I'd like to ask about other things that might affect Kate, such as friends, school, and family. Asking about these things might seem a bit strange, but they are important.*

The clinician just gently expanded the evaluation from a child–medical focus to a family–psychosocial focus as well. She moved away from the clinician's traditional biomedical role with the parent while emphasizing her concern for Kate's well being.

Mother: *Go ahead.*

Clinician: *Have there been any recent stresses at school?*

The clinician has deliberately chosen school, a less-threatening topic than family, to expand the focus of the interview.

Mother: *She is doing well. Her grades are good and her teachers report that she is well behaved. The sports thing is the only change.*

Clinician (still pursuing a less personal issue than the family): *How are things with her friends?*

Mother: *She remains popular and has several good friends. In fact, they want her to join the team again.*

The clinician now explores the family situation in a very general but indirect way.

Clinician: *I haven't seen Mr. Martin for a long time. What does he think about Kate's stomachaches?*

Mother: *He is so busy at work that he has hardly noticed. He cares, but he knows I am taking good care of Kate.*

Clinician (following up on mother's comment): *I know you are. Is he working more than ever?*

Mother: *Yes, it seems like he is. . . .*

The mother pauses and the clinician remains silent. Silence allows the mother to recognize her own feelings and to share them if she wishes.

Mother: *It seems like he is avoiding us . . . or me. When I ask for help, he always has an excuse. We argue a lot.*

The clinician now asks a more specific question that follows from the information just offered. This keeps the line of questioning nonthreatening but logically related to the conversation.

Clinician: *Have the arguments been more frequent over the past month or two?*

Mother: *Yes. They get quite unpleasant at times.*

The clinician's questions and the information received have revealed a possible connection between the family stress and the stomachaches and have confirmed the clinician's suspicion. Next, she makes the mother a partner in evaluating the problem within a family context.

Clinician: *Do you think that the stresses between you and your husband might be contributing to Kate's stomachaches?*

Mother: *I hadn't thought about that, but now that we have talked I think there is a connection. She does seem worried and spends more time in her room alone. Things at home are tense even if we aren't arguing.*

At this point, the clinician can suggest that a family meeting is the next logical and useful step.

Clinician: *A family meeting would be very helpful. It's apparent that there is a lot going on and that everyone is feeling some pain. The meeting would help everyone understand the issues. By working together, you could begin to resolve them. Your family is your greatest resource.*

The mother agrees to go home and discuss the possibility of a meeting with her husband. She will call the clinician next week.

Who Attends the Family Meeting and Who Leads it?

- Ideally, especially for the first visit, the immediate family should attend. If this is not feasible, the affected subunit of the family is sufficient. Others should attend future meetings as necessary.
- The clinician must identify the family leader, establish an alliance, and ensure that he or she attends the meeting.

B. **Arranging the office for a family meeting.** Having a roomy, comfortable, family-friendly meeting space available for use for the meeting is an important component of the family-systems approach. The clinician can do two things to arrange the office for the interview: find space (an ample, comfortable room) and obtain equipment (toys, tissues).

1. *Space for the interview.* Most offices and clinics contain only standard, narrow examining rooms. Although these rooms are not ideal, they can be made more family-friendly if the clinician provides small chairs and cushions for the children. A more suitable space is a room where the chairs can be arranged in a loose semicircle: a conference room, the clinician's office, or the waiting room if the meeting occurs after regular office hours. If the meeting takes place in the clinician's office, the clinician should not sit behind his or her desk because that arrangement appears too formal and thus creates a "barrier" between the clinician and the family, discouraging the sense of "joining."

   If the parent or clinician wants to discuss something privately, children might need to leave the room for a while. Parents invariably appreciate this time alone with the clinician. In this situation, children can sit in the hallway, the next room, the waiting area, or the playroom with a book, toy, or drawing material to keep them occupied while they wait. Teenagers appreciate the availability of a separate waiting room especially equipped for adolescents with appropriate age-level reading material.

   Exam rooms should have seating for everyone, including the clinician. Standing becomes uncomfortable and can convey to the family a sense of clinician dominance, impatience, or disinterest.

   If the family and clinician are seated at a table, an ideal table is a round one because the seating arrangement implies equality. If a round table is not available, seating the parent who needs to be perceived as the parent in charge at the head of the table is often helpful. Sometimes, placing no one at the head of the table works best if the family needs to encourage more expression and initiative from some members.

   A carpeted room is handy because the floor can be used as a place for the children to draw or play—it might actually be the only place available for this. At times, the clinician also needs to sit on the floor with the children to engage them.

2. *Equipment.* Toys and drawing materials to amuse and occupy the children during the visit should be available. More important, they are often useful because they help children express themselves. The clinician should observe the children during play to figure out what the children's actions and words communicate about their feelings. Some children actually can be interviewed better while they are drawing or playing. In addition, family drawing or hand puppet play can be used to help parents and children interact and communicate. Some suggested supplies includes large sheets of paper, crayons, pencils, felt tip pens, hand

puppets, books, and small toys. A box of tissues should also be kept handy because family meetings often evoke painful feelings.

C. **Planning the meeting.** Planning in advance results in an organized and time-efficient meeting. Therefore, the clinician should set a time schedule and then plan the final details in the pre-meeting phase.

1. *Scheduling.*

a. ***When should family sessions be scheduled?*** For working parents, family visits usually are most convenient when planned for the late afternoon or early evening. Some clinicians reserve a day or a half-day for behavioral–developmental problems and family sessions; others have regular weekend office hours. Another option for the clinician is to modify his or her schedule by blocking out more time for a single visit or by scheduling several closely spaced, shorter visits. This willingness to work around the family's schedule is important because finding a convenient time for the family greatly enhances the likelihood of its keeping the appointment. By being flexible with his or her scheduling, the clinician also shows his or her personal commitment to the family.

b. ***How much time should the clinician allot for the upcoming visit?*** Depending on the nature of the problems and on how well the clinician knows the family, the initial family meeting generally requires 40 to 50 minutes. For those clinicians who cannot devote that amount of time to one meeting, the initial family meeting can be divided into two visits. Follow-up visits usually take 20 to 30 minutes.

2. *The pre-meeting phase.* In the pre-meeting phase, the clinician should prepare a plan for the interview session. Organizing improves the chance that the upcoming meeting will be time-efficient, productive, and satisfying. Topics to consider in this phase include deciding which people should attend and forming a general hypothesis and plan.

a. ***Who should attend a family meeting?*** The clinician should first identify the family members and any others who live in the home. Ideally, the entire family (or all of those living in the home) should attend at least one meeting, usually the first. If that is not possible or if the family is too large, both parents (or parent figures), the "identified patient," and any other key family member(s) (e.g., sibling, grandparent) should attend the meetings. The clinician can insist that both parents attend the meetings; this should not be used as a threat but should emphasize the importance of their input for understanding the problem and of their cooperation for resolving it. Within a single-parent family, the parent might invite another person who either cares for the child or is influential (e.g., the parent's partner, another family member, or friend). If a single parent has a partner living in the house, that partner is considered part of the family and should be invited to the family meeting. The clinician should discuss this first with the parent to gain his or her approval.

If only a portion of the family attends, the clinician and the members present at the meeting must decide if the "partial" family meeting has been beneficial. If it has not been, the clinician should ask the family to bring the other members at the next visit. If this is not possible, the clinician may have to discontinue family meetings. However, he or she can still follow an individual child and can continue to advocate for that child.

b. ***How are a tentative hypothesis and plan formed?*** A clinician that has preliminary information should develop a general hypothesis and plan. The information might come from prior knowledge of the child and family, the parent's stated problem, records of past psychosocial evaluations, or parent and teacher questionnaires, like the ANSER system. In other situations, the clinician has little prior knowledge or background information, so he or she may have to use the first interview to obtain enough information to be able to come up with either. In both cases, the clinician can form a broad, tentative hypothesis but should guard against jumping to conclusions (e.g., *"This family needs marital therapy"* or *"The mother needs to agree with the father more"*).

Avoiding the "Either/Or" Pitfall

The clinician should avoid the "either/or" pitfall (e.g., *"Is this parental depression or a temperamentally difficult child?"*). With family relationship problems, the "and/and" approach provides a more accurate hypothesis and differential diagnosis and lessens the chance of missing something important (e.g., *"This may be parental depression and a difficult child and career stresses and. . . ."*). The clinician should also factor any known strengths and/or resources (e.g., the support of extended family) into his or her hypothesis.

D. **Reviewing the seven elements of the family meeting.** The family meeting is a dynamic, interactive process with seven key elements. The clinician is more likely to conduct a successful and effective meeting if he or she reviews these elements prior to the meeting to refresh an understanding of each element's influence on the clinician–child–parent relationship (Table 3.2).

Table 3.2. Seven elements of the family meeting

1. The therapeutic triad: child, family, and clinician
2. The clinician–child relationship
3. The clinician–family relationship
4. The child–family relationship
5. The clinician's feelings
6. The child's and parent's feelings
7. The clinician as leader

1. *The therapeutic triad: child, family, and clinician.* One of the best predictors of a successful outcome for the child and the family is a good relationship among the child, the parents, and the clinician. The family influence is always present (e.g., family beliefs about health and illness or about the role of the child in the family). "Family" is defined as the parent(s) or any other person who is a major supportive figure for the child.

The therapeutic triad is built on three simultaneous interactions/relationships: the clinician–child relationship; the clinician–family relationship; and the child–family relationship. The clinician supports the child–family relationship, and the family supports the clinician–child relationship (Fig. 3.1).

2. *The clinician–child relationship.* Clinicians traditionally are trained in the clinician–patient biomedical model. In these cases, the patient is a child, so the family strongly influences the clinician-child relationship. For example, if the family perceives the clinician as competent and caring, it supports the clinician's role and relationship with the child. The family reminds the child how much the clinician cares for him or her, and it encourages the child to speak with and to trust the clinician. However, if the clinician

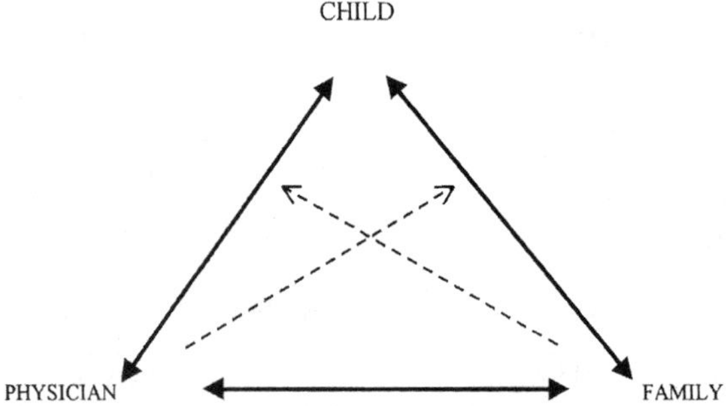

Figure 3.1. The therapeutic triad. (Adapted from Doherty W, Baird M. *Family therapy and family medicine*. New York: Guilford, 1983:13, with permission.)

focuses too intensely on the clinician–child relationship, he or she misses relevant family issues and fails to utilize family strengths, to gain the family's trust, and ultimately to help the family resolve the problem to its satisfaction.

3. *The clinician–family relationship.* For the clinician, developing and nurturing a good relationship with the family is critical for gaining its trust and cooperation. Because the therapeutic role of the family is an instrumental part in solving any problem, the clinician should cultivate its support. For example, a clinician that shows interest in the mother or father as a person is showing support for and expressing appreciation of their concerns and efforts. These parents will then be more likely to cooperate with the clinician's recommendations.

4. *The child–family relationship.* A major aim of the family interview is fostering the child–family relationship. This is best accomplished by supporting the dyadic relationships in the family (e.g., parent–child or parent–parent). Enlisting the support of significant others strengthens these dyadic relationships. For example, the mother–child relationship depends on the father's support, which in turn fosters the child–family relationship. As another example, one can look at the marital or parental relationship. A major influence on it is that of the in-laws, the child's grandparents. Parents can strengthen their own relationship by getting the grandparents' support. Grandparents can support the parents by taking the children for a night so that the parents could have time to themselves.

Strengthening Family Relationships

Family counseling is an admixture of family systems techniques and clinician-directed advice. If the grandparents criticize one or both parents, the clinician can suggest how they might all work together to change their behaviors and perceptions. He or she can help the grandparents realize how criticism weakens the child–family relationship and how support for the parents strengthens the child–family relationship.

5. *The clinician's feelings.* The clinician that is new to family interviewing might feel anxiety and self-doubt, fearing that he or she will be overwhelmed or unable to do enough or that intense feelings will be stirred up during the meeting.

The clinician can use the following tips to ease their own anxiety:

a. ***Select families carefully.*** The ideal family is one known from prior visits where a comfortable relationship exists.

b. ***Select problems carefully and focus only on one, such as tantrums or sleep problems.*** Do not attempt to solve all the family's problems.

c. ***Initially interview only the (seemingly) involved subsystem (e.g., mother and child or mother, father, and child), not all members of the household (e.g., siblings, grandparents).*** For the clinician who is just beginning at level 3 of family involvement, interviewing this subsystem may be sufficient. If it is not, the whole family may attend a later meeting when the clinician is more comfortable and skilled in his or her role.

d. ***Remember that progress will take time and effort.*** Informing the family of this sets realistic expectations and removes pressure from both the clinician and the family.

The clinician should also recall that experiencing a range of feelings about the family during the interview is normal. These can range from a "rescue fantasy" to respect and affection or even dislike. The clinician's role is to understand the nature of his or her own feelings and their origins, especially the negative ones, yet to support the family nonetheless. If those feelings interfere with the clinician–child–family relationship, the clinician should seek advice from more experienced colleagues. The clinician's effectiveness is enhanced when he or she remains aware of his or her own limitations. If the clinician's personal feelings remain problematic, the clinician should consider referring the family to another professional.

The Family's Feelings

The clinician should remain aware of the fact that the family members may feel one or more of the following ways:

- Worry about being perceived as incompetent or unreasonable;
- Anxiety about disclosing family secrets;
- Concern that the clinician won't like them or that he or she will disapprove of their parenting style;
- Uncomfortable because of a prior experience with another clinician or mental health worker;
- Vulnerable and exposed, which might make them defensive and guarded.

6. *The family's feelings.* Most families experience a variety of emotions in a family meeting. These can be put into two general categories, but the clinician should remember that many families experience both during the course of a family meeting.

a. ***Emotions associated with the family problems.*** Because family problems cause great emotional distress, families either bring these feelings to the meeting or find that they are stirred up during it. The emotions felt include resentment, fear, anger, depression, disappointment, sadness, and guilt. Families must ventilate or release these feelings and acknowledge them before they are willing or able to give an accurate history, to cooperate, or to follow the clinician's advice.

Some families ventilate spontaneously after sitting down; others require the aid of the clinician, who must acknowledge their mood and "invite" them to share their feelings, by saying something like the following: *"You look (sound) very worried (angry)," "How did that make you feel?"* or *"That must be very upsetting."* Many families feel better after venting, even if only for a few minutes, if they feel that they have been heard in a nonjudgmental way. After allowing the family to vent, the clinician should suggest that the family discuss its problem. *"I know this has been very sad for you; you have good reason to feel this way. Now I'd like to hear about your concern."*

b. ***Emotions associated with the meeting.*** Families fret about the visit. For families to feel ill at ease, guarded, or hesitant early in the session is very normal. Individual members may feel ashamed and embarrassed; they may wonder if they can really say what they want, if they can talk honestly with other family members, and if the discussion will remain confidential.

Members may also worry about what others will say about them and about what the clinician will think of them. Sometimes family members are anxious because they feel that that they will be blamed, be punished for, or be unloved because of the situation. Alternatively, an individual might be afraid of being hurt by or of hurting another's feelings. The family is also assessing the clinician for signs of support and openness or of disinterest or judgment. Each family member is asking himself or herself, *"Do I like and trust this person?"*

Responding to the Family's Feelings of Pain

Discussing family issues often evokes painful feelings (sadness, regret) from the members. When a member cries, the clinician should allow this individual to express his or her feelings without interruptions. Offering a tissue or making a reassuring statement too quickly might convey the impression that the crying should stop or that the clinician is uncomfortable. If the member attempts to downplay

continued on top of page

continued from bottom

his or her feelings or to stop the crying right away by saying something like, *"I'm so ashamed to be acting like this,"* or *"I didn't mean to be so emotional,"* the clinician should permit a few more moments of silence and/or encourage the member to share the feelings provoking the expression. The clinician can say, *"Stay with your feelings for a moment"* or *"You're doing fine."* This may be the first opportunity for this particular family member to share or express his or her feelings. Helping the family feel comfortable early on helps them express painful feelings later in the interview or in subsequent meetings.

To ease the family's worries, the clinician can offer the following words of encouragement:

"It's very normal for families to feel worried or nervous when they first arrive. I sense you are feeling that way, but I am certain you'll become a little more comfortable during our session."

"I want you to know that this meeting is a safe place in which each of you can share your personal feelings and can openly talk about what is important to you without being criticized or judged."

"I also want you to know that what happens here is confidential. You are certainly free to discuss this meeting with others who you trust, but that is your own personal family decision."

7. *The clinician as leader.* When a family agrees to a family meeting, it is admitting it needs guidance and support, which it looks for from the clinician. Therefore, the clinician must establish his or her leadership early in the first visit. Remaining passive and silent or deferring to the parent will not work; the clinician must actively lead, coach, and facilitate positive family interactions and problem solving. He or she demonstrates that leadership by organizing and structuring the session (with rules, if necessary), by interviewing effectively, and by adhering to the principles and goals of the interview. (See Chapter 5, "Facilitating a Successful Family Interview," for further discussion of this topic.) However, as families become more

Realization for the Clinician

The family interview is more than a set of applied skills and techniques. It is an intensely human experience that evokes strong feelings in the clinician and the family.

capable and confident, the clinician can transfer the leadership role to the parents, where it belongs.

V. **Summary**

Getting ready for a family meeting entails shifting the focus to a family context and organizing and preparing for the meeting. Five specific tasks follow:

- Detecting the problem—identifying a problem that would benefit from a family approach.
- Suggesting the meeting—explaining the purpose of the family meeting in a way that makes them willing to accept the suggestion.
- Arranging the office—finding adequate space for the meeting and having the right equipment.
- Planning the meeting—using the pre-meeting phase to plan who should attend and to form a tentative hypothesis.
- Reviewing the elements of the meeting, including the three components of the therapeutic triad: the clinician's feelings, the family's feelings, and the clinician as leader.

ADDITIONAL READINGS

Allmond B, Tanner JL. *The family is the patient*, 2nd ed. Baltimore: Williams & Wilkins, 1998.

ANSER system. Levine MD. Cambridge, MA: Education Publishing Service, 1997.

Barkley R. The families of ADHD children. In: *Attention deficit hyperactivity disorder*. New York: Guilford Press, 1990:130–168.

Coleman WL. The first interview with a family. In: Coleman WL, Taylor EH, eds. *Family focused pediatrics. Pediatr Clin N Am* 1995; 42(1):119–129.

Cummings EM, Davies P. *Children and marital conflict*. New York: Guilford Press, 1994.

Doherty WJ, Baird MA. *Family therapy and family medicine*. New York: Guilford Press, 1983.

Haley J. *Problem-solving therapy*. San Francisco: Jossey-Bass, 1976.

Hetherington EM, Cox M, Cox R. The effects of divorce on parents and children. In: Lamb ME, ed. *Nontraditional families*. Hillsdale, NJ: Erlbaum, 1982.

Levine MD. Attention and dysfunction of attention. In: Levine MD, Carey WB, Crocker AC, eds. *Developmental–behavioral pediatrics*, 3rd ed. Philadelphia: WB Saunders, 1999.

McDaniel S, Campbell TL, Seaburn DB. *Family-oriented primary care*. New York: Springer-Verlag, 1990.

Minichun S, Fishman HC. *Family therapy techniques*. Cambridge, MA: Harvard University Press, 1981.

Papp P. *The process of change*. New York: Guilford Press, 1983.

Richman JM, Chapman MV, Bowen GL. Recognizing the impact of marital discord and parental depression on children. In: Coleman WL, Taylor EH, eds. *Family-focused pediatrics. Pediatr Clin N Am* 1995;42(1):167–180.

Schmitt B. Pediatric counseling. In: Levine MD, Carey WB, Crocker AC, eds. *Developmental–behavioral pediatrics*, 3rd ed. Philadelphia: WB Saunders, 1999.

4 Coding and Documenting for Reimbursement*

Stephen B. Sulkes

I. Purpose

On first examination, coding and documentation may seem complex and arcane. Unquestionably, these issues distract the clinician. On the other hand, these keys to reimbursement, once mastered and individualized to the clinician's specific practice, become fairly automatic. The clinician can document and report in a standardized manner to provide maximum reimbursement while still providing optimal patient care.

Clinicians must be adequately reimbursed for their services. These problems, which often present initially as behavioral–interactional complaints (hereafter referred to as psychosocial pediatrics), on further investigation often reveal family–psychosocial issues necessitating a family-centered approach. Clinicians must adapt their practices to accommodate the growing number of children with psychosocial problems. These adaptations also must extend to billing functions so that the clinician is adequately reimbursed.

This chapter describes ways to convince insurance companies to reimburse the clinician, six methods of diagnostic and procedural coding, documentation procedures, board certification credentialing issues, use of a business manager, and consulting codes.

II. Convincing Insurance Companies to Reimburse Clinicians

As managed care is penetrating most communities, clinicians must work closely with health care insurers. Many insurers believe that clinicians provide only biomedical care in very short visits and that mental health professionals provide therapy in extended visits. Therefore, clinicians must inform insurers that they too work with families to resolve psychosocial problems and that doing so is time-efficient, clinically effective, and fiscally prudent.

The clinician must think like an insurer. When negotiating with insurers, his or her goal is to convince them that the care to be provided is of high quality and is offered at the same or lower cost as that of other providers dealing with the same problems. Insurers require efficient quality care in the primary setting and a justification of the clinician's utilization of services.

A. **Justifying the clinician's role in treating psychosocial problems.** Insurers want clinicians to see families in the primary setting. Clinicians should consider the following concerns of insurers:

1. *Insurers want to save money.* If a clinician did not manage the problem without assistance, who would and at what

*Stephen B. Sulkes, M.D., is in the Department of Pediatrics in the Strong Center for Developmental Disabilities, Children's Hospital at Strong, Box 671, 601 Elmwood Ave., Rochester, NY 14642.

costs? Therefore, providing quality care in the primary setting reduces costs.

2. *Insurers want mental health referrals to decrease.* They want patients with psychosocial problems to stay in the primary care setting. With an initial evaluation, a clinician can provide early and effective therapy without a mental health referral.

B. **Justifying the clinician's utilization of service.** Insurers want validation for the clinician's utilization of services. The clinician should consider the services that insurers are willing to pay for and address some of the following issues.

1. *The clinician must recognize that time is the main component for helping families resolve psychosocial problems.* The clinician must ask himself or herself, "How much time will I spend with the child and family?"

2. *Will the clinician reduce the number or types of lab tests?*

3. *Will the clinician prescribe less medication or lower cost medications* (e.g., generic or other lower cost equivalent medications)?

CASE 1: A TEENAGER WITH ATTENTION-DEFICIT/HYPERACTIVITY DISORDER, ADJUSTMENT DISORDER, AND ALCOHOL ABUSE

Jason, a 14-year-old eighth grader, has a history of good academic skills but also is demonstrating difficulty with attention focus. His clinician treated him with stimulant medication from age 10 with clear symptomatic improvement but noted that stress related to his younger sister's cystic fibrosis might affect his emerging learning difficulties. Because Jason's grades have recently declined, his parents have requested that his school psychologist conduct an evaluation. Jason's IQ is in the high average range, and his reading and math achievement scores are average to above average. Jason's mother notes that he is looking forward to entering the same competitive high school as his older brother, but she worries that he won't pass the entrance exam. She reports that the sister's cystic fibrosis is stable at the moment.

During the same visit, the clinician suggests that he and Jason talk privately without the mother. Jason expresses his dislike of taking medication but, at the same time, conveys his strong desire to enter the competitive high school with his brother and his friends. In response to confidential questioning, Jason acknowledges that, on weekends, he and his friends have been doing a "fair amount" of drinking involving "funneling 40-ouncers" of beer. He says that his mother does not know much about his drinking. The clinician performs a brief physical examination that focuses on stimulant side-effect checks and an abbreviated neurologic exam.

The clinician schedules two separate confidential counseling sessions for Jason and his mother, each 30 minutes long, to discuss the issues raised in this visit. In the session with Jason, the clinician focuses on the stresses that Jason is experiencing and elicits more details of the alcohol abuse. The session with the mother focuses on family system issues.

The clinician must then record procedural and diagnostic codes for these visits.

First Meeting

Procedural coding for the first session with this established patient, lasting 30 minutes and including 20 minutes of counseling and discussion, is coded by the clinician at the 99214 (detailed) level because the counseling was the major component. It could also be coded at the lower 99212 (problem-focused) level, based mainly on the history and examination performed.

Diagnostic coding might include 314.00 (Attention Deficit Disorder, predominantly inattentive type), 309.0 (Adjustment Disorder with Depressed Mood), and 303.02 (Alcohol Abuse, Episodic).

Second Meeting

Procedural coding is at the 99214 (comprehensive) level if it is based on the patient being an "established patient." If the clinician chooses to bill as a psychotherapist, the 30-minute counseling session with Jason could be coded 90804, and the session with the mother could be coded 90805 (30-minute therapy session, with/without patient present).

Diagnostic coding would be the same for all follow-up counseling sessions.

Maximizing Reimbursement

The clinician maximizes his or her reimbursement by using the most descriptive and appropriate codes when submitting charges to insurers.

III. **Methods of Diagnostic and Procedural Coding Systems**

Insurers have standardized codes, called diagnostic codes and procedure codes, to keep track of their expenses. Doing so allows them to maintain a uniform measure of information from different types of claims and to determine reimbursement.

A. **Diagnostic coding.**

1. *International Classification of Disease, Clinical Modification, 9th edition (ICD-9-CM).* The World Health Organization has developed the *International Classification of Disease, Clinical Modification*, which is currently in its ninth edition (ICD-9-CM). This reference is organized by affected organ systems and by subclassifications of acquired injuries.

The ICD-9-CM is published in three volumes. Volume I is a numeric listing of codes organized by conditions in various organ systems. Volume II, the alphabetic index, is the most useful one for clinical coding. The clinician routinely uses this volume to look up codes for specific clinical diagnoses. Volume III is devoted to surgical and diagnostic procedures (based on anatomy) and is of limited value to the clinician treating psychosocial problems (see "Procedural Coding" following Case 2 below).

Insurers generally accept ICD-9-CM codes for billing purposes. For quick reference clinicians can review their records and compile a list of the most frequently used codes from Volume II of the ICD-9-CM. In addition, lists of codes in alphabetically searchable forms are available for personal digital assistants (PDA) and other hand-held computing devices.

Figure 4.1, an example of an encounter form, lists commonly used diagnostic codes grouped by problem category. It also lists *Current procedural terminology* (CPT) codes.

Specifying the diagnosis helps ensure adequate reimbursement. The digits before (to the left of) the decimal point in an ICD-9-CM code indicate a general range of diagnoses. Adding at least one digit after (to the right of) the decimal point provides diagnostic specificity. Additional digits can be added to describe whether the condition is acute or chronic and/or active or residual. For example, for maximal specificity of an attention-deficit/hyperactivity disorder (ADHD), the second digit after the decimal point in codes 314.00 (Attention-Deficit/Hyperactivity Disorder, predominantly inattentive type) and 314.01 (Attention-Deficit/Hyperactivity Disorder, predominantly hyperactive-impulsive type or combined type) indicates a more exact diagnosis than if that digit were removed (Fig. 4.2B). An overall guide to ICD-9-CM coding is provided in Fig. 4.2A.

Diagnostic Codes

DSM-IV diagnostic codes are carried over to the ICD-9-CM. The clinician should ensure that the definition of a code in ICD-9-CM matches that in DSM-IV, since insurers depend on the ICD-9-CM.

2. *Diagnostic and Statistical Manual, 4th edition (DSM-IV).*

The American Psychiatric Association's *Diagnostic and statistical manual*, 4th edition (DSM-IV) is familiar to all those who deal with mental health problems. The DSM-IV is especially useful for specifying the diagnostic criteria for various classifications of mental health conditions. The clinician can identify the complexity of mental and behavioral

(*text continues on page 52*)

Encounter Form						No Show:		
Patient Name:			Unit #:			Date of Service		
Insert coinciding Clinical/Specialist # (C/S#) next to Diagnosis AND Procedure Code C/S# Please Initial			C/S# Please Initial					
1 Pediatrics:			4 Education:			7 Psychiatry:		
2 Psychology:			5 Nursing:			8 Other:		
3 Social Work:			6 Speech:					
C/S#	**Consultation CPT Code**		**C/S#**	**Established Patient Code**		**C/S#**	**Proc. / Tsting CPT Code**	
	99245	High Complexity		99215	Comprehensive		64640	Botox Injection
	99244	Moderate Complexity		99214	Detailed HX		43760	G-Tube Change
	99243	Low Complexity		99213	Expanded Problem Focused		96100	Psych Testing
	99242	Expanded Problem Focused		99212	Problem Focused		96115	Neurobehavior status exam
	99241	Problem Focused					90887	Parent Interpretive Conf
	Attention Deficit Disorder			*Cognition*			*Sleep Disorders*	
	314.01	ADHD		783.4	Global Delay (psychological)		307.41	Sleep Disorder – Insomnia
	314.00	ADD Without Hyperactivity		317	MR Mild (50-70)		307.45	Sleep Cycle disruption
	314.1	Hyperkinesis W/ Devel. Delay		318.0	MR Moderate (35-49)		780.59	Sleep Apnea
	314.2	Hyperkinetic Conduct Disord.		318.2	MR Profound (under 20)		307.46	Night Terrors
	314	Unspec. Hyperkinetic Synd.		318.1	MR Severe (20-34)		307.46	Sleepwalking
	Behavior Disorder			319	MR Unspecified		780.54	Excessive Sleepiness
	312.81	Conduct Disord, Childhood		315.5	Mixed Dvlpmntl. Disability		292.89	Sleep Disord-medication induced
	312.82	Conduct Disord, Adolescent		315.8	Other Spec. delays in Dev.		*Tic Disorders*	
	312.0	Conduct Disord, Aggressive		315.9	Unspec. Dvlpmntl. Disability		307.20	Tic Disorder Unspec.
	312.1	Conduct Disord, Unaggress.		*Feeding/Eating/Elimination*			307.21	Tic Disorder Transient
	313.81	Oppositional Disorder		307.6	Enuresis		307.22	Tic Disorder Chronic
	299.8	Other Spec. Chldhd. Psych.		307.7	Encopresis w/o constipation		307.23	Tourette's Syndrome

	Code	Diagnosis		Code	Diagnosis		Code	Diagnosis
	312.34	Explosive Disorder		787.6	Encopresis w/ constipation		*Adjustment Disorders*	
	307.3	Stereotypic Behavior (SIB)		783.4	Failure to Thrive		303	with Depressed Mood
	307.52	Pica Disorder		783.3	Feeding Disorder		309.24	with Anxiety
	312.39	Trichotillomania		783.0	Loss of Appetite		309.28	+ Mixed Anxiety/Depressed Mood
	312.9	Delinquency		564.0	Constipation		309.30	With Conduct Disturbance
		Tantrums		787.2	Dysphagia		309.9	Unspecified
	Autism Spectrum Disorders			278.00	Obesity		742.1	Microcephaly
	299.80	Asperger's/PDD		*Depression*			237.72	Neurofibromatosis Type I
	299.00	Autism		296.2	Depression, single episode			
	Learning Disorders			296.3	Depression, recurrent			
	313.83	Acad. Underachive. Disord.		311	Depression NOS			
	315.01	Alexia		300.4	Dysthymic Disorder			
	315.02	Developmental Dyslexia		309.0	Adjustmt. Dis., Depresd mood			
	315.2	Other Spec. Learng Difficult.		*Anxiety*				
	315	Reading Disord. Unspec.		313.0	Overanxious Disorder			
	315.1	Specific Arithmetic Disorder		300.29	School Phobia			
	315.4	Coordination Disorder		309.21	Separation Anxiety			
	315.2	Written Expression Disorder		300.3	OCD			
	315.9	Learning Disorder NOS		300.00	Anxiety State, unspecified			
	Speech/Language Disorders			300.01	Panic Disorder			
	315.32	Receptive Lang. Disorder		300.02	Generalized anxiety disorder			
	315.39	Dev. Articulation Disorder		*Sensory Impairment*				
	315.31	Dvlpmtl. Lang. Disorder		389.00	Hearing Loss Conductive			
	313.23	Elective Mutism		389.1	Hearing Loss Sensorineural		**Primary DX:**	
	307.0	Fluency Disorder		389.2	Mixed Conductive&Sensorineural		**Secondary DX:**	
	307.9	Communication Disorder NOS		369.20	Visual Impairmnt/Low Vision		**Other DX:**	
				369.9	Vision Loss/Blindness			

Figure 4.1. A developmental–behavioral practice encounter form, showing commonly used *International Classification of Disease, Clinical Modification*, 9th edition codes.

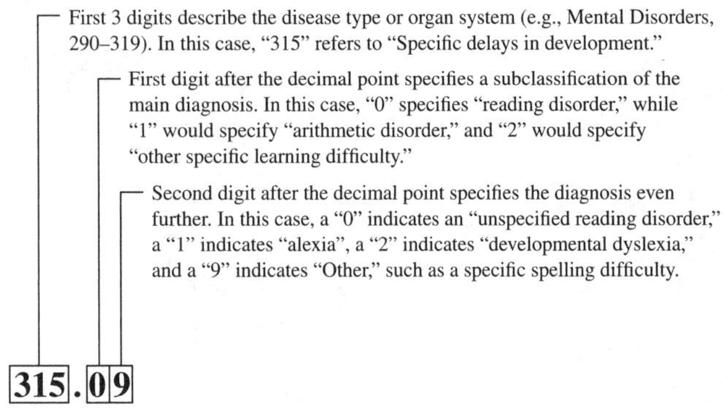

Anatomy of an ICD-9-CM code
First 3 digits describe the disease type or organ system (e.g., Mental Disorders, 290–319). In this case, "315" refers to "Specific delays in development."
First digit after the decimal point specifies a subclassification of the main diagnosis. In this case, "0" specifies "reading disorder," while "1" would specify "arithmetic disorder," and "2" would specify "other specific learning difficulty."
Second digit after the decimal point specifies the diagnosis even further. In this case, a "0" indicates an "unspecified reading disorder," a "1" indicates "alexia", a "2" indicates "developmental dyslexia," and a "9" indicates "Other," such as a specific spelling difficulty.
315.09

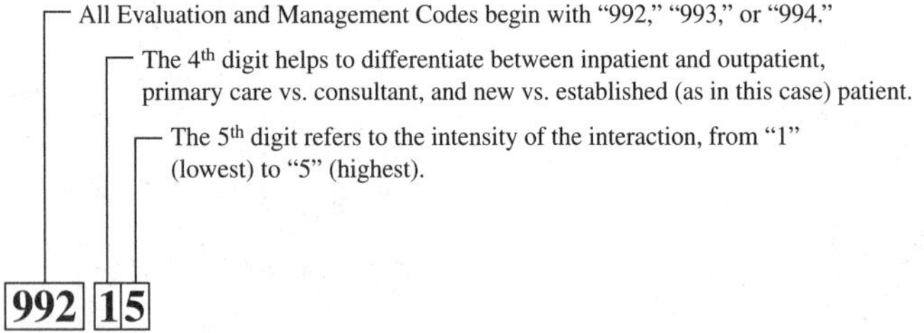

Anatomy of an Evaluation and Management (E&M) CPT code
All Evaluation and Management Codes begin with "992," "993," or "994."
The 4th digit helps to differentiate between inpatient and outpatient, primary care vs. consultant, and new vs. established (as in this case) patient.
The 5th digit refers to the intensity of the interaction, from "1" (lowest) to "5" (highest).
992 15

Figure 4.2. A: Anatomy of an *International classification of disease, clinical modification*, 9th edition (ICD-9-CM) code and of a *Current procedural terminology* (CPT) code.

diagnoses by using the DSM-IV's well-known "multiaxial" system to consider all the factors going into a diagnosis.

Axis I	Clinical disorders and other conditions that may be a focus of clinical attention
Axis II	Personality disorders and mental retardation
Axis III	General medical conditions
Axis IV	Psychosocial and environmental problems
Axis V	Global assessment of functioning

3. *Classification of Child and Adolescent Mental Diagnoses in Primary Care (DSM-PC).* In 1996, the American Academy of Pediatrics, collaborating with the American Psychiatric Association, published the *Classification of child*

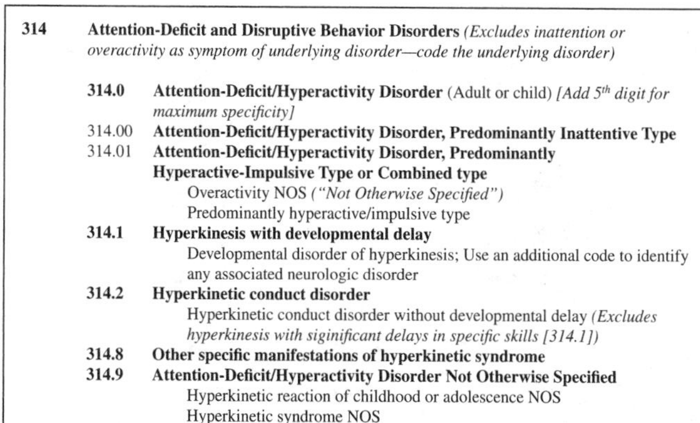

314 **Attention-Deficit and Disruptive Behavior Disorders** *(Excludes inattention or overactivity as symptom of underlying disorder—code the underlying disorder)*

314.0 **Attention-Deficit/Hyperactivity Disorder** (Adult or child) *[Add 5th digit for maximum specificity]*

314.00 **Attention-Deficit/Hyperactivity Disorder, Predominantly Inattentive Type**

314.01 **Attention-Deficit/Hyperactivity Disorder, Predominantly Hyperactive-Impulsive Type or Combined type**

Overactivity NOS *("Not Otherwise Specified")*

Predominantly hyperactive/impulsive type

314.1 **Hyperkinesis with developmental delay**

Developmental disorder of hyperkinesis; Use an additional code to identify any associated neurologic disorder

314.2 **Hyperkinetic conduct disorder**

Hyperkinetic conduct disorder without developmental delay *(Excludes hyperkinesis with siginificant delays in specific skills [314.1])*

314.8 **Other specific manifestations of hyperkinetic syndrome**

314.9 **Attention-Deficit/Hyperactivity Disorder Not Otherwise Specified**

Hyperkinetic reaction of childhood or adolescence NOS

Hyperkinetic syndrome NOS

Figure 4.2. B: ICD-9-CM coding structure for attention-deficit/hyperactivity disorder.

and adolescent mental diagnoses in primary care, known as the DSM-PC Child and Adolescent version. The book's introduction states that it "is intended to help primary care clinicians better identify psychosocial factors affecting their patients so that they can provide interventions when appropriate, be reimbursed for those interventions, and identify and refer patients who require more sophisticated mental health care." Table 4.1 illustrates the DSM-PC categorization of manifestations (presenting complaints).

The following two aspects of the DSM-PC are noteworthy:

a. ***Recognition that developmental and behavioral conditions are classified by three levels of function, ranging from "normal" to "problem" to "disordered."***

b. ***Recognition that social–environmental factors ("V" codes) impact a child's mental health (e.g., a child's family, school, social, and physical factors).***

The clinician determines a diagnosis for a child's problem using the DSM-PC to consider first whether the manifestation represents normal developmental variation, a problem (the dysfunction is more persistent and begins to interfere with other aspects of life), or a disorder (problem meets DSM-IV diagnostic criteria). Second, the clinician considers other environmental factors that might exacerbate or ameliorate the situation. Codes for both manifestations and environmental factors can be listed to portray the child's status with maximum accuracy. Table 4.2 describes DSM-PC codes for environmental situations (represented in ICD-9-CM as "V" codes).

(*text continues on page 57*)

Table 4.1. The *Classification of child and adolescent mental diagnoses in primary care* (DSM-PC) categorization of manifestations (presenting complaints)

Manifestation	Variation Codes	Problem Codes	Disorder Codes
1. Developmental competencies	V65.4 (Developmental Variation) V65.49 (Learning Variation) V65.49 (Coordination Variation) V65.49 (Language Variation)	V62.3 (Developmental Problem) V40.0 (Learning Problem) 781.3 (Coordination Problem) V40.1 (Language Problem)	317, 318.x, 319 (Mental Retardation) 315.x (Learning Disabilities) 315.4 (Coordination Disorder) 315.3x, 307.9, 307.0 (Speech–Language Disorders)
2. Impulsive, overactive, and inattentive behaviors	V65.49 (Overactive Variation) V65.49 (Inattention Variation)	V40.3 (Hyperactive/Impulsive Behavior Problem) V40.3 (Inattention Problem)	314.x (Attention Deficit/ Hyperactivity Disorders)
3. Negative, antisocial behaviors	V65.49 (Negative Emotional Behavior Variation) V65.49, V65.4 (Aggressive/Oppositional Variation) V65.49 (Secretive Antisocial Behavior Variation)	V71.02 (Negative Emotional Behavior Problem) V71.02 (Oppositional or Aggressive Problem V71.02 (Secretive Antisocial Behavior Problem)	No specific disorder; consider Adjustment Disorder 313.81, 312.8x (Oppositional Defiant, Conduct Disorder) 312.8x, 309.3, 312.9 (Conduct, Adjustment, or Disruptive Disorder)
4. Substance use/abuse	V65.49 (Substance Use Variation)	V71.09 (Substance Abuse Problem)	305.xx, 303.xx (Substance Abuse/Intoxication, Substance Dependence)

5. Emotions and moods	V65.49 (Anxious Variation)	V40.2 (Anxiety Problem)	300.2, 300.23, 309.21, 300.31, 309.81 (Anxiety Disorder, Phobias, Separation Anxiety Disorder, Panic Disorder, Posttraumatic Stress Disorder)
	V65.49, V62.82 (Sadness Variation, Bereavement)	V40.3 (Sadness Problem)	296.2x, 296.3x, 300.4, 311, 296.0x, 296.89 (Major Depression, Dysthymia, Bipolar Disorders)
	V65.49 (Ritual Variation)	V40.3 (Ritual, Obsessive, Compulsive Problem)	300.3 (Obsessive-Compulsive Disorder)
	V65.49 (Thoughts of Death Variation)	V40.2 (Thoughts of Death Problem)	313.89 (Suicidal Ideation/Attempts)
6. Somatic and sleep behaviors	V65.49 (Somatic Complaint Variation)	V40.3 (Somatic Complaint Problem)	300.8x, 300.1x (Somatoform, Pain, Conversion Disorder)
	V65.49 (Excessive Sleepiness Variation)	V40.3 (Excessive Sleepiness Problem)	307.44, 307.45, 347 (Excess Sleep Disorders)
	V65.49 (Insomnia Variation)	V40.3 (Sleeplessness Problem)	307.42, 307.47, 307.45 (Insomnia, Dyssomnia, Circadian Rhythm Disorders)
	V65.49 (Nocturnal Arousals Variation)	V40.3 (Nocturnal Arousals Problem)	307.46, 307.47 (Sleep Terror, Sleepwalking Disorders, Other Parasomnia)
7. Feeding, eating, elimination behaviors	V65.49 (Soiling Variation)	V40.3 (Soiling Problem)	787.6, 307.7 (Encopresis with/without Constipation)

(continued)

Table 4.1. *Continued*

Manifestation	Variation Codes	Problem Codes	Disorder Codes
	V65.49 (Day or Nighttime Wetting Variation)	V40.3 (Wetting Problem)	307.6 (Enuresis)
	V65.49 (Purging/Binge-Eating Variation)	V69.19 (Purging/Binge-Eating Problem)	307.51 (Bulimia Nervosa)
	V65.49 (Dieting/Body Image Variation)	V65.49 (Dieting/Body Image Problem)	307.1 (Anorexia Nervosa)
	V65.49 (Inadequate or Excessive Nutrition Intake Variation)	V40.3 (Inadequate or Excessive Nutrition Intake Problem)	307.59 (Feeding Disorder of Infancy or Childhood)
8. Illness-related behaviors	V65.49 (Health-related Behaviors Variation)	V15.81 (Health-related Behaviors Problem)	316 (Psychological Factors Affecting Medical Condition)
9. Sexual behaviors	V65.49 (Cross-Gender Behavior Variation)	V40.3 (Cross-Gender Behavior Problem)	302.6, 302.85 (Gender Identity Disorder, Childhood or Adolescent)
	V65.49 (Sexual Behavior Variation)	V40.3 (Sexual Behavior Problem)	302.9 (Sexual Disorder, Not Otherwise Specified)
10. Atypical behaviors	V65.49 (Repetitive Behaviors Variation)	V65.49 (Repetitive Behaviors Problem)	307.3 (Stereotypic Movement Disorder)
	V65.49 (Social Interaction Variation)	V40.3 (Social Interaction Problem)	312.39 (Trichotillomania) 307.2x (Tic Disorders)
	293.0 (Delirium Due to a General Medical Condition)	—	299.x (Autism Spectrum Disorders)

Tables 4.1–4.3, 4.5, and 4.6 have all been adapted from *Diagnostic and statistical manual for primary care* (DSM-PC). *Child and adolescent version*. Elk Grove Village, IL: American Academy of Pediatrics, 1996.

Table 4.2. ***Classification of child and adolescent mental diagnoses in primary care*** **(DSM-PC) codes for environmental situations**[a]

1. Challenges to primary support group (e.g., death of a parent, marital discord, domestic violence) (V61.20, others)
2. Changes in caregiving (e.g., foster care/adoption, abuse/neglect, parental substance abuse, parental physical/mental illness) (V61.20, others)
3. Other functional changes in a family (e.g., addition of a sibling or a stepparent) (V61.2, others)
4. Community or social challenges (e.g., acculturation, religious problems) (V62.4, others)
5. Educational challenges (e.g., parental illiteracy, inadequate school facilities, discord with teachers) (V62.3)
6. Occupational challenges for parents or adolescents (V62.2, others)
7. Housing challenges (e.g., homelessness, unsafe neighborhood, dislocation) (V60.0, others)
8. Economic challenges (e.g., poverty) (V60.2)
9. Inadequate access to health/mental health services (V61.9)
10. Legal system problem for parent or child (V62.5)
11. Other environmental situations (e.g., natural disasters, witness of violence) (V62.8)
12. Acute or chronic health conditions (V61.49)

[a] Represented in *International classification of diseases, clinical modification,* 9th edition, as "V" codes.

CASE 2: A CHILD WITH A SLEEP DISORDER AND FAMILY STRESSES

Jami, a 4-year-old girl, will sleep only in her parents' bed. History reveals that she falls asleep on the sofa each evening while her parents watch television. They transfer her to her own bed when she is sound asleep. At about 1 A.M., she appears in the parents' room and refuses to go back to her own bed. This began about a year ago, coincident with a bout of reactive airway disease during which Jami's parents closely monitored her for several nights. Her current medications include oral bronchodilators. Review of systems is negative for headaches, rashes, abdominal pain, bowel or bladder problems, sore throat, and vision/hearing problems. Recent family stresses include her mother's new job and declining health of the paternal grandmother, who lives in the same community. Jami attends a preschool/daycare center 5 days a week; no problems have been identified in that environment.

Physical examination shows normal growth. Skin; head, eyes, ears, nose, and throat (HEENT); chest (no wheezes); heart; abdomen; extremity; and neurologic exams are normal. The clinician does not order any lab studies.

The clinician spends 25 minutes exploring the stresses the family is experiencing as well as discussing bedtime management. A bedtime behavior management plan, which includes Jami starting the night in her own bed as well as reinforcements for staying there all night, is developed. A follow-up visit is scheduled in 2 weeks.

The clinician must now record diagnostic and procedural codes.

Diagnostic Coding

Using the DSM-PC, the clinician could apply several diagnostic codes:

- 307.42 (primary insomnia), if the problem is viewed as persistent and highly stressful to patient and family;
- 780.52 (secondary insomnia, due to a medical condition), if the medication effects are felt to be predominant;
- V40.3 (insomnia/sleeplessness problem, with partial arousals), if this is not causing clinically significant distress or impairment during daytime functioning;
- V65.49 (insomnia/sleeplessness variation), if the problem is different from the usual pattern for this child, does not appear to be medication-related, and is not affecting daytime behavior.

Procedural Coding

Since Jami is an established patient and the clinician spent 25 minutes on counseling and 15 minutes for the history and physical examination, the clinician could use a procedure code of 99215 (comprehensive outpatient visit, established patient).

B. **Procedural coding.**

1. *Current Procedural Terminology, 4th edition.* Each year the American Medical Association updates its list of procedural codes. This listing of services, *Current Procedural Terminology*, 4th edition (CPT-4), is designed "to provide a uniform language that will accurately describe medical, surgical, and diagnostic services . . . for reliable nationwide communication among clinicians, patients, and third parties." Virtually all insurers, including Medicaid, base their reimbursement schedules on CPT-4 codes.

CPT-4 is broadly organized into organ systems, with thousands of codes for a myriad of surgical and other technical procedures. It devotes little space to interactions that require interviewing, examining, and talking with patients and families.

Procedural Codes

All insurers, including Medicaid, base their reimbursement schedules on CPT-4 codes.

2. *Evaluation and Management codes.* Most procedures related to psychosocial problems, such as interviewing and counseling, fall into the group of codes called Evaluation

and Management (E&M) Codes. E&M codes are classified based on the following factors:

a. ***Whether the patient is new to the clinician.***

b. ***Where the interaction occurred*** (e.g., hospital inpatient, emergency department, outpatient, intensive care unit, neonatal intensive care unit, the patient's home, skilled nursing facility, or other residential setting).

c. ***Whether the clinician is the primary clinician or a consultant.***

The good news regarding E&M codes is that they are universally recognized. However, all insurers do not accept all codes. If a procedure does not have a CPT code assigned to it, getting an insurer to reimburse the physician for it will be hard. On the other hand, a CPT code's existence does not guarantee that a given insurer will be willing to reimburse for it.

A notable example of this situation is CPT code 99361 for an interdisciplinary team conference lasting 30 minutes. The insurer may have never been billed for this service and thus may hesitate to add it to its list of reimbursable procedures, even though the service is a regular part of the clinician's practice. The clinician can justify the addition of this code to the insurer's approved list by explaining to the insurer that no other CPT code definition describes such interdisciplinary conferences. The alternative for the insurer would be to receive individual bills from each member of the team, a more costly alternative.

Evaluation and Management (E&M) Codes

Most procedures related to psychosocial problems fall under E&M codes.

Another reason that insurers often hesitate to add a new code to their list is their fear that it will be widely used by clinicians from numerous specialties. Consequently, insurers limit the use of E&M codes to specific individual clinicians or situations. An example is CPT code 90887, which covers a review of records. Since all kinds of physicians might want to bill for record review, a special justification for its use in psychosocial pediatrics might be that, upon reviewing records from a school or other source, evaluations might be referred to other sites rather than to the developmental-behavioral pediatrician (e.g., to a school in the case of a complete school-based evaluation given under special education law or to a mental health professional for therapy when the primary physician's psychosocial evaluation would only delay inevitable and necessary therapy).

(*text continues on page 64*)

Table 4.3. Common evaluation and management codes

CPT* Code	Site	Relationship	History	Exam (1995 rules)	Decision Complexity	Approx. Time
99201	Outpt.	New (Primary)	Problem-Focused	Problem-Focused	Straightforward	10
99202	Outpt.	New (Primary)	Expanded Problem-Focused	Expanded Problem-Focused	Straightforward	20
99203	Outpt.	New (Primary)	Detailed	Detailed	Low	30
99204	Outpt.	New (Primary)	Comprehensive	Comprehensive	Moderate	45
99205	Outpt.	New (Primary)	Comprehensive	Comprehensive	High	60
99241	Outpt.	Consultant	Problem-Focused	Problem-Focused	Straightforward	15
99242	Outpt.	Consultant	Expanded Problem-Focused	Expanded Problem-Focused	Straightforward	30
99243	Outpt.	Consultant	Detailed	Detailed	Low	40
99244	Outpt.	Consultant	Comprehensive	Comprehensive	Moderate	60
99245	Outpt.	Consultant	Comprehensive	Comprehensive	High	80
99211	Outpt.	Established (Primary or Consultant)	M.D. presence may not be needed			5
99212	Outpt.	Established (Primary or Consultant)	Problem-Focused	Problem-Focused	Straightforward	10
99213	Outpt.	Established (Primary or Consultant)	Expanded Problem-Focused	Expanded Problem-Focused	Low	15

99214	Outpt.	Established (Primary or Consultant)	Detailed	Detailed	Moderate	25
99215	Outpt.	Established (Primary or Consultant)	Comprehensive	Comprehensive	High	40
99221	Inpt.	New (Attending)	Detailed	Detailed	Low	30
99222	Inpt.	New (Attending)	Comprehensive	Comprehensive	Moderate	50
99223	Inpt.	New (Attending)	Comprehensive	Comprehensive	High	70
99251	Inpt.	New (Consultant)	Problem-Focused	Problem-Focused	Straightforward	20
99252	Inpt.	New (Consultant)	Expanded Problem-Focused	Expanded Problem-Focused	Straightforward	40
99253	Inpt.	New (Consultant)	Detailed	Detailed	Low	55
99254	Inpt.	New (Consultant)	Comprehensive	Comprehensive	Moderate	80
99255	Inpt.	New (Consultant)	Comprehensive	Comprehensive	High	110
99231/61	Inpt.	Subsequent (Attending/Consultant)	Problem-Focused	Problem-Focused	Low	15/10
99232/62	Inpt.	Subsequent (Attending/Consultant)	Expanded Problem-Focused	Expanded Problem-Focused	Moderate	25/20
99233/63	Inpt.	Subsequent (Attending/Consultant)	Detailed	Detailed	High	35/30
90804	Outpt.	Psychotherapy (Face-to-face)				20–30
90805	Outpt.	Psychotherapy (Face-to-face) with medical evaluation/management				20–30

continued

Table 4.3. *Continued*

CPT* Code	Site	Relationship	History	Exam (1995 rules)	Decision Complexity	Approx. Time
90806	Outpt.	Psychotherapy (Face-to-face)				45–50
90807	Outpt.	Psychotherapy (Face-to-face) with medical evaluation/ management				45–50
90808	Outpt.	Psychotherapy (Face-to-face)				75–80
90809	Outpt.	Psychotherapy (Face-to-face) with medical evaluation/ management				75–80
90887	N/A	Review of testing performed by others				
99358	All	Prolonged MD services (Patient not present)				First 60 min.
99359	All	Prolonged MD services (Patient not present)				Each addt'l. 30 min.
99354	All	Prolonged MD services (Patient present)				First 60 min.
99355	All	Prolonged MD services (Patient present)				Each addt'l. 30 min.
99371	All	Telephone case management	Brief			**

99372	All	Telephone case management	Intermediate	**
99373	All	Telephone case management	Complex	**
99374	All	MD supervision of multi-disciplinary team (review care plan, review reports, communications, etc.)		15–29
99375	All	MD supervision of multi-disciplinary team (review care plan, review reports, communications, etc.)		30+
99401	All	Preventive Counseling		15
99402	All	Preventive Counseling		30
99403	All	Preventive Counseling		45
99404	All	Preventive Counseling		60
90801	All	Psychiatric Diagnostic Interview		—
99802	All	Psychiatric Diagnostic Interview with play equipment, physical devices, language interpreter, or other communication aid		—

*Note—not all codes will be accepted by all insurers for all physicians. Credentialing and local insurer decision-making may apply.
**Specific time frames for these codes have not been established.

3. *Resource-Based Relative Value Scale.* The latest addition to the coding instruments is the Resource-Based Relative Value Scale (RBRVS). This scale was developed in response to a request from clinicians and the United States government (Medicare). RBRVS puts medical, surgical, radiological, and mental health issues on the same scale. The RBRVS attempts to shift compensation to reward primary care activities, such as interviewing, counseling, and prevention, more and to reward the performance of procedures less. It has been widely implemented and has proven to be a boon to clinicians working with families with psychosocial problems.

Each CPT-4 procedural code carries a value measured in Relative Value Units (RVUs). The number of RVUs applied to each CPT-4 code is determined by several factors, including the following:

a. ***The amount of clinician work involved.***
b. ***The associated practice costs.***
c. ***Liability (i.e., the risk of the procedure).***
d. ***Geographic adjustments.***

Insurers generally accept the American Medical Association's latest revision of the RBRVS tables for each procedural code. Insurers can negotiate a single dollar number with participating clinicians, the reimbursement rate per single RVU. Once this is established, each service is priced based on its accepted RVU level. This has resulted in comparable reimbursement for comparable clinician work and has made primary care providers closer in reimbursement parity to other specialty groups.

The clinician can estimate an RVU. For example, a middle-intensity primary care office visit for a problem of low to moderate severity that takes about 15 minutes (CPT code 99213) yields roughly one RVU. Again, an extended visit that requires 40 minutes with an established patient for a problem of moderate to high severity would have an RVU of about 2.4, representing the increased work, the increased practice costs (i.e., more time in an exam room), and slightly higher risks. A comparison of RVUs for psychosocial procedures to other procedures is shown in Table 4.4.

IV. Documenting Services

To get reimbursed, clinicians must document their services. In addition to evaluating records to determine the quality of the interaction, insurers have begun to adopt the federal government's rules for documentation for Medicare to determine payment level. To determine the level of E&M for coding, the clinician must document the history, examination, and complexity of medical decision making.

A. **Determining the level of Evaluation and Management for Coding.** Many psychosocial interviewing and counseling activities fall under E&M codes. Because not all insurers reimburse based on counseling time, the clinician must understand the standard E&M documentation require-

Table 4.4. Comparing relative value units for psychosocial procedures with other procedures

RVU	Psychosocial Pediatrics Procedure	Other Specialty Procedure
2.00	99204—New patient, 45 minutes	9005—Drainage external ear abscess, complicated
1.77	99215—Est. pt., 40-minute conference	70552-26—Interpretation of brain MRI
2.81	99245—Consult, new pt., 80 min.	43219—Esophageal endoscopy with stent insertion

ments. Table 4.3 shows the E&M codes most commonly used for psychosocial problems.

The key elements for documentation are history, examination, and complexity of medical decision making.

1. *History.* To determine the appropriate coding level for the interaction, the level of history depends on the information gathered for each of the following four major elements:

- Chief Complaint (CC)
- History of Present Illness (HPI)
- Review of Systems (ROS)
- Past, Family, and/or Social History (PFSH)

The four corresponding levels of history which exist are the following:

- Problem-focused
- Expanded problem-focused
- Detailed
- Comprehensive

The requirements for each level of history are listed in Table 4.5.

Extended History of Present Illness (HPI)

The complexity of the history of psychosocial problems usually meets the criteria for an extended HPI.

a. ***Chief Complaint (CC).*** The CC is usually a statement, in the patient's words, giving the reason for the encounter.

Table 4.5. History requirements

History Level	Problem-Focused	Expanded Problem-Focused	Detailed	Comprehensive
CC	Required	Required	Required	Required
HPI	Brief 1–3	Brief 1–3	Extended (4)	Extended (4)
ROS	N/A	Problem Pertinent 1	Extended (2–9)	Complete (10)
PFSH	N/A	N/A	Pertinent (1/3)	Complete (2–3/3)

b. ***History of Present Illness (HPI).*** HPI is composed of eight potential elements:

(1) Location
(2) Severity
(3) Timing
(4) Modifying factors
(5) Quality
(6) Duration
(7) Context
(8) Associated signs and symptoms.

Describing any one, two, or three of the above HPI elements constitutes a *Brief HPI.* Documenting four or more of these elements (or the status of at least three chronic or inactive conditions) constitutes an *Extended HPI.*

c. ***Review of systems (ROS).*** Documenting the ROS can be challenging as it includes the 14 "systems" listed below:

(1) **Description.**

(a) *Constitutional symptoms* (e.g., fever, weight loss).
(b) *Eyes.*
(c) *Ears, nose, mouth, and throat (ENT)* (together these constitute one organ system).
(d) *Cardiovascular.*
(e) *Respiratory.*
(f) *Gastrointestinal.*
(g) *Genitourinary.*
(h) *Musculoskeletal.*
(i) *Integumentary (skin and/or breast).*
(j) *Neurologic.*
(k) *Psychiatric.*
(l) *Endocrine.*
(m) *Hematologic / lymphatic.*
(n) *Allergic / immunologic.*

(2). **Classification.** ROS is classified as one of the following three levels:

(a) *Problem pertinent.* Only the system related to the present illness is reviewed.

(b) *Extended.* Two to nine systems related to the illness are reviewed.

(c) *Complete.* Ten or more systems related to the illness are reviewed.

Note: These standards, which were established for the care of older adults, do not consider many factors relevant to children and are currently being reviewed by the American Academy of Pediatrics.

d. ***Past, Family, and/or Social History (PFSH).*** The PFSH consists of a review of the following areas:

(1) **Past (medical) history**

(2) **Family history**

(3) **Social history**

Taking the history of a new patient with a psychosocial problem requires a complete PFSH, making meeting the requirements in this area for a comprehensive history relatively easy (Table 4.5). With established patients, two of the three areas must be addressed. This is not difficult if social and interval medical history are addressed. They must be addressed specifically, however, to differentiate them from HPI elements.

CASE 3: A CHILD WITH ENURESIS

Joshua, a 5-year-old boy, is seeing his primary clinician for a chief complaint of new onset nocturnal enuresis. The clinician documents Joshua's history. He was initially toilet trained successfully at 30 months of age and had been dry until 3 weeks ago (HPI-duration) when nocturnal wetting episodes began occurring about three times a week (HPI-timing), 1 month after starting kindergarten (HPI-context). Other data obtained in the HPI include sleep habits (HPI-associated signs and symptoms), evening fluid consumption, toileting habits, Joshua's parents' response to his wetting, and their success at modifying it (HPI-modifying factors).

Review of systems documentation addresses appetite, growth, and fevers (ROS-constitutional factors), earaches and sore throats (ROS-ENT), coughs (ROS-respiratory), stooling patterns (ROS-gastrointestinal), dysuria (ROS-genitourinary), headaches and/or seizures (ROS-neurologic), and school-related anxieties (ROS-psychiatric). The interval medical history, which is reviewed, indicates that Joshua was seen in the emergency room for a sprained ankle 2 months ago but otherwise has been healthy and that he takes no medications (PFSH–past medical history). From the family history, the clinician discovers that Joshua's father had primary enuresis that resolved at age 7 years (PFSH-family history). The social history reveals that Joshua's family is intact but that his father has been working evening shifts for the past

6 months. This has left Joshua's mother in charge of all bedtime activities (PFSH-social history). A physical examination is performed with the eight organ systems mentioned above.

This is a very complete interaction. The Chief Complaint (CC) is present, as are five elements of HPI and three elements of PFSH. All of these make coding this a "comprehensive" history possible. However, only seven ROS elements are mentioned, downgrading the classification to an "extended ROS." This drops the overall history to the "detailed" level. The clinician can include enough ROS elements in the HPI to qualify a child for the "complete" level by mentioning symptoms relevant to fatigue (a constitutional symptom), vision, hearing, bowel problems, enuresis (a genitourinary symptom), joint pain, seizures/tics, depression, possible thyroid disease, and allergies to meet the ten-system requirement.

The highest E&M code that can be considered for this visit as it now stands would be 99214 (typically a visit totaling 25 minutes) even if the total time of the visit was longer. If the clinician had mentioned three more organ systems (choosing from eyes, cardiovascular, musculoskeletal, endocrine, integumentary, hematologic, or allergic), the ROS would have been characterized as "Complete"; the entire history could be considered "Comprehensive"; and the total visit could be coded at the highest level (99215).

2. *Examination.* The examination is the second element in documenting for the level of E&M coding. The examination can be either complete or problem-focused; the number of physical exam elements determines the type of examination. The examination has the following four levels:

- Problem-focused
- Expanded problem-focused
- Detailed
- Comprehensive

The number of elements examined determines the level of coding for the exam. Two different sets of examination element criteria are described in Table 4.6 and Table 4.7.

a. ***Examination elements can either be entire organ systems or multiple components of a given organ system.*** The following eleven organ systems are recognized:

(1) **Skin.**
(2) **Eyes.**
(3) **Ears, nose, mouth, and throat** (again, these are considered together).
(4) **Respiratory.**
(5) **Cardiovascular.**
(6) **Gastrointestinal.**
(7) **Genitourinary.**
(8) **Hematologic/lymphatic/immunologic.**
(9) **Musculoskeletal.**
(10) **Neurologic.**
(11) **Psychiatric.**

Table 4.6. Determining the level of physical examination for coding purposes (1997 rules)

Type	General	Multisystem	Single System
Problem-focused	1–5 elements	1–5 elements	1–5 elements
Expanded problem-focused	6 elements	6 elements	6 elements
Detailed	12 elements or 2 items from at least 6 organ systems or body areas	12 elements	9 elements
Comprehensive	9 organ systems or body areas, all elements of examination performed with 2 elements for each documented	All elements performed with documentation of every major element and at least one minor element	
Eye & psych.	Same as single system		

Table 4.7. Determining the level of physical examination for coding purposes (1995 rules)

System/Body Area	Number	Elements of Exam
Problem-focused examination	1	Limited examination of affected body area or organ system
Expanded problem-focused examination	2–4	Limited examination of affected body area or organ system and other symptomatic or related organ system(s)
Detailed examination	5–7	Extended examination of affected body area(s) and other symptomatic or related organ system(s)
Comprehensive examination	8	General multisystem examination (8 or more organ systems) or complete examination of a single organ system

b. ***Example of examination element criteria.*** If the clinician documents having examined the patient's skin, eyes, ears, lungs, heart, abdomen, and genitalia (seven organ systems) plus five elements of a neurologic exam, this examination would be coded as "Detailed."

A different (and easier to follow) set of examination element criteria were outlined in 1995. Many insurers also accept these (Table 4.7).

3. *Complexity of medical decision making.* Complexity of medical decision making is the third factor in documenting for the level of E&M coding. The complexity of medical decision making has the following four levels:

- Straightforward
- Low
- Moderate
- High

Table 4.8 describes the method for determining the level of complexity of medical decision making. To qualify for a given level of decision making, two out of the three criteria must be met or exceeded.

a. ***Documenting the visit.*** The clinician must consider the following question: Who will be the primary consumer of the clinician's written report? As the clinician documents his or her thoughts in order to maximize readability to the patient, family, or school, the resulting narrative reports may be difficult for insurance company reviewers to screen for relevant information for coding. Using checklists of major items can help the clinician achieve completeness without sacrificing clarity. Sometimes, summaries for insurers, as shown in Fig. 4.3, may also be needed.

Table 4.8. Determining the level of complexity of medical decision making

	Criteria		
Type of Decision Making	Number of diagnoses or management options	Amount and/or complexity of data to be reviewed	Risk of complications and/or morbidity or mortality
Straightforward	Minimal	Minimal/none	Minimal
Low complexity	Limited	Limited	Low
Moderate complexity	Multiple	Moderate	Moderate
High complexity	Extensive	Extensive	High

RE: *Patient Name*
DOB:
Insurance Number:

To Whom It May Concern:

I saw [Patient Name] on [Service Date] for [Diagnoses].

This letter documents the components of the services provided and billed with the diagnosis code of [ICD or DSM code(s)].

The following services were provided:

_______ Parent conference regarding the diagnosis, etiology, management, and medical treatments of [Diagnosis]. This conference lasted approximately _____ minutes.

_______ Face-to-face visit with [Patient Name] for additional discussion and initiation of therapy; _______ minutes.

_______ Correspondence to the school [Patient Name] attends.

_______ Review of school records.

_______ Phone consultation(s); ______ minutes.

_______ Other: ____

Should you have any additional questions or wish these services to be coded in a different way, please contact _________ in my office.

Thank you for your consideration.

Sincerely,

Figure 4.3. Sample letter detailing behavioral services to insurance company.

b. ***Determining the coding level for Evaluation and Management: complexity versus time.*** The coding level for an E&M procedure can be determined in either of the following two ways:

(1) **The complexity of the activity, as documented by the history, exam, and medical decision making.**

(2) **The time spent with the patient.** In addition to documenting complexity, the clinician must document time spent with the patient. Some insurers do not allow time to be a determinant of coding level; when they do, the allowance may only be for select codes. In codes referable to psychiatric and other mental health services, insurers may accept time as the major determinant. This acceptance is of particular benefit when coding for feedback sessions in which counseling is provided.

Billing Using Time Spent with Patient

In general, to bill using time as the major determinant of a session's coding level, counseling must have constituted over 50% of the time spent with the patient/family.

For example, to code at the 99245 comprehensive consultant level, estimated by *Current procedural terminology* (CPT) to require 80 minutes of face-to-face time with the patient, over 40 minutes must be spent in counseling activity. Documentation must include both the length of time spent with the patient and the issues discussed.

The continuum of services provided under various coding levels is well illustrated by looking at attention deficit/hyperactivity disorder (ADHD). In addressing this condition, interactions can range from complex evaluation down to simple follow-up (Table 4.9).

V. **Other Issues**

A. **Consultant codes versus adapted primary care codes.** Some E&M codes are reserved for consultations. These are most readily accepted when the billing clinician's practice is solely specialty, but they can also be used when a pediatrician provides specialty consultation to a patient whose primary clinician is not a pediatrician (e.g., family practitioner). Unless he or she can demonstrate special skills to the insurer, a pediatrician will have difficulty using consultant codes when the patient's primary physician is also a pediatrician.

For clinicians with a special interest in psychosocial pediatrics, using higher level codes at the _____4 or _____5 level for services that are more complex or require extra time (e.g., if the patient is familiar to the practitioner, codes for established patient interactions must be used) (Table 4.3) is entirely justifiable. Insurers often question an increase in high-end codes since they expect most interactions to be at the middle end of the complexity range or lower (i.e., at the _____2 or _____3 level).

Use of Higher Level Codes

As long as documentation matches the criteria for a higher level code, either in terms of time spent in counseling or in terms of complexity, the clinician can use the higher level codes.

B. **Coding for interdisciplinary work.** When the clinician is a member of an interdisciplinary team, coding for all of the services provided by each team member is reasonable. At the same time, clarifying with insurers whether professionals from other disciplines (e.g., education, occupational therapy) are working for the clinician or are separately employed consultants is necessary. If they are separately employed, the insurer may require them to be separately credentialed and billed. Insurers may need help in differentiating psychologists who only perform psychoeducational testing from those who also provide counseling services. However, once this differentiation has taken place, such psychologists may be exempt from mental health benefit limits. Seeking reimbursement from schools for non-physician team members under the provisions of special education law may be most effective, depending on local regulations.

C. **The hiring of a business manager.** Given the complexity and mercurial nature of the current health care reimbursement world, clinicians may choose to hire a business manager who has expertise in dealing with insurers and who can keep up with changing rules. Since insurers typically update their lists of reimbursable codes and documentation procedures at least yearly, having a business manager who can deal directly with insurers is worthwhile. The business manager can ensure appropriate reimbursement for the clinician's services, leaving the clinician free to focus on providing quality care.

D. **Board certification issues.** The American Board of Pediatrics and American Board of Medical Specialties have now approved board certifications for Developmental–Behavioral Pediatrics and Neurodevelopmental Pediatrics. Fellowship curricula and training/practice requirements are being established by representative organizations, including the Society for Developmental–Behavioral Pediatrics and the Society for Developmental Pediatrics. At present, in order to justify consideration as a specialist in psychosocial pediatrics, a clinician must have pursued post-residency training in this area and must spend a substantial portion of professional time focusing on service, training, or research in the areas of developmental and behavioral pediatrics. See Chapter 15, "Getting More Training," for further discussion.

VI. **Summary**

This chapter described the complex world of coding and documenting and various methods that clinicians can use to get maximum reimbursement for their services. These methods require the mastery of a new language and the "cracking of codes." This chapter focused on ways to convince insurers to pay, methods of diagnostic and procedural coding, documentation of services, and other issues (e.g., hiring a business manager).

A. **Key points to remember include the following:**

1. *Diagnostic codes are the ICD-9-CM, DSM-IV, and DSM-PC.*

(*text continues on page 76*)

Table 4.9. Sample continuum of coding for established patient with attention-deficit/hyperactivity disorder (ADHD)

99211	99212	99213	99214	99215
Face-to-face encounter with a parent discussing a child's school progress prior to writing a prescription for a psychoactive drug, such as methylphenidate, for a child doing well in school **Or** Scoring of Conners or other behavior rating scale to assess therapy	Face-to-face parental prescription renewal for a child *not* doing well in school **Or** Review with a parent of information from other care sources regarding the child (e.g., behavioralist, psychiatrist)	6-month follow-up without other problems. **Documentation might include:** • Reason for the visit. • Medication review. • Medication effects. • Quality of school work. • Absence of tics. • Pertinent physical exam with special reference	Review of patient having difficulty in school, home, or social situations. **Documentation might include:** All of data in **99213** plus review of past medical history. **Exam of Other Pertinent Organ Systems:** • Vision. • Hearing.	Comprehensive evaluation of a child with suspected ADHD. **Documentation might include:** All data in **99214**, Plus review of HPI, Family history, Social history, ROS, Medication history, Educational history. **Comprehensive Physical examination, includ-**

to neuro exam and growth parameters. • Pertinent lab work. • Discussion of 6-month treatment plan with medication adjustment. • Plan for further monitoring.	• Endocrine (e.g., thyroid). • Neurologic (e.g., seizures). **Plus:** Discussion of possible interventions, including, but not limited to: • Educational interventions. • Medication alterations. • Lab studies. • Psychiatric intervention. • Behavior program.	**ing 8+ organ systems** with special focus on neurologic and mental status exams. **Decision making:** analyzing differential diagnosis, treatment options, and coordination of services as necessary with school, family, and mental health providers.

Adapted from Suchyta R, 1994.

2. *Procedural codes are CPT-4, E&M, and RBRVS.*
3. *Documentation procedures require history, examination, and complexity of medical decision making.*

B. **Insurance companies will want to determine the following:**

1. *The clinician is the patient's primary physician or a consultant.*
2. *The patient is new or established.*
3. *The clinician spent most of his or her time counseling the patient.* If the answer to this question is "Yes," the code is based on the documented time spent; if the answer is "No," the code is based on accurate documentation that includes the following areas:
   a. ***The full history*** (including Chief Complaint, History of Present Illness, Review of Systems, and Past, Family, and/or Social History).
   b. ***The complete physical examination.***
   c. ***The degree of complexity of decision making.***

ADDITIONAL READING

American Medical Association. *Current procedural terminology.* Chicago: American Medical Association, 2000.

American Medical Association. *Medicare RBRVS: the physician's guide, 1994.* Chicago: American Medical Association, Department of Health Care Financing, 1994.

American Psychiatric Association. *Diagnostic and statistical manual of mental disorders,* 4th ed. Washington, DC: American Psychiatric Association, 1994.

Bradley J, Risley T. *Coding for pediatrics. A manual for pediatric documentation and reimbursement for use with current procedural terminology,* 4th ed. Elk Grove Village, IL: American Academy of Pediatrics, Committee on Practice and Ambulatory Medicine, 1999.

Wolraich MI, Felice ME, Drotar D, eds. The classification of child and adolescent mental diagnoses in primary care. In: *Diagnostic and statistical manual for primary care (DSM-PC). Child and adolescent version.* Elk Grove Village, IL: American Academy of Pediatrics, 1996.

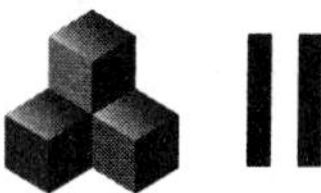

II

Interviewing the Family: Practical Strategies

5 Facilitating a Successful Family Interview

I. **Purpose**

Because the interview is the cornerstone of family counseling, effective interviewing skills are key for a successful interview and a good outcome for the family. Chances of having a successful interview are further increased when the clinician adheres to the principles and goals of a family interview. This chapter describes these interviewing skills, principles, and goals, as well as two techniques for facilitating the interview. For other useful suggestions, see Chapter 3, "Getting Ready for a Family Meeting."

II. **Principles of the Family Interview**

The family interview differs from the traditional patient–clinician interview because it emphasizes understanding the problem within the family–social context and helping the family adapt, develop its own interaction, and mobilize its resources to resolve the problem. To accomplish this, the family interview must be centered on certain principles that will help the clinician remain focused on the family perspective and the family's strengths.

A. **Assess the problem within the family–social context in which it arises.** Family and social factors affect the child, the child's problem/symptom, the parents, and the family interactions. Some family factors are the parents' psychosocial health, their parenting practices and perceptions of the problem, and the family structure and function (hierarchy, roles, relationships). The clinician must consider the impact of these factors on the child and the family and its ability to adapt. (See Chapter 2, "Determining Which Problems Are Suitable For Family Counseling," and Chapter 7, "Assessing Family Functioning: Additional Methods," for further discussion.)

B. **Mobilize the particular strengths and competence of the family (all families have them!) to change the behavior and improve the lives of the family members.** Some strengths might be the love and respect of family members for one another, an intact marriage/partnership, their religious beliefs and practices, and their network of support. Focusing on their strengths reduces the inclination of family members to judge or blame each other and instead helps them discover how they have coped thus far and how they are their own greatest resource. Thus, the search for strengths is a major component of the interview.

C. **Respect the family's chief complaint, and give the members time to describe the problem as they see it.** No matter what their complaint is, the family members have their own interpretations and beliefs about their presenting problem. They need to tell their stories and have their concerns acknowledged.

D. **Enhance the family's motivation by a steady emphasis on its strengths, adaptability, and cooperation.**

Emphasizing a family's problems engenders feelings of blame, shame, and incompetence. When a family has a negative self-image, that becomes a self-fulfilling prophecy, and the family becomes discouraged. The clinician helps the family move beyond the problem by focusing on ways to help the members work together, change their interactions, and achieve their goals. Moving beyond the problem and negative self-image increases their motivation and hope, two essential factors for a good outcome.

E. **Repeat preexisting successful behavioral patterns instead of trying to stop or change existing problematic behaviors.** Using the successful behaviors that the family has utilized in the past is often an easier way to help it cope with the present problem or difficulty than changing would be. These successful behaviors, often unique to each individual family, fit and/or stem from its cultural values. Thus the therapeutic plan must correspond to the family; the family should not be expected to match a therapeutic formula. With the clinician's encouragement, the family can focus on what it can do for itself, not on what the clinician can do for it. The clinician can help it identify these patterns so that the family can envision and recreate them.

III. Goals of the Family Interview

Identifying and reviewing the goals before the family meeting and following them during it provides substance and purpose to the interview. A few selected goals are listed below.

A. **Form a trusting and supportive alliance with every family member.** The clinician "joins" with the family and "touches" every member in a supportive, nonjudgmental manner in an ongoing process that begins at the first meeting and continues throughout the relationship. Without this alliance, the meetings will not succeed. (See Chapter 1, "The Family-Oriented Approach," and Chapter 6, "The Four Steps of a Family Interview," for further discussion.)

B. **Assess the family structure and function.** The clinician observes the family's structure: the family membership, the hierarchy, the boundaries and subunits, and the members' roles, relationships with one another, and coping abilities. (See Chapter 6, "The Four Steps of a Family Interview," for further discussion.)

C. **Help the family adapt and cooperate.** The clinician facilitates the family's efforts to change its perceptions of the problem and its interactions, to set appropriate expectations/goals, and to cooperate in developing and practicing new interactions.

D. **Provide appropriate suggestions and interventions when needed.** These suggestions should complement the family's attempts to develop its own problem-solving strategies. Interventions can also be directed to an individual or subunit (e.g., counseling for the parents or medication for the child).

E. **Assist in identifying and maintaining the family's strengths and resources.** To do so, the clinician inquires about family traditions and rituals, extended family support, friends and neighbors, religious beliefs, community resources, and other strengths, such as the parents' job security and satisfaction or the children's academic, athletic, or artistic skills. These strengths bolster the family's and individual's sense of competence and also serve as buffers against disappointments or stresses and as specific interventions (e.g., the parents can ask relatives to watch the children, so they can get some respite and time for themselves). The clinician helps the family utilize these strengths.

F. **Model the healthy, adaptive behaviors.** The family observes the clinician as closely as he or she observes it. Thus, the clinician becomes a role model to "teach" healthy, adaptive behaviors, such as the following:

1. *View a problem without blaming.*
2. *Acknowledge others' thoughts and feelings.*
3. *Share thoughts and feelings.*
4. *Ask for help.*
5. *Express appreciation.*
6. *Demonstrate affection or approval.*

G. **Establish the clinician as the leader.** When a family seeks help, it looks to the clinician for leadership and guidance. Therefore, initially the clinician must assume control, guide the families to their goals, and facilitate the process of changing family interactions. Eventually, as the family becomes more competent and less dependent on the clinician, the clinician gives the family the leadership.

H. **Make each session sufficiently satisfying to the family.** The clinician must conduct the interviews in a manner that leaves the family feeling better or more hopeful so that it is willing to return for the other scheduled visits. Thus the family members must feel that the clinician respected them, listened to them, helped them change their behaviors, and offered appropriate advice and guidance.

I. **Help the family to achieve competence and independence.** The clinician must remember that the ultimate goal of the family meetings is to help the family develop its own skills so that it does not need to return to or depend on the clinician. Following a successful intervention, the family is ready to prevent and/or solve problems (both present and future) on its own.

IV. **Interviewing the Family: 15 Skills**

The following interviewing skills are the key elements of the successful interview.

A. **Listening empathetically.**

Listening with empathy is the most important skill for the clinician. It can be defined as the ability to listen and to respond to the family's emotions with compassion and understanding. Without filtering or judging what the family is saying, the empathetic clinician conveys a genuine interest and respect for the family.

The clinician can develop and convey empathy by reflective listening, which means the clinician acknowledges the family members' feelings and concerns so that they sense that the clinician shares their feelings. Some examples of responses that the clinician may offer include the following:

"That must have been difficult for you."
"You must feel proud of your son."
"You look sad when you mention this topic."
"I don't know how you did it."

B. **Listening actively.** Active listening is listening and then responding to the family in verbal and nonverbal ways. Verbally, the clinician actively listens by making brief comments every once in a while. He also paraphrases. Paraphrasing condenses and clarifies information and assures the speaker that he or she is understood. Paraphrasing can be done at several points in the interview. These mini-summaries also help the family retain information (e.g., *"Let me be sure I follow you. You have said that . . ."*). Nonverbal active listening involves leaning forward slightly, minimizing movement of hands or feet, making appropriate eye contact, and assuming a facial expression and tone of voice that match the happy or sad mood of the family.

C. **Ensuring clear communication.** The clinician must be sure that what he or she says to the family, what the family says in response, and what the family says to each other contains no ambiguity or misunderstanding. Accomplishing this improves the clinician's understanding of the family and also helps the family members communicate more clearly and effectively with one another. The following items help ensure clear communication.

1. *Avoid medical or technical jargon (e.g., "family dysfunction" or "mood disorders").* These terms often make families feel stigmatized. The family often doesn't understand these terms or misinterprets them to mean that the family is "crazy" or "abnormal."
2. *Stay away from dispensing too much information at one time (e.g., talking at length or giving too many details).* This overwhelms the family's ability to retain the information or to determine the most important points. It also reduces the available time for the family members to talk, communicate with each other, or ask their own questions.
3. *Keep away from speaking too rapidly (e.g., at a fast, pressured pace).* Speaking rapidly reduces the family's ability to "follow" the conversation, to remember, and to understand the information. It also makes the clinician seem hurried and disinterested.
4. *Offer to clarify the message for the family.* For example, the clinician might follow a comment with, *"Does this*

make sense to you?" or *"Would you like me to repeat it or say it another way?"*

5. *Make sure that family members understand each other.* One of the most common family problems is poor communication, even in the clinician's office. The clinician can help the family members communicate better during the family meeting. Asking questions, such as *"Did you understand what your mother said?"* or *"Would you like her to say it again?"* helps clarify misunderstandings.

6. *Clarify any vague or subjective words or phrases.* For example, if the speaker uses words like *"lazy," "slow learner,"* or *"not so good,"* the clinician should guarantee that everyone in the room (including the clinician) understands what the speaker is saying by asking questions, such as, *"What do you mean by 'lazy'?"* or *"Can you explain what you mean by 'bad attitude'"*

7. *Encourage elaboration to get a more detailed description of the problem.* For example, respond with, *"Tell me more,"* or *"Describing in more detail would help me and the others to understand better."*

8. *Ask the family to specify references to others.* For example, if the speaker says, *"She says . . .,"* the clinician can ask, *"Who do you mean by 'she'?"*

9. *Ask the family to specify behavior.* For example, if a family member says, *"He never does what he's told,"* the clinician asks a question to define that reference, such as, *"What is he told?"* or *"Never?"*

D. **Permitting silence.** The family interview often evokes strong feelings and thoughts, which can be difficult or painful to discuss. Permitting silence, far from wasting time, allows the family to reflect on its feelings, to organize its thoughts and feelings, and to regain its composure. Silence also provides an opportunity for a quiet or hesitant family member to speak. If the family appears uncomfortable with silence, the clinician should start with brief periods of silence (5 to 10 seconds) and gradually extend them (15 to 30 seconds) if they prove appropriate and productive.

E. **Listening without interrupting.** When the clinician listens without interrupting, he or she helps the family tell its story and conveys respect and interest. Frequent interruptions fragment the interview, frustrate the family, and lessen the chance of gaining important information. A speaker usually pauses spontaneously after talking for about a minute to let the listener respond. At this point, the clinician can ask questions, offer comments, or encourage another member to speak (e.g., *"Susan, would you like to respond to your father?"* or [to the speaker or another member] *"What are you feeling now?"*).

F. **Listening to the family's story with an open mind.** Keeping an open mind while listening to the family's story conveys impartiality and acceptance to the family members. By understanding, respecting, and incorporating aspects of the family's story into the diagnosis and treatment, the clinician enhances the understanding of the family context.

G. **Complimenting the family.** Compliments express respect for and recognition of the family's efforts, strengths, and commitment to and affection for one another. Giving compliments also models good parenting skills. When the clinician compliments a child in the meeting, he or she is showing the parent how to praise the child for good behavior, thus reinforcing it.

Compliments should be given in the interview as opportunities arise. The entire family can be complimented on past actions or for behaviors in the meeting. The clinician should recognize that parents need and deserve compliments as much as children do.

Compliments can be:

1. *Verbal.* (*"Nice job. You're a really hard-working parent."*)
2. *Nonverbal.* (A smile, nod of the head, a handshake, or a "high five".)
3. *Notetaking.* The clinician very deliberately jots a note in the chart while exclaiming, *"Wow, that's impressive!"*
4. *Direct.* (Giving the compliment directly to the person.)
5. *Indirect.* (Asking another member, *"Did you hear that?"* or *"Wasn't that nice?"*)

Giving compliments also ends the interview on a positive note and leaves the family with hope, a sense of accomplishment, and a willingness to return.

Giving Compliments

Compliments should be genuine and should be given several times during the meeting.

H. **Remaining neutral/not taking sides.** Staying in "the middle of the road" removes the focus (and implied blame) from "the identified patient" (usually the child). It conveys respect for and acceptance of each member's perspective and also eliminates the formation of a coalition between the clinician and a family member. Everyone is then assured that the clinician is working for the family's well being. This perception of impartiality ("fairness") helps the clinician gain each member's trust and increases their willingness to comply with suggested interventions. Clinicians should be especially vigilant in the following situations:

1. *Parents who don't agree on discipline.*

2. *A parent who feels that he or she has too much responsibility for child-care.*
3. *A parent who feels unappreciated by his or her spouse/partner.*
4. *A disgruntled parent or child who tries to persuade the clinician to take his or her side.*
5. *A parent and child who disagree about family rules (e.g., curfew hours).*

In these situations, the clinician must remain neutral if he or she is to gain the trust and cooperation of all the family members. However, remaining neutral is often not easy. For example, a father who is excessively and unfairly criticized by his in-laws needs the support of the clinician in a way that does not antagonize the in-laws. One way a clinician might accomplish this is to form a stronger alliance between the father and the mother so that they support each other.

Telling the Story

Letting the family tell its own story helps the clinician understand how each family member's subjective experience influences his or her response to the clinician's assessment and suggestions.

I. **Confronting.** When the clinician feels that confrontation is the only way or the last chance to gain a more truthful answer, to interpret or resolve an apparent contradiction, or to challenge an assumption, he or she should confront that family member. The clinician can try to determine if a challenge will succeed (e.g., get a truthful answer) or if it will backfire (e.g., antagonize the member), but often he or she will not know until the challenge actually occurs. It can be done by asking the family member a direct question or by making a statement, sometimes in an abrupt manner. Below are examples of situations when the clinician might confront a family member or the whole family.

1. *To emphasize the importance of particular information.*

Clinician: *Parent stresses strongly influence children.*

If the parent does not respond then, the clinician may repeat or rephrase the statement/question later in the interview when the parent is more comfortable:

Clinician: *As I said earlier, parents often experience stressful situations that affect their children. Have you experienced any stresses recently that might be affecting your child?*

2. *To confront generalizations.*

Father: *We never have any peace.*
Clinician: *Never?*

3. *To challenge assumptions.*

Mother: *My 3-year-old should know better.*
Clinician: *He should?*

4. *To resolve an apparent contradiction.*

Clinician: *When we spoke on the phone, you were very worried; however, now you appear very happy. I am confused. I need to know how you really feel and what you want.*

5. *To resolve inconsistencies between feelings and body language or between content and affect.*

Clinician: *You sound very worried, but I can't tell by looking at you. You seem so at ease.*
Clinician: *You are discussing your child's school failure, but you don't sound very worried.*

J. **Reframing.** Reframing is a method used to change the family's incorrect, negative perception of one member's mood or behavior to a positive, more correct perception by explaining or "demystifying" it. The process also gives new meaning to one's own behavior or role in a relationship. For example, a clinician might reframe a "bad" child as one who "has poor impulse control," which is a symptom of his particular type of attention-deficit/hyperactivity disorder. In the same way, an "irritable" or "mean" parent is reinterpreted as a "sad" parent, who is depressed and tired.

K. **Normalizing.** When a family has a problem, it often thinks that it is the only one with this problem. It labels itself as "abnormal," which only adds to its feelings of stress, shame, or secrecy. The clinician can correct this false impression by normalizing the problem in one of two ways. One method places the family's problem within the range of normal variation—a common, nonsevere problem that is experienced by others. For example, a family makes an appointment with the clinician because the 7-year-old son is experiencing encopresis. Both the parents and child are ashamed. The clinician can allay the boy's worries a bit by saying, *"I take care of many kids with the same problem. It's a common problem, and it's normal to feel embarrassed."*

Another mode of normalizing occurs when parents call because of intense parenting disagreements. The clinician can respond by saying, *"It is normal to feel this intense stress under these conditions. The harmony and stability within families comes and goes. The problem does need attention, but your willingness to seek help is a measure of your ability to cope and restore harmony."* In this instance, normalizing does not mean that this situation is a normal occurrence; however, it does mean that the problem, although severe, is a normal reaction and that the family needs help.

L. **Avoiding the parent role.** Parents sometimes expect or want the clinician to assume the role of a parent (e.g., *"Can you talk some sense into our son?"*). However, the clinician should sidestep this role because it presents several problems:

1. *The child may perceive the clinician as another parent instead of as a neutral figure.* He or she may then reject the clinician's advice.
2. *The clinician's role is to help the parents cope and adapt, not to convince the child to do something.*
3. *It removes parental authority from the parents.* Therefore, the child may continue to disobey them.
4. *The clinician may be perceived as intrusive and paternalistic if he or she acts as parent without being asked.*
5. *The clinician should instead provide leadership without becoming the parent.* As stated above, being the "parent" undermines parental authority.
6. *The clinician should give extra support to the parents, as though he or she were parenting the parents, when they have weak parenting skills.* The following examples show how the clinician can do this without usurping parental authority and without being overly directive or obvious.
   a. ***In a meeting, the clinician can excuse the child so that the clinician and parent can have a private talk.*** This conveys a sense of hierarchy and adult–parental authority to the child. With the child out of the room, the clinician can make suggestions to the parents who then communicate them to the child when he or she rejoins the meeting.
   b. ***Sometimes, if a child is disrespectful (swearing at or belittling the parent), the parent is unable to reestablish proper parental authority.*** In this case, the clinician temporarily forms an alliance with the parent and acts as a coparent to help the parent regain control and establish rules, limits, and consequences.

The Physician as Expert Problem Solver

Clinicians trained in the biomedical, problem-solving model are taught to see themselves as the "experts" who are expected to solve every problem. Families also see clinicians as "experts" and encourage this role. The clinician's "fix it" response undermines the family system's ability to resolve the problem, invariably causing it to recur or to intensify. Therefore the physician must resist the urge to be the expert problem solver and to rush in with inadequate or inappropriate advice.

M. **Taking brief, selective notes.** Clinicians should not take detailed notes as this "removes" them from the family. Brief and selective note taking instead can be very useful for the following reasons.

1. *Selective notetaking lets the clinician pay attention and communicate with the family.* For example, it gives the clinician more opportunity to observe family interactions and to demonstrate active and empathetic listening.
2. *It allows the clinician to emphasize and to communicate important points to the family as he or she jots something down* (e.g., *"That's important,"* or *"I agree with you."*).
3. *It also permits the clinician to give a compliment as he or she writes something down* (e.g., *"Now that is really impressive!"*).
4. *It lets the family better observe the clinician's reactions as it looks for support, understanding, and respect.* To the family, excessive note taking may appear to be a way for the clinician to "hide" his or her own feelings, or it may make the clinician appear distant and uninterested.
5. *Brief notetaking appears friendlier and less clinical.* In family meetings, the family usually wants a warm, supportive relationship in which the clinician "joins" the family as part of the therapeutic process. Excessive note taking can prohibit the formation of this relationship. When the members see that everything they say or do is recorded, they often feel uneasy, hesitant, and/or self-conscious. They may even feel that the session isn't "confidential."

N. **Using humor.** A stressed family is often somber and intent on solving its problem. This seriousness can make it lose perspective so that the problem appears worse than it is. The family members may not have laughed together for a long time, or they may have lost their sense of humor. Clinicians, in their attempt to be professional, sometimes contribute to the problem by taking themselves and their positions too seriously. Humor is used most effectively when the clinician can make fun of himself or herself. When the clinician models this concept to the family, the family members learn not to take themselves so seriously all the time and to "lighten up" and feel better, even temporarily.

Laughter and humor can change the family's perspective of the problem (e.g., members might laugh at their efforts to resolve a problem or for being so worried over *"such a little problem"*). Parents often say, *"It feels good to laugh; we haven't done that for a long time."* If the clinician is uncertain about whether to use humor, he or she should not use it because the use of humor must be natural and spontaneous. It should also fit the family's mood and the clinician's style. Examples of appropriate times to use humor are listed below.

1. *During the family meeting, members may joke or say humorous things that elicit laughter from the others.* The clinician should note this and encourage it, as follows:

Clinician: *It's good to see you laugh. Do you all laugh much at home? What kinds of things make you laugh? Who has the sense of humor?*

2. *Families say might say things that the clinician can use to promote laughter, such as:*

Parent: *I was so mad, I told him he was grounded for a month.*

Clinician: *A month? How could you stand having him in the house all that time?*

Humor serves other purposes. A family can use humor to avoid pain or because family members do not recognize the severity of a problem. Humor is also used in hurtful ways (e.g., making fun of another or playing practical jokes). Sometimes, the family scapegoat is the target of jokes. When the clinician detects these situations, he or she should respond appropriately by gently confronting the family to help it adopt a different perspective and a more healthy response to the family member who is the target.

O. **Self-disclosure.** The clinician might disclose past or current personal experiences selectively and with discretion to demonstrate empathy and understanding. The clinician must first decide that sharing an experience really is appropriate for the situation and is beneficial to the family and that it does not harm the clinician–family relationship. The advantage of self-disclosure is that it can establish a more personal and trusting relationship between the clinician and the family. For example, the family with a parent–adolescent conflict might stimulate the clinician to disclose his or her own similar experience, as the following situation illustrates.

Clinician: *I can understand your problem because I had a similar problem with my teenager a few years ago.*

Parents (thinking to themselves): *He's been through this himself. He knows the pain we are feeling. He can understand where we're coming from.*

The Downside of Self-Disclosure

The clinician's self-disclosure can be problematic. The family may perceive the disclosure as a weakness, which, in turn, may alter its view of the physician as the expert or the leader. Also, if the clinician talks too much about his or her own past, he or she is taking time and attention away from the family. If the clinician has any question or doubt about self-disclosure, he or she should avoid it.

In another situation, a child might have a particular problem, such as poor athletic skills. The clinician might share that she also experienced this problem and how she learned to develop other interests and skills that earned her satisfaction and praise.

V. Two Techniques to Initiate a Conversation

Sometimes, families or individuals are reluctant to begin a conversation. In these cases, a semi-structured, semi-verbal task to help the members organize their thoughts is often beneficial. It is especially helpful for adolescents who feel self-conscious, embarrassed, or angry with the meeting. This section gives two techniques to help initiate a discussion and facilitate the interview—the list of concerns and the issues checklist. In using these in the family meeting, the clinician first explains the mechanics and purpose of the task to the family.

A. **The list of concerns.** The clinician gives each family member paper and a pencil and ask them to list three concerns that are important to them or issues that they want to discuss and settle. Then each member ranks them according to importance. After these two steps have been followed, each member reads his or her list to the others or passes it around to the rest of the family. Then the family negotiates, often with the help of the clinician, the issue(s) to be discussed at this meeting. Others can be discussed at another meeting.

B. **Issues checklist.** The Issues Checklist (Robin, 1989, abridged version) is a tool for facilitating family discussion. It has been used successfully for separating distressed families from nondistressed families. The parent (or both parents, if possible) and the child/adolescent should complete this checklist independently of one another. Each member is asked to circle "Yes" for topics they have discussed with parents/son or daughter during the last 4 weeks and "No" for those that have not come up. For topics where "Yes" was circled, the accompanying intensity rating scale of 1 to 5 should be completed (Table 5.1).

The checklist is scored as follows:

1. *Quantity of issues.* Count the number of issues marked "Yes."
2. *Intensity.* For "Yes" issues, add the intensity ratings and divide by the number of "Yes" issues to obtain mean intensity rating.

Examples of positive scores include a parent who reports 15 or more "Yes" items and/or has a mean intensity rating of 2 or higher or a child/adolescent who reports 13 or more "Yes" items and/or has a mean intensity rating of 1.7 or higher. In addition to calculating the number of "Yes" items and mean intensity on both parent and child/adolescent checklists, comparing areas where child/adolescent and parent ratings do not agree can be helpful. As with any screening tool, the clinician should conduct further clinical assessment when the screen is positive.

Table 5.1. Issues checklist (abridged)

Directions: Circle "Yes" for topics you have discussed with your parents/son or daughter during the last 4 weeks and "No" for those that have not come up. For those circled "Yes," use the rating scale from 1 = calm to 5 = angry to answer the question, "How did you feel when you discussed this topic?"

			How Did You Feel When You Discussed This Topic?				
Have You Discussed?			**Calm**	**A little Angry**			**Angry**
1. Telephone calls	Yes	No	1	2	3	4	5
2. Bedtime	Yes	No	1	2	3	4	5
3. Cleaning bedroom	Yes	No	1	2	3	4	5
4. Doing homework	Yes	No	1	2	3	4	5
5. Putting away clothes	Yes	No	1	2	3	4	5
6. Using the television	Yes	No	1	2	3	4	5
7. Cleanliness (washing, showers, brushing teeth)	Yes	No	1	2	3	4	5
8. Which clothes to wear	Yes	No	1	2	3	4	5
9. How neat clothing looks	Yes	No	1	2	3	4	5
10. Making too much noise at home	Yes	No	1	2	3	4	5
11. Table manners	Yes	No	1	2	3	4	5
12. Fighting	Yes	No	1	2	3	4	5
13. Cursing	Yes	No	1	2	3	4	5
14. How money is spent	Yes	No	1	2	3	4	5
15. Picking books or movies	Yes	No	1	2	3	4	5
16. Allowance	Yes	No	1	2	3	4	5
17. Going places without parents (shopping, movies, etc.)	Yes	No	1	2	3	4	5
18. Playing stereo or radio too loudly	Yes	No	1	2	3	4	5
19. Turning off lights in house	Yes	No	1	2	3	4	5
20. Drugs	Yes	No	1	2	3	4	5
21. Taking care of records, games, bikes, pets, and other things	Yes	No	1	2	3	4	5
22. Drinking beer or other liquor	Yes	No	1	2	3	4	5
23. Buying records, games, toys, and things	Yes	No	1	2	3	4	5

(continued)

Table 5.1. ***Continued***

			How Did You Feel When You Discussed This Topic?				
Have You Discussed?			**Calm**		**A little Angry**		**Angry**
24. Going on dates	Yes	No	1	2	3	4	5
25. Who should be friends	Yes	No	1	2	3	4	5
26. Selecting new clothes	Yes	No	1	2	3	4	5
27. Sex	Yes	No	1	2	3	4	5
28. Coming home on time	Yes	No	1	2	3	4	5
29. Getting to school on time	Yes	No	1	2	3	4	5
30. Getting low grades in school	Yes	No	1	2	3	4	5
31. Getting in trouble at school	Yes	No	1	2	3	4	5
32. Lying	Yes	No	1	2	3	4	5
33. Helping out around the house	Yes	No	1	2	3	4	5
34. Talking back to parents	Yes	No	1	2	3	4	5
35. Getting up in the morning	Yes	No	1	2	3	4	5
36. Bothering parents when they want to be left alone	Yes	No	1	2	3	4	5
37. Bothering adolescent when he/she wants to be left alone	Yes	No	1	2	3	4	5
38. Putting feet on furniture	Yes	No	1	2	3	4	5
39. Messing up the house	Yes	No	1	2	3	4	5
40. What time to have meals	Yes	No	1	2	3	4	5
41. How to spend free time	Yes	No	1	2	3	4	5
42. Smoking	Yes	No	1	2	3	4	5
43. Earning money away from the house	Yes	No	1	2	3	4	5
44. What adolescent eats	Yes	No	1	2	3	4	5

The clinician can use this checklist informally (without formal scoring) as a way to initiate a discussion. For example, he or she might note a topic that concerns the parent (e.g., '34. Talking back to parents') or a topic on which both parent and child/adolescent agree (e.g., '6. Using the television'). (See Chapter 2, "Determining Which Problems are Suitable for Family Counseling," for further discussion.)

VI. **Summary**

The interview is the centerpiece of the family meeting. The clinician can prepare for the interview and enhance the likelihood of a successful meeting by (a) reviewing the principles of the interview, which supply a guiding framework; (b) following the goals of the meeting, which define the purposes of the interview; and (c) using specific interviewing skills or methods to achieve these purposes. The chapter also describes two techniques to initiate a family meeting, "the list of concerns" and the "issues checklist."

ADDITIONAL READING

Allmond B, Tanner JL. *The family is the patient.* Baltimore: Williams & Wilkins, 1998.

Doherty WJ, Baird MA. *Family therapy and family medicine.* New York: Guilford Press, 1983.

Goldstein JH. Therapeutic effects of laughter. In: Fry WF, Salameh WA, eds. *Handbook of humor and psychotherapy: advances in the clinical use of humor.* Sarasota, FL: Professional Resources Exchange, 1987.

Green M. Seminal articles with commentaries. *Pediatrics* 1998; 102:201–202.

King M, Novik L, Citrenbaum C. *Irresistible communication: creative skills for the health professional.* Philadelphia: WB Saunders, 1983.

Korsch BM, Gozz EK, Vida F. Gaps in doctor–patient communication: doctor–patient interaction and patient satisfaction. *Pediatrics* 1971;45:855.

Lefcourt HM, Martin RA. *Humor and life stress.* New York: Springer-Verlag, 1986.

Minichun S, Fishman HC. *Family therapy techniques.* Cambridge MA: Harvard University Press, 1981.

Napier AY, Whitaker CA. *The family crucible.* New York: Harper & Row, 1978.

Parish AB. It only hurts when I don't laugh. *Am J Nursing* 1994; 8:46–47.

Robin AL. *Communication training: a problem-solving approach to parent–adolescent conflict.* Unpublished doctoral dissertation. State University of New York, Stony Brook, 1975.

Robin AL, Foster SL. *Negotiating parent–adolescent conflict: a behavioral–family systems approach.* New York: Guilford Press, 1989.

Satir V. *Conjoint family therapy.* Palo Alto, CA: Science and Behavior Books, 1983.

Scarf M. *Intimate worlds: life inside the family.* New York: Random House, 1995.

Senn MJE. The psychotherapeutic role of the pediatrician. *Pediatrics* 1948;2:147–152.

Stinnett N, Stinnett N, DeFrain J, DeFrain N. *Creating a strong family.* West Monroe, LA: Howard, 1999.

Young KT, Davis K, Schoen C, et al. Listening to parents: a national survey of parents with young children. *Arch Pediatr Adolesc Med* 1998;152:255–262.

6 The Four Steps of a Family Interview

I. Purpose

Interviewing is a very individualized process for each clinician. The content and process of the interview are determined by the clinician's style and preferences, by the family's problem and communication style, by the nature of the clinician–family relationship, and by the time constraints of the visit. Furthermore, spontaneous revelations of information and emotional outbursts also contribute to the shape of the interview.

The family interview is both a semi-structured diagnostic and psychotherapeutic, goal-oriented conversation between the clinician and the family and also a conversation among family members. The interview generally follows a four-step sequence: (a) engaging the family; (b) understanding the family; (c) working with the family; and (d) concluding the interview. Each step contains its own set of questions and specific elements.

This chapter uses a case study to illustrate and describe the four steps of the family interview and the various questions/elements of each step (Table 6.1). This general guide will help the beginning family counselor–clinician organize the interview so that it is productive, satisfying, and time-efficient.

No One Way to Conduct a Family Interview

The interview is an individualized, dynamic, flexible process shaped by a variety of clinician and family factors. The steps and questions outlined in this chapter are only as a general guide. No "one size fits all" interview approach exists. Therefore, each clinician must develop his or her own interviewing style.

A. **Modifying the interview.** Even though many questions are listed in this case study, asking all of them is often not necessary or feasible. The clinician should modify the content and sequence of the interview appropriately as conditions dictate. The clinician can select particular questions (or add new ones) for use in particular situations. He or she must also acknowledge that carrying out a complete, initial interview in one session may not be possible. The clinician may use two visits as follows: the first two steps (engaging the family and understanding the family) might be completed in the first visit, and the next two steps (working with the family and concluding the meeting) might be finished in the second visit. Several follow-up visits occur later.

Table 6.1. The four steps of the family interview

1. Engaging the family (alliance formation).
2. Understanding the family and its concerns (the assessment phase: understanding the problem within the family context).
3. Working with the family (the therapeutic phase: direct interventions; helping the family develop its own solutions).
4. Concluding the family meeting (summarizing; complimenting; planning the next meeting).

CASE STUDY: THE FAMILY WITH TWO SONS EXPERIENCING INTENSE SIBLING RIVALRY

The father of two boys, Alex (9) and Rodney (11), called the clinician, stating, *"My sons are always fighting. It's gotten so bad that I worry about them having a good relationship; it's really strained our home life. We don't know what to do."* After ascertaining that the boys were not in physical danger, the clinician said that this problem would be best resolved with a family meeting. The father agreed, so the clinician set the appointment for 10 days later. She told the father to call her if the boys physically harmed each other in the interim.

II. Step One: Engaging the Family

The first step in the family interview is engaging the family. Engaging the family requires forging a trusting alliance with every member of the family—the clinician "joins" with the family as part of the problem-solving process. This step is critical because the nature of the relationship between the clinician and the family strongly influences the outcome. Although the clinician may already have a trusting relationship with the mother and child from prior visits, often he or she is meeting other family members for the first time in the family interview. (See Chapter 1, "The Family-Oriented Approach: Why and How It Works," pg. 7)

In this step of the interview, the clinician employs several interviewing strategies. (See Chapter 5, "Facilitating a Successful Family Interview.") Four selected aspects, partnership, respect, validation, and support (Table 6.2), are especially helpful in establishing the therapeutic alliance in this step.

Table 6.2. Establishing the alliance: four key aspects of engaging the family

1. Partnership
2. Respect
3. Validation
4. Support

1. *Partnership means working together.* From the beginning, the clinician works with the family in a problem solving-partnership, which he or she establishes by saying, *"How can I help you?"* or *"We'll work on this together."*

2. *Respect is conveyed by nonjudgmental acknowledgment and acceptance of the family's complaint, efforts, values, strengths, resilience, and other qualities.* A compliment, such as, *"I admire your commitment to your family,"* or *"I respect your family values,"* communicates respect.

3. *Validation implies legitimizing the family's concerns, feelings, and actions.* The clinician ensures that the family does not perceive itself or its problems as abnormal, unrealistic, or hysterical. He or she emphasizes this in responses to the family by making comments like, *"You have a right to feel as you do,"* or *"Anyone would have done the same thing."*

4. *Support indicates ongoing help.* The clinician needs to assure the family that he or she will work with it until things are better and that the family members can depend on his or her continuing support and advocacy. The clinician should let the family know this by making statements, such as, *"I will help you as long as it takes"* or *"You can always call me whenever you need to."*

Engaging the Family

Engaging the family includes building the relationship and developing the therapeutic alliance between the family and the clinician. Relationship building, which is the first step, continues and develops throughout all subsequent interviews. It is an ongoing process.

The five elements of engaging the family are the greeting, social conversation, identifying the family leader, explaining the purpose of the meeting, and estimating the number of visits (Table 6.3).

A. **The greeting.** The greeting, the first contact between the family and the clinician, should be warm and welcoming to help put the family at ease. Every member must be greeted by name and with a smile, eye contact, and physical contact. Children are called by their first names (not "your son," "he," or "she") and should be acknowledged with either a pat on the shoulder or a handshake. Parents and other adults should be greeted with formal names or titles and handshakes. At this point, the clinician also introduces himself or herself using the name or title with which he or she would prefer to be addressed.

If the clinician greets the family members in the waiting room and then escorts them to the room that is going

Table 6.3. Engaging the family
Allow 3 to 5 minutes for this step[a]

1. **The greeting:** Be warm and welcoming; address everyone by name; invite the family members to sit where they wish.
2. **Social conversation:** Talk briefly to each member; make each feel involved and respected; join with the family.
3. **Identifying the family leader:** Identify who is in charge.
4. **Explaining the purpose of the meeting:** Appreciate the family context; use the family as a resource; explain to the family how this is different from the typical medical visit.
5. **Estimating the number of visits:** Decide how many visits will be needed and how much time each visit will require. This relieves the pressure the family feels to get the problem solved in one visit.

[a] The 3- to 5-minute time allotment for this step of the visit is only an approximation.

to be used for the family meeting, he or she should start the social conversation at that point. He or she could say, *"It's good to see you," "How are you doing?"* or *"Thank you for being so prompt."* The clinician should not hurry down the hall several paces in front of the family, silently leading them to the room while glancing through the chart. Taking a few minutes to review the chart before greeting the family or reviewing it with the family members in the office is preferable.

Once in the room where the chairs are arranged in a loose semi-circle, the family members should be invited to sit where they wish. A child may prefer to sit on a parent's lap. The seating arrangement itself may reveal something about family relationships (e.g., the child who sits next to his father and far from the mother may be indicating his emotional closeness to the father and distance from the mother).

CASE STUDY (CONTINUED)

The clinician has followed the boys for several years so she felt she knew them. She doesn't feel that she knows the mother well, and she has never met the father in previous visits.

B. **Social conversation.** In this step, the clinician talks with each family member, making a connection with each individual so that each one feels important, involved, and acknowledged. These few minutes of social conversation, which are especially useful in the first meeting when the family is the most nervous and hesitant, establish personal contact between the clinician and each member, help the clinician begin to know them, and relax the family. This time of informal "living room talk" permits the family members to settle down, to gather their thoughts, and to feel comfortable in the family session.

Families often enter the room already engaged in conversation (e.g., the traffic conditions it encountered driving to

Initiating the Social Conversation

Starting with someone other than the "identified patient" (the member with "the problem") is best. Starting with members who are the least well known to the clinician makes them feel involved early in the session. The clinician might preface his or her questions with the following statement, "Before we start, I'd like to get to know you a little."

the office, daily activities, or plans following the visit). The clinician can often use those topics to begin the social conversation. For example, overhearing an ongoing conversation, he or she could say, *"I heard you talking about playing sports after school. Are you enjoying that?"*

CASE STUDY (CONTINUED)

Clinician (to the father): *I'm glad we have a chance to meet. I've enjoyed knowing your family.*

C. **Identifying the family leader in the hierarchy.** The clinician must identify the family leader and make an alliance with him or her. The mother usually makes most of the child-rearing decisions and may also be the leader (the member who is ultimately in charge). However, the leader can also be the father, a parent's partner, or a grandparent who lives with or near the family. The alliance is crucial because this individual's support greatly influences the family's adaptability and cooperation. If the family leader is not yet known or is not present, he or she must be identified early in the interview.

CASE STUDY (CONTINUED)

Clinician (to the parents): *Mr. Brown, you and I spoke on the phone about this appointment, but who generally makes decisions about the children?*

Father: *We both do.*

Mother: *I do more of the day-to-day things, but we are both concerned about this issue and agree on seeking help.*

D. **Explaining the purpose of the meeting.** Explaining that the purpose of the meeting is to understand the family context in which the problem arises helps the family realize how this meeting differs from a typical medical visit. The clinician must clearly explain that the discussion will not center on the child and the problem. The members must understand that everyone's input is needed to yield a better understanding of the problem and to provide better solutions. Sometimes, children have not been told the purpose of the meeting, or they think it is "to make them behave." The clinician should correct these assumptions and should assure them that the focus is not on the symptoms or to blame any one family member. The clinician should not proceed with the meeting until the family clearly understands its purpose and appears comfortable with the shift from the "identified patient" to the family context. (See Chapter 3, "Getting Ready for a Family Meeting," Six Ways to Suggest a Family Meeting, page 31, for further discussion.

CASE STUDY (CONTINUED)

Clinician: *Does everyone know why we are meeting?*

Rodney: *Because I have a problem, and they want you to fix me.*

Clinician: (to parents): *Did you explain the purpose of the meeting to the boys?*

Mother: *No I didn't. I was afraid they'd make a big fuss.*

Father: *The boys know that we are at our wit's end, but we never did sit down and talk about it.*

Clinician: *Alex, why do you think we are meeting?*

Alex: *I'm not sure.*

Explaining the Purpose of the Family Meeting

Families (understandably) are uncertain and nervous about the purpose of the family meeting. The clinician can explain the purpose in the following way, *"I'd like to explain the purpose of the family meeting. All families face problems from time to time and need help solving them. We're having this meeting so that everyone can understand the problem and can work together to make things better. As a family you have many strengths that can help each other. We're not here to blame anyone. This meeting has two parts. In the first part, everyone will talk about the concern that brings the family here; and I'll ask questions too. Then, we'll talk about how you can work together to solve the problem or at least start to make things better. Everyone needs to participate. If you don't want to talk at first, that is okay; but after awhile, I do want to hear from everyone."*

E. **Estimating the number of visits.** Most clinicians do not have enough time to conduct a complete initial interview in one visit. Early in the first visit, the clinician should estimate the number of visits that will be necessary and then should tell the family. This approximation might be based on prior knowledge of the family, on the parent's phone call, or on the nature of the presenting problem from the early discussion in the first meeting. Informing the family that sufficient time exists to discuss the problem and possible solutions (e.g., two visits for the complete initial interview and a number of follow-up visits) removes considerable pressure and strain from both the family and the clinician. (See Chapter 3, "Getting Ready For a Family Meeting," Planning the Meeting, page 38, for further discussion.)

Length and Duration

Generally, an initial interview requires 40 to 50 minutes depending on the (apparent) complexity of the problem. The clinician can schedule this interview either in one visit or as two visits of 20 to 25 minutes each. The number of follow-up visits varies. Each requires 20 to 30 minutes.

CASE STUDY (CONTINUED)

Clinician: *We'll need two visits to start off with and then schedule a few shorter visits afterwards.*

III. Step Two: Understanding the Family and Its Concern

The centerpiece of this step is understanding both the family and its concern. This step of the family meeting contains two parts: exploring the family structure and function and exploring the family's problem or concern within the family context (Table 6.4).

A. **Exploring the family structure and function.** To explore the family structure and function, the clinician must observe the family's interactions and ask about the family composition and activities (e.g., the hierarchy, boundaries, coalitions, communication patterns, and family perceptions) (Table 6.5). (See Chapter 1, "The Family-Oriented Approach: Why and How It Works," for further discussion.)

Table 6.4. Understanding the family
Allow 20 to 25 minutes for this step[a]

1. Explore the family structure and function.
2. Explore the family's problem.

[a] These time limits are only an approximation.

Table 6.5. Exploring the family structure and function

1. Observe the family's pattern of interactions.
   a. Content
   b. Process
2. Ask about the family.

1. *Observing the family.* The clinician's observations should begin when he or she greets the family and should continue throughout the visit(s). Observations also include information and impressions provided by the parent's initial phone call. The clinician should note both the content and the process of the family's interactions and communication. *Content* is defined as the verbal message, or the "what," of the communication. *Process* is the way in which the content is delivered—both the verbal and nonverbal message—or the "how" of the communication and interaction. The clinician should observe the family with the following questions in mind:

a. ***What is the leader's style?***

(1) How does he or she assert leadership (authoritarian, authoritative, loud, quiet, permissive)?

(2) Is this person the most appropriate leader in this situation?

(3) How does this person accept alternative suggestions, disagreement, praise, cooperation, and lack of cooperation?

b. ***What is the family hierarchy?*** Hierarchy can be established by the following information:

(1) Who attends the meeting? Who makes decisions?

(2) How do the other family members react to the leader?

(3) Are "power," decision making, and leadership shared appropriately?

(4) Does sharing change the hierarchy or family subsystems?

(5) Do power struggles for leadership occur?

c. ***What do the family's nonverbal communications reveal about it?*** The clinician should closely observe the following behaviors and interactions:

(1) How do the family members enter the room and greet the clinician?

(2) What is the seating arrangement? Who is sitting next to whom?

(3) Are the parents sitting together or apart?

(4) How is each member dressed? What is the general appearance?

(5) What do facial expressions, eye contact, body postures communicate?

(6) Do the members touch one another?

(7) Are the family members relaxed or tense?

(8) Do the members drift off, sit still, pay attention, or become fidgety?

(9) How does the family send nonverbal messages to each other?

(10) How do they respond to each other and to the clinician (e.g., behaviors, moods, facial expressions)?
(11) How does the family conclude the meeting and "say" goodbye?

d. ***What do the family's verbal communications reveal?*** The clinician should note the following aspects.
(1) Who initiates the communications?
(2) How are the communications received by other family members?
(3) What happens immediately after the communication? What does each family member do?
(4) Do members need "permission" to communicate certain topics?
(5) What types of communication are cut off?
(6) Who cuts off the communication?
(7) How do family members both listen and speak to the clinician?
(8) Do they all volunteer to talk?
(9) Do they listen to one another?
(10) Do they listen with empathy?
(11) Do they acknowledge each other's feelings?
(12) Do they talk to each other or only to the clinician?
(13) How do they handle interruptions and disruptions?
(14) What is not said in the meeting?

e. ***How does the family carry out tasks in the meeting?*** (Tasks can include discussing a problem, sharing feelings, negotiating a goal, planning an activity, or [re]assigning roles.)
(1) Does everyone participate, or does one person do everything?
(2) Can the family create a plan for doing the task?
(3) How are rules for doing the task formed and communicated?
(4) Who participates in forming the plan?
(5) Does sharing power and responsibility cause a breakdown in completing the task?
(6) How does the family react to suggestions?
(7) How age-appropriate and constructive are "duties" or work assignments?
(8) Who assigns them and how?
(9) Is the performance of the task basically leaderless?

f. ***What "roles" does each family member play during a task?***
(1) By what process were they assigned or assumed?
(2) Do these roles remain set, or do they change?
(3) Does anyone sabotage the task? If so, who?

(4) Who provides minimal support for the task?
(5) Who does most of the work?

g. ***How does the family adapt during the task?***

(1) How does the leader of the task adapt to new task requirements and changes in the participants' behavior?
(2) Is the family flexible while doing the task?
(3) Can family members correctly determine that the task should end for one or more of the following reasons?

- Someone is not feeling good.
- They cannot perform an assigned "job."
- Time is running out.

(4) How does the family (and each member in it) react when a task cannot be completed?
(5) How does the family treat the one who does not do his or her part?
(6) Were harmful coalitions formed (did two or more members side against other family members)?
(7) Does one (or more) family member(s) appropriately or inappropriately "rescue" another family member while doing the task?

h. ***What are the family's emotions during the task?***

(1) Does the family experience joy or accomplishment?
(2) Do the members express or demonstrate joy, approval, affection, anger, and/or sadness?
(3) How do they express these feelings?"
(4) How do they respond to one another's feelings?

CASE STUDY (CONTINUED)

The clinician notes that the parents sit together and that Alex is sitting close to his mother. Rodney, however, moved his chair to be as far as possible from the rest of the family. The family mood is serious, and the boys seem hesitant to talk. The father sighs as he sits down and says, *"I feel relieved that we are finally sitting down together to deal with this."* The mother initiates most of the conversation and appears to be the leader.

2. *Asking about the family.* In addition to observing the family's interactions, the clinician learns more about the family structure and function with the judicious use of just a few questions. Comprehensive fact-gathering questioning is neither necessary nor advisable as the family usually divulges information in the course of the meeting without needing to be asked. (See Chapter 1, "The Family-Oriented Approach: Why and How It Works.) Examples of questions that can be asked include the following:

a. Who lives at home?
b. Who is in charge at home?
c. How do the siblings get along?
d. How is the marriage/partnership?
e. Is the marriage/partnership affected by the problem?
f. Is the problem affected by the marriage/partnership?
g. Who else cares for the children?
h. Who are the extended family members?
i. Where do extended family members live, and what is their relationship with the family?
j. What does the family do together? Evenings? Vacations? For fun?
k. Do they have any traditions? Holidays? Church or temple?

CASE STUDY (CONTINUED)

Clinician: *Does anyone else live at home?*
Mother: *Just us. But all of the boys' grandparents live close by.*
Clinician: *Are they supportive? Do they help out?*
Father: *Very. My father always offers advice.*
Clinician (seeking clarification): *What kind of advice?*
Father: *How to raise the kids.*

The clinician makes a mental note to follow-up on this comment because it seems related to the stated problem. But she has noted the family's mood and wants to acknowledge and understand it.

Clinician (exploring the mood): *I notice that everyone seems very serious.*
Mother: *Home life is tense.*
Clinician (acknowledging the tension): *Yes, I can see that. This must be a very difficult time for the family.*
Father: *It is. This fighting is not what we want as a family.*
Clinician (emphasizing the family context and being supportive): *That's why we're meeting as a family. We want to understand the issues better. It's apparent that everyone is affected. And as a family, you have the resources to resolve this problem.*

B. **Exploring the family's problem or concern.** The five components of exploring the family's problem or concern are (a) stating the problem or concern and negotiating a goal, (b) describing the problem, (c) identifying family patterns that maintain the problem, (d) exploring past attempts/advice to resolve the problem, and (e) identifying family and social changes that influence the problem (Table 6.6).

1. *Stating the problem or concern and negotiating a goal.* The clinician should have already discussed the purpose of the meeting. Now family members should state their own perceptions of the problem and should set a goal for the meeting(s). Stating the problem and setting a goal with the aid of the clinician's leadership and experience helps the family define and agree upon both its concern and goal.

Table 6.6. Exploring the problem

1. State the problem and negotiate a goal.
2. Describe the problem.
3. Identify family patterns that maintain the problem.
4. Explore past attempts/advice to resolve the problem.
5. Identify family and social changes that influence the problem.

CASE STUDY (CONTINUED)

Clinician: First, *I'd like each of you to briefly state the problem in just a few words. We'll discuss it in more detail in a few minutes. Who would like to begin?*

The clinician deliberately does not want to ask the boys first because she does not want to focus initially on the 'identified patients'.

Both parents: *The kids are always fighting.*

Clinician (inviting one of the boys to get involved): *What do you think, Alex?*

Alex: *I don't like fighting, but I have to.*

Clinician (clarifying): *You "have to"?*

Alex: *He picks on me. He starts it.*

Rodney: *We're just playing, but it's not my fault.*

Clinician: *Rodney, what do you think the problem is?*

Rodney: *The fighting and the lousy feelings.*

Father: *Maybe it's just a boy thing. I fought with my brother when I was young. But they fight too much.*

Clinician (attempting to be sure they agree about the "problem"): *Although you all seem to have different views, do you all feel that "fighting" is a concern and that "home life is tense"* (using the mother's phrase)?

The family agrees that these are the problems.

The clinician should now ask them about their goal(s) for the meeting(s). Negotiating a goal serves two purposes.

a. ***The goal helps the family members share with one another the behavior they want or need.*** The clinician might say, *"What would you like to achieve with these meetings?"*

b. ***The goal helps the clinician redirect the interview if and when the interview becomes too problem-focused or too acrimonious, divisive, and accusatory.*** For example, the clinician might get the meeting back on track by saying, *"Remember that your goal is to have the boys play together. Let's go back to discussing how that can happen."* Some families become so fixated on the problem that they do not think about a goal. In those cases, the clinician needs to make an extra effort to help the family determine a goal. For a detailed description of setting a goal, see Chapter 8, "Three Models of Brief Family Interviews," The Solution-Oriented Interview, page 170.

CASE STUDY (CONTINUED)

Clinician: *Now that you've stated the problem, I'd like to ask about your goal for this meeting(s). What would you like to happen in your family?*

The family was silent. The clinician waited about 15 seconds.

Father: *What do you mean?*

Clinician: *If "home life" weren't so tense, what would be happening instead?*

Mother: *The kids would not be fighting.*

Clinician (helping the family restate the goal as a desirable behavior): *What would you see if they were not fighting?*

Father: *There would be peace in the house.*

Clinician (helping the family specify the behaviors of the goal): *What would you all be doing if there were peace in the house?*

Father: *We'd be doing chores and activities together. We'd feel comfortable.*

Alex: *I want Rodney to stop beating me up.*

Rodney: *I wouldn't be blamed for the fighting.*

Clinician (to help the mother, Alex, and Rodney state their goals in positive terms): *Could you tell us all what you want instead of fighting, instead of being beat up, and instead of being blamed?*

Mother: *I'd like the boys to play together after school.*

Alex: *I wish Rodney would play with me and not beat me up.*

Rodney: *I want Dad to know it's not my fault.*

Clinician: (attempting to be sure they agree on a goal): *It sounds like you all want the same things: the boys playing together, feeling comfortable, and no one being blamed. Is that right?*

Rodney: *I want to play with Alex, not fight with him.*

Clinician (emphasizing the family meeting purpose): *That's one reason you're all here.*

The members look at each other silently.

Father (asking the family): *Is that right?*

The mother, Rodney and Alex all nod.

In this exchange, the clinician helps the family focus on one goal. Since the boys' fighting appears to be the central problem, the logical goal is having the boys play together. After brief conversation, the family agrees that this is their current goal.

2. *Describing the problem.* Once the goal has been established, the clinician can focus on a more detailed problem description. Describing the problem in depth helps the clinician to understand it within the family–social context, to explore recent changes or stresses that influence it, and to identify family patterns of interactions that maintain it.

In family meetings, members often talk to the clinician, not to each other. When this occurs, the clinician must remind them to speak to each other. The clinician can say, *"I'd like you to look at Rodney and tell him what you'd like to see happen."*

Promoting Family Communication

Family members often talk to the clinician about another's behaviors. They "report" their perceptions and feelings to the clinician. A major goal of the meeting is to get the members to communicate with each other. The clinician must remind them to look at and talk to each other.

CASE STUDY (CONTINUED)

Clinician (seeking clarification): *What exactly do you all mean by "fighting"?*

The family explains that fighting means name calling and pushing. These activities have been going on for about a month; they used to occur only once or twice a week, but now they are happening almost daily. Most occurrences are after school during the few hours that the boys are home alone, so the parents are not sure who starts things. Lately, the disagreements have intensified to occasional punching; Alex often comes to his parents in tears.

Father (speaking to the clinician): *I've really had it. This is not what I want family life to be like.*

Clinician: *I'd like to ask all of you to address each other, not me. Could you look at your family and tell them that?*

The father does so. They are quiet.

The father's expression of his feelings is important. He has expressed both his frustration and his disappointment. The family 'heard' him.

Mother: *I am sure we can do something, but I must admit that I'm lost. For a while, I spanked Rodney, but I felt badly afterwards so I stopped.*

Clinician (exploring this spontaneous disclosure of behavior and feelings): *Does Rodney know that?*

Mother: *This is the first time I've said this.*

Clinician (encouraging family communication): *Could you tell him now?*

Mother: *Rodney, I am sorry for the spanking. I feel badly for both of us.*

Rodney's eyes well up with tears. The mother reaches out and takes his hand. The clinician and family are silent.

This interaction was significant. The mother and son shared feelings verbally (Mother) and nonverbally (Rodney).

3. *Identifying family behavior patterns that maintain the problem.* In attempts to resolve a problem, families repeat behaviors that maintain the problem. As they work harder, louder, and longer, they become tired, impatient, and frustrated. These patterns for interactions often pass from one generation to another. To help the family change these entrenched patterns, the clinician should identify them and share his or her observations with the family.

CASE STUDY (CONTINUED)

Clinician: *What do you do when the fighting occurs?*

The parents describe their patterns of behavior. When a fight has occurred, Alex usually comes to the mother; she, feeling that this is a father-son issue, asks her husband to "do something." The father, remembering how his father had raised him, tells Alex to "be tough and fight back."

However, recently when Alex came to him in tears, the father began to feel that Rodney was being too rough, so he has begun to scold him.

Mother: *I know spanking doesn't help. My parents spanked me too, and I hated it.*

Rodney: *You yell at me too!*

The clinician made a mental note of the fact that, although the spanking had ceased, the yelling continues and that it is both a symptom and a cause of family stress.

Clinician (using an insight-oriented question): *Do you see a connection between how you were raised and your own parenting practices?*

The mother states that she does now that it has been pointed out.

Clinician (to the mother): *Does your behavior change anything?*

Mother: *It only makes things more unhappy.*

Clinician (to the boys): *Let's hear from you.*

The boys start to argue and blame each other for the fighting. To help them refocus, the clinician reminds them of the stated goal to play together. Alex says that he felt that he was being picked on, so he usually told his father that Rodney was starting the fights.

Rodney says that he felt that he was unfairly blamed. He resented the spanking and the scolding and would tell Alex afterwards, *"I'm going to get you for tattling to Dad."*

The clinician encourages a dialogue between Rodney and his father about Rodney's feelings. Then she acknowledges Rodney's feelings towards Alex and emphasizes again the purpose of the meeting, which is not to hurt or blame but to work together to achieve their goal.

Clinician (exploring the father's parenting history to understand the family context and the father's behaviors better): *Could you tell me more about how your parents raised you?*

Father: *My father always told us to settle our differences ourselves, even if it meant fighting. He wanted us to be "tough" and not "sissies."*

4. *Exploring past attempts / advice to resolve the problem.* This line of inquiry seeks to determine what, if any, attempts or advice the family has used in the past. The answers inform the clinician about the appropriateness of the attempts/advice, each member's efforts, and the outcomes. Did each member cooperate with and follow the advice, or did one or more member(s)disagree with it?

CASE STUDY (CONTINUED)

Clinician: *What else have you tried in the past?*

The parents state that they had punished Rodney by taking away TV time because he seems to be "starting the fights" but that it didn't help.

Rodney appears to be the scapegoat, the one who is usually blamed; and consequently, the clinician thinks he might have a negative self-image.

Clinician: *Have you spoken with the Rodney's and Alex's teachers or sought professional help?*

The family has not sought any outside help.

Clinician (following up on the father's statement that he followed his father's advice. She is trying to find out if this maintained or eased the problem.): *Has anyone offered advice?*

Father: *My father gives us advice. We don't really ask him, but we go along with it when he offers it.*

The paternal grandfather had strongly advised the father to *"let the boys fight it out."* He wanted grandsons who could *"handle things like strong men do."*

Clinician: *How does the advice change the problem?*

The father laughs uncomfortably and shrugs his shoulders.

Mother: *They fought even harder and hurt each other. That's what's happened.*

Clinician: *Has anything helped?*

Mother (sounding very discouraged): *Nothing I can think of.*

5. *Identifying family or social changes that influence the problem.* This inquiry looks for changes (stresses, transitions, losses) within or outside of the family that may have influenced the problem. Problems often emerge or, if preexisting, intensify during these changes.

CASE STUDY (CONTINUED)

Clinician: *Were there any changes in the family about the time the fighting started or intensified? Any recent stresses like health or job problems or marital tensions?*

The family denies any changes.

Clinician (to Alex and then Rodney): *Have you had any difficulties at school or with friends?*

Alex denies any problems.

The clinician looks at Rodney. Rodney looks down at the floor and is quiet. The clinician allows about 15 seconds of silence. The rest of the family follows her lead and remains quiet too.

Clinician: *Rodney, you seem pretty quiet. Do you have something you might want to share?*

Rodney remains silent but glances at his parents.

Mother (after a pause): *During the past month or so, he missed some school. He said he didn't feel good.*

Clinician (wondering whether a connection between a school stress and the fighting at home can be made): *Rodney, I know this might be hard to talk about, but it's important to know what's going on at school. Can you tell us a little more?*

With gentle coaxing and encouragement from his parents and the clinician, Rodney reveals that he is being bullied at school during recess. He has not told the teacher because he felt she would tell his father, and he does not want to disappoint his father who has always urged the boys to be "tough."

Clinician (in acknowledgement of Rodney's feelings, paraphrases his story and attempts to help him express his feelings): *Rodney, thank you for sharing this. You've been through a lot. You had to see this bully every day. You couldn't tell the teachers or Mom or Dad. How did this make you feel?*

Rodney tells the family that he felt scared and sad. He restates again that he didn't want to disappoint his father because he is not fighting the bully. He feels his father might be angry with him.

Rodney: *Sometimes I don't want to go to school.*

Clinician (acknowledging Rodney's feelings again in an attempt to encourage elaboration): *So when you do go to school and then come home, you must feel pretty upset.*

Rodney: *Alex knows about the bully. When I come home, Alex teases me about being bullied and calls me a "wimp." Then I get mad at him and really want to beat him up.*

Father: *You never told us this.*

Rodney: *I didn't want to tell you. I thought you'd get mad at me. I made Alex promise he wouldn't tell.*

Mother: *This breaks my heart.*

Clinician: *It must be hard to hear this, but it helps all of us understand why the boys are fighting.*

IV. **Step Three: Working with the Family**

Working with the family, the "therapeutic" phase of the interview, consists mainly of the clinician facilitating changes in family behaviors and of helping them develop solutions. The clinician can make suggestions when necessary and appropriate. This step has four elements: (a) identifying family strengths, support systems, and past successes; (b) engaging the family in developing a plan of action; (c) suggesting interventions/offering advice; and (d) assigning homework tasks (Table 6.7).

A. **Identifying family strengths, support systems, and past successes.** Families often become so involved with the problem that they forget their strengths, support systems, or

Table 6.7. Working with the family
Allow 20 to 25 minutes for this step[a]

1. Identify family strengths, support systems, and past successes.
2. Engage the family in developing a plan of action and encourage collaboration.
3. Suggest interventions/advice.
4. Assign homework tasks.

[a] These time limits are only approximations.

past successes. The clinician's job is to help the family rediscover and utilize these strengths and supports effectively.

CASE STUDY (CONTINUED)

Clinician (pointing out the family's strengths): *I want to remind you that you are a family with many strengths. You are caring and very supportive of each other. Coming here and talking with each other make that clear. You also have support from relatives.*

Father: *That's good to hear.*

Clinician (searching for other successes): *What else have you done in the past that worked and might be tried again?*

The family recalled that, when the boys had been enrolled in after-school sports, they were very happy and got along well.

Clinician (looking for more specific supports): *Who provided transportation?*

Father (identifying another support): *A neighbor whose son also plays sports.*

B. **Engaging the family in developing a plan of action and encouraging collaboration.** The clinician helps the family develop a plan of action that facilitates a change in the family's behaviors by combining its strengths, past successes, its new insights, and its goals. The plan requires the cooperation of all relevant family members.

CASE STUDY (CONTINUED)

Clinician (reminding the family of its cooperation in the meeting): *You've shown that you are willing to work together. What can you do as a family that will help you achieve your goal?*

The mother states she will listen to the boys when they come to her with their problems and will not automatically send them to their father. The father states that he too could spend more time listening to the boys and that he will not be so insistent that they be "tough." He also fees he had relied too much on his own father's advice.

Clinician: *Do you think explaining this to the boys' grandfather would help? Once he understands, would he be supportive of you?*

The parents are not sure if the grandfather would understand and support them.

Clinician (to the boys): *What would you like to do instead of fighting?*

The boys state their wish to participate again in after-school sports.

Mother (identifying a strength): *The boys are good at sports. We let that slide. But when they play, they feel good and so do we.*

Clinician: *How can you make that happen?*

Father (demonstrating initiative and leadership): *I could speak with our neighbor again. Maybe we can take turns driving to ensure it really happens.*

Clinician: *How are you feeling about this?*

Father: *This all sounds good, but I'm not sure we can do all of this. It's not that easy.*

Clinician: *You have a right to be cautious, but your goal is clear and realistic. Is everyone willing to cooperate?*

The family's mood brightens a bit, and the family members state their willingness.

Offering Advice

Suggestions and advice are helpful if the family:

- wants them and is ready to listen;
- understands them;
- is prepared to try them;
- agrees to them as a family;
- feels they fit the problem and its family values; and
- has the capabilities and resources to carry them out.

C. **Suggesting interventions/offering advice.** The clinician can also be directive and can suggest specific interventions aimed at the family as a whole and/or at individuals. Sometimes, parents request specific advice. The advice that the clinician gives must respect the family hierarchy, fit the family's coping ability, and support its goals. This intervention/advice generally consists of the traditional recommendations (the five R's—reassurance, resources, readings, recipes, and Rxs [medications]), tailored to fit that particular family. (See Chapter 2, "Determining Which Problems Are Suitable for Family Counseling," for further discussion.)

CASE STUDY (CONTINUED)

Mother: *We need your advice about the bullying at school.*

The clinician could offer to call the school, but she wants the family to take the initiative to act and to create its own solutions. She does offer some advice.

Clinician: *I suggest that you call the teacher tomorrow and tell her the situation. Ask to arrange a meeting with her, the school counselor, and the two of you (looking at both parents). Rodney should be there too. The meeting should take place after school in a quiet, private room. Tell her that I will dictate a letter to her with copies also going to the principal and the school counselor. The school has a good policy regarding bullying. Both the bully and Rodney will get help and support. I will call, if necessary.*

The parents thank the clinician. Rodney looks grateful and relieved.

Clinician: *Rodney, how does this sound to you?*

Rodney: *Okay.*

Clinician (complimenting the family and supporting them): *I like the idea of signing up the boys for after-school sports.*
Father: *Maybe Grandpa could help out here. He loves watching the boys play sports.*

D. **Assigning homework tasks.** After a family meeting, the clinician can assign the family a homework task of practicing the new tasks/behaviors/interactions. If these changes are to become the new reality, they must take place in the home, not just in the meeting. Because changing behavioral patterns takes time, practice, work, reminders, and encouragement, having a task helps to reinforce the new perceptions and the agreed-upon behaviors. The task should be geared to the goal that has been discussed (and that may have been practiced) in the session.

CASE STUDY (CONTINUED)

Clinician: *I'd like to suggest a homework task for the family. One of the best things you did here today was to listen to each other. You have stated that was something you want to do, so I'd like to suggest a weekly family meeting. If you can't do it weekly, twice a month would be okay. Try it and see how it works.*

The clinician explains how to conduct a family meeting at home and gives the family a handout with more details.

Clinician (getting feedback from the family): *Do you think this might help?*
Mother: *We'll try it.*
Father: *It can't hurt.*
The boys shrug their shoulders.

Chapter 12, "Strategies to Enhance Family Functioning," Home Family Meetings, page 240, offers more insight into conducting a home family meeting.

Pitfalls to Avoid When Offering Advice

When offering advice, the clinician must avoid two common pitfalls:

1. Failure to "join" with the family and gain its trust.
2. Failure to understand the problem within the family context.

Clinicians often fall into these pitfalls because they feel pressured to "do something" quickly (e.g., write a prescription) and "fix" the child's symptoms; thus they ignore family issues and influences.

V. Step Four: Concluding the Session

Concluding the session in a controlled, non-abrupt manner conveys a sense of order, professionalism, and clinician leadership and also gives the family members time to compose themselves and to consider final thoughts, feelings, and questions. The six elements of the concluding step are (a) making a transition to the conclusion, (b) summarizing the meeting, (c) letting the family respond, (d) getting family feedback, (e) scheduling the next visit, and (f) complimenting and thanking the family (Table 6.8).

A. **Making the transition to the conclusion.** The clinician must watch the time and allow 3 to 5 minutes to conclude the meeting. The clinician's manner of making the transition to the conclusion tells the family that the meeting is ending. He or she initiates the transition with a phrase, change of voice, and/or action. For example, he or she may say, *"It's been a very good session,"* while putting down notes or *"Let's begin to wrap things up for this meeting,"* and shift position.

CASE STUDY (CONTINUED)

Clinician (glancing at the clock): *I see it's almost time to end our session.*

B. **Summarizing the meeting.** The clinician uses the summarization to highlight and clarify the essential aspects of the meeting. The family is better able to remember the relevant aspects if they are condensed into a few succinct, clear statements. When this is done, the family is also more likely to respond with any remaining questions and comments. In addition, a clear summary conveys that the clinician has heard the family's concerns and that he or she respects and understands them.

CASE STUDY (CONTINUED)

Clinician: *Let me take just a few minutes to summarize things, and then I'd like to hear from you. You came here because the boys were fighting. As we discussed, a combination of factors has kept the problem going. No one is to blame. You've demonstrated some real strengths, like your commitment to work together and your willingness to change your behaviors. You have supportive relatives and a*

Table 6.8. Concluding the session
Allow 3 to 5 minutes for this step[a]

1. Make the transition to the conclusion.
2. Summarize the meeting.
3. Let the family respond.
4. Schedule the next visit.
5. Compliment and thank the family.

[a] These time limits are only an approximation.

helpful neighbor. You've come up with some excellent solutions, such as changing your responses to the boys, arranging a school meeting, providing after-school sports, sharing the driving, and even asking the boys' grandfather to help out. I've also suggested the family meetings at home. That's a lot.

C. **Letting the family respond.** The family members will invariably have final thoughts and questions. They need to have time and to feel that they have "permission" to voice their thoughts and feelings. When the clinician invites the family to speak, it has the opportunity to do so. Members may wish to speak to the clinician, to the whole family, or to an individual. The responses also give the clinician information about how the members felt about the meeting (e.g., *"Being here really helped"* or *"This meeting was a waste of time"*).

D. **Getting family feedback.** If the family does not offer feedback about the meeting, the clinician should ask (as a family and individually) if the meeting was useful or satisfying, (e.g., *"Did this meeting help?"* or *"Did we address your concerns satisfactorily?"*). If anyone expresses a concern, the clinician should respectfully ask him or her to elaborate.

CASE STUDY (CONTINUED)

Clinician: *Do you have any questions or comments for me or for other members of the family?*

Mother to the family: *I am glad we came here.*

Rodney: *Will the bully bother me again?*

The clinician looks over to the father to give him the chance to respond and to demonstrate his support for his son.

Father: *Rodney, don't worry. We are going do everything possible to take care of that. And I want to tell both of you* (looking at the boys) *that you can always come and talk to me, and I will not tell you to just tough it out.*

Sometimes when families express feelings, such as affection, remorse, pride, or sorrow, they want to touch each other (e.g., kissing, hugging, squeezing the shoulder, holding hands, patting the back); but they may feel hesitant or unsure about whether or not doing so is "okay." The clinician should show sensitivity to these special moments. If appropriate, he or she might encourage this demonstration by remaining silent or by saying something like *"Show him how much you care."*

E. **Scheduling the next visit.** The clinician schedules follow-up visits at this time. The first should be scheduled 2 to 3 weeks later, if possible. Subsequent visits can be scheduled farther apart as progress is made. The follow-up visit provides the clinician with information on how the family is doing and on whether or not the meeting was successful. Families need the follow-up visit to discuss their progress or lack thereof and to get feedback and encouragement from the clinician. If a family isn't progressing, it needs additional intervention and support. The clinician should use this meeting to determine if he or she missed something or moved too quickly. The family might also have a new problem that requires the physician's attention. Scheduling a follow-up visit(s) also demonstrates the clinician's ongoing interest in and support for the family. (See Chapter 9, "After the Interview: The Post-Interview Phase, Follow-Up, and When to Terminate the Meetings," for further detail.)

CASE STUDY (CONTINUED)

Clinician: *I'd like to schedule a follow-up meeting in 2 to 3 weeks. Will that work for you? If anything comes up before that, please give me a call.*

F. **Complimenting and thanking the family.** Compliments should be offered in a genuine and generous manner that recognizes the family's positive attributes and strengths. Compliments help the family "reframe" others, itself, or its internal interactions by replacing a negative perception of others or a negative self-image with a positive one. (See Chapter 5, "Facilitating a Successful Family Interview," for more information,)

CASE STUDY (CONTINUED)

Clinician: *This has been a good visit. Your commitment to one another is very apparent. Look at all you accomplished today. Each of you contributed to the success of this meeting. Rodney, you were very brave in sharing your story about school. Alex, you said you want to be friends with Rodney. That was very kind. And* (to the father) *I think it was very important that you told the boys they can come and talk to you and that they don't always need to be tough. And* (to the mother) *sharing your feelings with Rodney about spanking him was also very significant. Thank you for coming in. I look forward to our next visit.*

VI. **Summary**

No one "correct" way to interview a family exists. Each clinician develops his or her own style based upon personal skills and preferences, the presenting problem, the family's coping abilities, its communication patterns, the family–clinician relationship, and the time constraints of the office/clinic setting. Family interviews generally follow this four-step sequence: (a)engaging the family, (b) understanding the family and its concern, (c) working with the family, and (d) concluding the session. Following these steps helps make the family meeting organized, effective, satisfying, and time-efficient.

ADDITIONAL READING

Allmond B, Tanner JL. *The family is the patient.* Baltimore: Williams & Wilkins, 1998.

Campbell TL, McDaniel S. Conducting a family interview. In: Lipkin M, Putman SM, Lazare AR, eds. *The medical interview.* New York: Springer-Verlag, 1995:178–186.

Coleman WL. The first interview with a family. In: Coleman WL, Taylor EH, eds. *Family focused pediatrics. Pediatr Clin N Am* 1995;42(1):119–129.

Coleman WL, Howard BJ. Family-focused behavioral pediatrics: clinical techniques for primary care. *Pediatr Rev* 1995;16(12):448–455.

Doherty WJ, Baird MA. *Family therapy and family medicine.* New York: Guilford Press, 1983.

King M, Novik L, Citrenbaum C. *Irresistible communication: creative skills for the health professional.* Philadelphia: WB Saunders, 1983.

Korsch BM. *The intelligent patient's guide to the doctor–patient relationship.* New York: Oxford University Press, 1997.

McDaniel S, Campbell TL, Seaburn DB. *Family-oriented primary care.* New York: Springer-Verlag, 1990.

Minichun S, Fishman HC. *Family therapy techniques.* Cambridge, MA: Harvard University Press, 1981.

Morrison J. *The first interview.* New York: Guilford Press, 1995.

Nichols MP, Schwartz RC. *Family therapy: concepts and methods,* 2nd ed. New York: Allyn and Bacon, 1991.

Weber T, McKeever JE, McDaniel SH. A beginner's guide to the problem-oriented first family interview. *Fam Process* 1985:24:357.

7 Assessing Family Functioning: Additional Methods

I. **Purpose**

In assessing family functioning, a major facet of family counseling, the clinician should consider family membership, hierarchy, patterns of interaction and communication, and medical–psychosocial health of the family members.

In addition to the strategies discussed in the previous chapter, the clinician can use several other strategies to assess family functioning, including the following:

- Observing assigned family activities in the meeting.
- Gathering additional information with questions and tools.
- Using screening questionnaires to explore family–psychosocial problems and overall family function.
- Noting information that the family spontaneously shares during the meetings.

Having so much information can easily overwhelm the clinician. However, often assessing all components of family functioning is not necessary. Gathering it all in one meeting is certainly not feasible. The clinician selects a few components to evaluate by observing/listening to the family and using his or her "clinical judgment."

I. **Observing Assigned Family Activities in the Meeting**

One method that the clinician can use to gauge family function is to assign the family an activity and then to observe its interaction. Five suggested activities are described below.

A. **The family draws a picture together.** The family drawing lets the clinician observe the nonverbal family interaction. The game-like feeling of this activity helps young children and/or hesitant, less verbal family members relax and get involved. In the 5 to 10 minutes allotted for this brief activity, the clinician observes both the content (what each member draws) and the process (how they share space and cooperate) of the drawing.

For the activity, the family sits at a table and is given a large sheet of paper. Each member chooses a single crayon of a different color.

The clinician gives the family directions in the following way:

Clinician: *I would like each of you to draw something. You may draw whatever you want. Please don't talk to anyone, including me, during this exercise. You have 5 minutes.*

1. *Observing family interactions.* The clinician observes the family interactions during the process. When time is up, the clinician asks each member to describe his/her drawing (content). The clinician encourages members to comment on the process: how he or she interacted, how others interacted, and the feelings he or she experienced. The clinician may ask the following questions:

- "How did you draw your picture?"
- "How did others draw theirs?"
- "Were you working together or alone?"
- "Would you like to have done it differently?"
- "What were you feeling during this task (game)?"

From the activity and responses, the clinician gains initial, general impressions about the family interactions. One must emphasize and remember that these conclusions are only preliminary and thus that they may be confirmed or altered as the clinician learns more about the family. Below are some observations and their possible interpretations (in parenthesis).

2. *Possible interpretations*

a. ***Did the family members draw thick lines to enclose their space*** (rigid boundaries) ***or give "intruders"*** (those who draw in their "space") ***a stern look*** ("forbids" others to enter)?

b. ***Did they "hide" their drawing from others*** (keeps secrets, wants privacy, avoids criticism)?

c. ***Did individual members extend their drawings*** (a ray of sunshine, a tree branch, a straight line) ***into others' space*** (reaches out, invites others to cooperate)?

d. ***Did members make eye contact, smile, and want others to look at their drawing*** (open, friendly, shares, wants praise)?

e. ***Did members look at others' drawings and smile and nod*** (approving, accepting)?

f. ***Did they scowl and grimace when looking at the drawings of others*** (disapproving, rejecting)?

g. ***Did they begin right away*** (initiative, confidence)?

h. ***Did they wait and watch before beginning*** (hesitancy, dependency)?

i. ***Did one member act as a leader and the others as followers*** (hierarchy)?

j. ***Did any members seem to join together against another*** (coalition)?

k. ***Did any members work together in a positive manner*** (alliance)?

B. **The child draws a picture.** Having the child draw a picture provides an opportunity for the child to describe his or her feelings and perceptions about himself or herself, family members, and family problems. To start this activity, the clinician gives the child a piece of paper (on a clipboard or table) and a single crayon, pencil, or felt tip pen. The clinician instructs the child by saying, *"Draw a picture of you and your family doing something."* While the child draws the picture, the clinician speaks with the parents, observes how the child carries out the task (the process), and assesses the following items:

- works independently?
- pesters the parent?

- needs reassurance?
- experiences any particular feeling(s)?

The clinician also observes how the parents respond to the child during this process. Did they allow the child to work independently or did they help and advise the child?

The clinician then asks the child about the content:

- "What did you draw?"
- "Can you tell us about your drawing?"
- "Who are the people?"
- "What are they doing?"

The clinician encourages the following responses from the parents:

- sharing their reactions to the child's drawing;
- asking questions about the child's drawing;
- complimenting the child on his or her picture.

Picture Drawing

The picture drawing can be used in well-child visits and consultations (e.g., enuresis or learning problems) to help the child share feelings, reveal a concern, or describe a recent experience. To do so, the clinician should ask the child to draw a picture about the relevant subject.

C. **Role playing.**

Role playing allows the parent and child to reenact a problematic interaction, to practice a desired interaction, and to express related emotions. For some families, role playing "breaks the ice" and helps them shift to a family focus. For example, a mother might present with the chief complaint that "the child doesn't mind me." After a few minutes of problem description and goal negotiation, the clinician asks the mother and daughter to role play.

1. *The problem.*

Clinician: *I need you to help me understand the issue better. I'd like to have each of you pretend you are home. I'd like you* (mother) *to enter Susan's* (daughter) *room and ask her to pick up her clothes. And then Susan, I want you to act like you do when mom asks you to clean up your room. I'd like you both to act and talk and look and sound just like you do at home. I'll help you.*

2. *The feelings associated with the problem.* After a few minutes of role playing the problematic situation, the clinician asks the mother and daughter to discuss their feelings.

Clinician: *How did each of you feel? How do you think the other person was feeling?*

3. *The desired interaction.* In this use of the technique, the clinician asks the mother and daughter to describe their goal or what they'd like to happen.

Clinician: *Now let's go through this again but now both of you act and talk as if the goal you just described has been reached.*

4. *The feelings associated with the desired interaction.* After a few minutes of role playing the desired behavior, the clinician asks the mother and daughter to discuss their feelings as they role-played their goal-behavior.

Clinician: *How did each of you feel? How do you think the other was feeling?*

D. **Hand puppets.** Like role playing, hand puppets can be used to recreate a problematic interaction, to rehearse a desired interaction, and to communicate associated feelings. Members can either play themselves or assume the identity of the hand puppet (e.g., a bear, a clown, or an identity of their own choice). Acting as a "character" instead of as oneself often makes expressing oneself easier (for children especially) because the individual can pretend he or she is someone else in this "make believe" game. The hand puppet game should be conducted like the role-playing exercise.

E. **The magic wand.** The magic wand provides an easy, effective way to help children express their feelings, thoughts, or wishes. This activity works well with children because they think imaginatively and express themselves more easily by playing and making wishes. This activity helps the clinician and the parents understand their feelings, therefore promoting a family discussion. The magic wand, which can be purchased in most toy stores, is a clear plastic tube filled with clear oil and little bits of sparkle, stars, moons, or other figures. The clinician does not even need to use a real wand; a pen or pencil can be substituted and the clinician can instruct the child to "pretend this is a magic wand."

The clinician would conduct this activity in the following ways.

1. *Hands the magic wand to the child and says, "Now wave the magic wand and make a wish."*
2. *Asks the child to make a general wish or a wish that is more specific to the child's or family's needs.* The clinician could say, "Make a wish about what you would like to see happen at home," or "Make a wish about what would make you happy."
3. *Encourages children to hold the wand and to express their feelings.* The clinician could ask, "When you made that wish what were you feeling?" Alternatively, the clinician could have the child "fill in the blanks" for the following sentence "When I am _______, I feel ________."
4. *Uses the child's wish to initiate a family discussion.* The clinician starts the discussion with a statement, like

"Ms. Miller, what do you think about Sandra's wish?" or "How did you feel when you heard Sandra's wish?"

5. *Invites other members to wave the wand and make a wish.* Parents often participate to be supportive of the child, but it also allows them to share their wishes and feelings with the rest of the family in a nonthreatening way. They can say, "My wish is ______" or "When I see us ______, I feel ______."

III. **Gathering Additional Information**

To gather valuable information about specific components of the family function, the clinician should make inquiries in a respectful and sensitive manner. Parents with a family history of alcohol abuse, for instance, usually do not volunteer that information unless specifically asked (even then, they may deny it). Six sources/strategies for assessing selected components of family functioning are described in Table 7.1.

A. **Family history.** The family history (e.g., medical and psychosocial history) provides valuable information about family functioning. The following principles guide the clinician in exploring family history.

1. *Explore after a good relationship with the family has been established.*

2. *Remember that the exploration does not have to be completed in one visit.*

3. *Introduce it in a respectful manner that emphasizes its importance.* The clinician might say, *"I'd like to ask a few questions about your health and the health of other family members. This will help me understand the family."* Family history has many components, some of which families are used to (questions about medical problems—cancer, hypertension) and which are not perceived as threatening or intrusive. However, necessary inquiries about mental health and personal problems are more sensitive to the family and sometimes are perceived as intrusive or irrelevant. Therefore, the clinician should start with medical illnesses before psychosocial issues.

a. ***Medical illness.*** The clinician can inquire about grandparents, aunts, uncles, and "any other relative" as well as immediate family. Questioning might begin as follows, *"Let's start with you, the parents. Do either of you*

Table 7.1. Gathering additional information: six sources/strategies

1. Family history
2. Stressors that affect the family
3. Parenting history
4. The family life cycle
5. The brief family genogram
6. Child and family evaluation form (CAFÉ)

have medical problems? Are you receiving care? How have these problems affected you and your family?"

b. ***Psychosocial problems.***

(1) **Behavior problems.** Specific questions to ask include, *"Does your child remind you of yourself or of another relative?" "How would you describe your behavior as a child or teenager?"* and *"Did you or any relatives have any problems?"*

(2) **Mental health problems.** Queries can include, *"Have you or any relative ever been diagnosed with anxiety, depression, or any other mental health problem?" "What kind of treatment was suggested?" "Medication?" "Counseling?" "Was it helpful?"* and *"How has this affected you and your family?"*

(3) **Alcohol or drug problems.** Examples of questions include, *"Have you or any other family members ever had a problem with alcohol or drug use either now or in the past?" "Have you or another family member received help?"* and *"How has this affected you and your family?"*

If parents state they are currently affected by any of these problems, the clinician should **always** ask if they are getting treatment and if it is helpful. If the treatment is not helpful or if parents who wish to receive treatment are not getting it, the clinician can offer assistance by suggesting a referral in the following way.

Clinician: *Would you be interested in getting help? Do you have a primary care provider who could help or who could make a referral? Would you like me to help with a referral?*

See Chapter 14, "Making a Mental Health Referral," for further discussion.

B. **Stressors that affect the family.** Stressors are influences that negatively affect family functioning. Stressors can be internal (within the family) and/or external (outside the family). Although clinician does not have to explore all possible stressors, he or she should explore issues that are raised by the family or that the clinician thinks pertain to the problem. For example, if a parent spontaneously states, *"This problem has really affected my marriage,"* the clinician might ask, *"How has it affected your marriage?" "How would you describe your marriage?"* or *"Have you considered getting help?"*

External stressors can even include lack of transportation to attend an appointment at the clinic or hospital or lack of access to health care. In these cases the clinician might refer the family to a hospital or to the county Department of Social Services. Some internal stressors might include the same problems the clinician finds with a family history; however, both the clinician and the family might feel that discussing "stressors" instead of "family history" is easier. The use of "stressors" is often perceived as less intrusive and less personal. Other stressors might include marital discord or domestic violence.

The clinician can help the family feel comfortable in answering these questions by making a statement, such as, *"Every family experiences stress from time to time. I'd like to ask if you or a relative/partner has experienced any stresses or changes recently, especially around the time that the problems started."*

If the family seems hesitant or unsure in response to this question, the clinician can follow with a more specific question, such as, *"For example, has anyone experienced any new stress recently, like changes at work or drinking problems at home?"* or *"Has anyone tried to find help for this issue?"* (Table 7.2).

C. **Parenting history.** Asking parents about their upbringing and the ways that they were raised helps the clinician understand their parenting practices and beliefs. Parents' tendencies are to treat their children as they themselves were treated. A brief discussion between the parents and the clinician often gives both parties insight into how and why the parents act the way they do towards their children. With this understanding, changing parenting practices and parent–parent or parent–child interactions are two of the most common goals in family counseling. The clinician should first explain the reason for asking the parents about their parenting history. An example of how to do so follows.

Clinician: *The way we were raised as children strongly influences how we raise our own children. I'd like to ask you a few questions about your parents and how they raised you.*

The questions are intended to elicit descriptions of the following components of parenting style:

- expression and demonstration of positive and negative emotions;
- openness of communication; and
- amount of parenting control.

Table 7.2. Stressors that affect family functioning: selected examples

Internal	External
Divorce, marital conflict	Change in family income; poverty
Extra time and energy needed for a family member with a medical or emotional problem	Job or career stress
Alcohol–substance abuse	Lack of access to health care
Formation of a stepfamily	Lack of community resources
Domestic violence	Lack of social support (e.g., extended family, friends)

Influences on Parenting Style

When parents reflect about their own upbringing, they often gain insight into their own parenting practices. Sometimes this understanding motivates them to change undesirable practices and habits.

1. *Expression and demonstration of positive* emotions (affection, pride, warmth, acceptance, approval, and love) *and negative emotions* (withholding affection, belittling, humiliating, criticizing, scolding, nagging, blaming):
   a. ***"Did your own parents readily express their love, pleasure, and approval? Their displeasure?"***
   b. ***"How did they show these feelings?"***
   c. ***"Did they give you praise and encouragement?"***
   d. ***"How would you describe your relationship with your mother? Father? Siblings?"***
2. *Openness of communication* (thoughts and feelings) *between parents and children:*
   a. ***"How did your parents communicate with you?"***
   b. ***"Did they encourage you to express your feelings and thoughts?"***
   c. ***"Were some topics or feelings never discussed?"***
   d. ***"How does that affect you and your communication with your children?"***
   e. ***"Would you like to have more open communication with your children?"***
   f. ***"How did your parents resolve their conflicts*** (settle their arguments) ***between themselves or with you?"***
3. *Amount of parental control.* Control can range from restrictive/controlling/highly supervised to lax/permissive/loosely supervised:
   a. ***"How would you describe your parents' main parenting style?"***
   b. ***"Were they strict? Permissive? In between?"***
   c. ***"What were your parents' shortcomings and strengths?"***
   d. ***"How do their behaviors and parenting styles affect you and your children?"***
   e. ***"How did your parents reward you or acknowledge good effort and behavior?"***
   f. ***"How did they punish you or show disapproval for undesirable behaviors?"***
   g. ***"Were they fair?"***
   h. ***"Did your mother and father have different parenting styles? How did they resolve their differences?"***

i. ***"Do you parent differently from your parents? Does your style work for your family now?"***

D. **The family life cycle.** All families grow through stages of development, the family life cycle. For most families, it is a series of normal transitions and transformations which follow a predictable pattern that begins with marriage or a committed relationship, continues through pregnancy and childbirth; becomes a family with young children, then adolescents, and then adult children; and progresses to middle years, old age, and finally death. Specific developmental tasks are accomplished in each transition. Exploring the family's stage in the life cycle provides much information about the family.

Family life cycle changes, such as becoming a family with adolescents or with elderly grandparents, require adjustments that can be stressful. These changes are internal stressors or "growing pains of families;" although families respond to help and guidance with them, the stresses of these transitional phases are often temporary and thus are not necessarily indicative of serious dysfunction. The clinician should use the family life cycle to pinpoint the family's stage of development in order to help the parents understand and adapt to the challenges facing them. Many families cope well with these transitions unless additional changes are imposed upon the family life cycle (e.g., internal stressors, such as divorce or the formation of a stepfamily, or external stressors, such as the loss of a job or the move to a new city or state). Then the family's coping ability may be overwhelmed. To evaluate these additional factors, different forms have been developed. For more information, see the "Child And Family Evaluation (CAFÉ) form" below (see Table 7.3).

E. **How to use the family life cycle to assess family functioning.** The clinician should review the family's stage in the life cycle and then inquire about its adaptation to the corresponding developmental task/challenge. Examples of appropriate questioning for different stages appear below.

1. *The arrival of a baby.*
   a. ***What developmental task/challenge most affects the family?***
   b. ***How are new parents adjusting to their new parent roles?***
   c. ***Are they learning to share the parenting responsibilities?***
   d. ***What else is happening in the lives of the parents, the grandparents, and other children*** (if the family includes older children)?
      (1) **Parents.**
         (a) *Describe their physical and social–emotional health.*
         (b) *How are they doing with their marriage/partner relationship and jobs?*

(c) *How is their relationship with their parents?*
(d) *Do they have a support network?*

(2) **Grandparents.**
(a) *Describe their physical and social–emotional health.*
(b) *If they have problems (e.g., physical, emotional, or social), how do they impact the new parents/family?*
(c) *How is their relationship with their children and grandchildren?*
(d) *Are they a support for the family?*

(3) **Children.**
(a) *If an older sibling(s) is present, describe her/his health and social–emotional development.*
(b) *How is he or she adjusting to the new baby?*
(c) *Is he or she receiving appropriate attention?*

F. **The brief family genogram.** The brief family genogram rapidly diagrams and visualizes the family relationships of a nuclear family. The clinician uses it both to understand the family's problem ("current" situation) and to discover what they want to accomplish ("desired" situation) (Fig. 7.1). Once a genogram is created, it should be kept in the patient's chart, updated with new information as necessary, and expanded to include other members. A more detailed genogram is described in the "Child And Family Evaluation (CAFÉ)" form later in this chapter.

The following two cases illustrate how the clinician can use a brief genogram to understand the family functioning.

CASE 1: THE WELL-CHILD VISIT—THE FAMILY WITH A TODDLER WHOSE PARENTS CANNOT SET LIMITS

During a well-child visit David, a 2-year-old, is out of control. He runs all around the office, pulling open drawers, spilling supplies

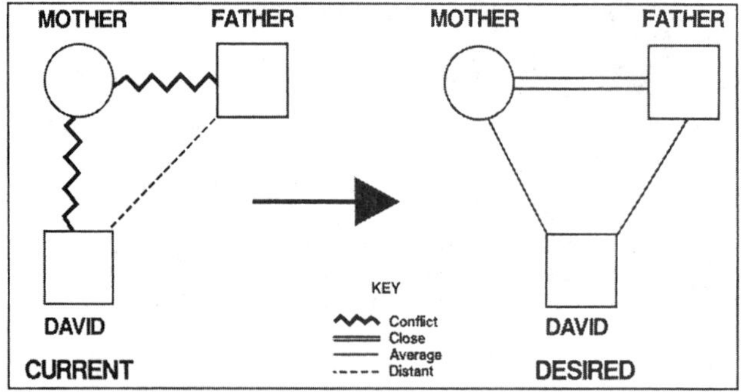

Figure 7.1. David's family: current and desired relationships.

on the floor, and opening and closing the door. His passive, depressed-looking mother angrily and repeatedly, yet ineffectively, tells him to stop; but she is unable to enforce her commands. Although the mother does not voice a concern, the clinician raises the subject of the toddler's noncompliance and the need to set limits and suggests a family meeting with both parents.

The Family Meeting

During the family meeting, the mother again appears unable to set limits, and David runs all around the room as he had before. The clinician asks the parents if this happened at home and in public (multiple settings). It had. The father's interactions with David are minimal, but he openly criticizes the mother for not setting limits. The mother's inability to manage David's behavior and the corresponding criticism she receives from her husband leaves her feeling depressed and discouraged, which is apparent to the clinician. In response to the clinician's inquiry, the mother reveals that she has felt depressed for several years but that she has not sought help. See Fig. 7.1, Current situation, and Chapter 11, "Supporting Parents," for further details.

The clinician helps the parents agree on a goal, discusses how they could cooperate with each other, and offers advice on appropriate behavior management techniques. Because the mother's difficulty in setting limits seems associated with her long-standing depression, the father becomes more sympathetic to his wife's struggles. The clinician also suggests a referral to a therapist for the mother, which she accepts (Fig. 7.1, Desired situation).

Other possible desired situations might include forging a "close" relationship between the father and David and/or between the mother and David or maintaining an "average" relationship between the parents while they both improve their relationship with David.

CASE 2: A 13-YEAR-OLD WHO IS "DEPRESSED"

First Adolescent Visit

A mother brings in Jimmy, her 13-year-old son, because of his "angry outbursts" at school. Jimmy sits far from his mother with his arms crossed and makes little eye contact with her. This the clinician attributes to "normal teenage behavior." Jimmy's symptoms began approximately 2 months ago when he began slamming doors, kicking walls, and arguing with classmates. His mother feels he is "depressed" because of his "father's illness" and urges the clinician to prescribe antidepressant medication. The clinician carefully interviews Jimmy, who is quiet but cooperative. He has several good friends, and is earning C's in school. A search for stressors reveals that approximately 3 months ago Jimmy's father had a serious heart attack and was forced into temporary retirement. He is spending his days at home and is participating in a cardiac rehabilitation program. Jimmy is concerned about his father but is glad that his father is "getting better." With the loss of the father's income, the mother has taken a full-time job and doesn't get home for dinner until 6 P.M. This leaves Jimmy and his father home together in the afternoons. Jimmy reports that they watch television together for an hour and that Jimmy then leaves to join his friends.

The family history reveals no mental illness, but the mother's father had died of a heart attack in mid-life when she was a young girl. In a private discussion with the clinician, Jimmy denies sexual activity or other romantic stressors and alcohol or drug use.

The clinician agrees with the mother's assessment—that Jimmy probably is "mildly depressed" because of his father's illness. He decides against medication for the present but does suggest that the parents try to schedule "more family time together." He schedules a follow-up appointment in 2 weeks.

Second Adolescent Visit

Jimmy and his mother return to the clinic. Jimmy sits far from his mother again and looks sullen. Following the clinician's advice, the mother has tried to schedule "more family time," but "no one wants it." Jimmy reports, *"Nothing has changed,"* and gives no explanation for his outbursts. The father is continuing his cardiac program and is making slow progress. The mother, who is "very worried about Jimmy," urges the clinician to "do something." The clinician, sensing Jimmy now might be depressed, prescribes an antidepressant, explains the purpose to Jimmy, and assures him he'll "feel better." He schedules another appointment in 4 weeks.

Third Adolescent Visit

The mother reports that Jimmy's "depression" has not improved. When asked about Jimmy's compliance, she states that she gives Jimmy the pill every morning at breakfast. When the clinician questions him, Jimmy admits that he is not swallowing the medication. He tucks the pill into his cheek and spits it out later. When the clinician tries again to convince him to take the medication, Jimmy says that it "wasn't fair." When asked to explain what he means, he refuses, and the mother has no idea of what he is talking about. The clinician is also confused. He feels that he is lacking important information about the family, so he asks the mother about scheduling a family meeting, which would also include the father. He explains the purpose of the meeting. The mother agrees and feels that her husband will too.

First Family Visit

The mother and father sit close together; Jimmy sits some distance from them both (Fig. 7.2). The clinician again explains the purpose of the meeting and reviews the history up to this point. He asks Jimmy again what he means by "It's not fair." Jimmy answers, *"It's not fair that I take the medication. I'm not the one with problems in this family."* When asked what he means by that, he looks at his father but says nothing. The clinician asks the father about his relationship with Jimmy. The father admits that it is *"not as peaceful as you've been told."* The father reveals that when Jimmy comes home from school, he makes many requests of

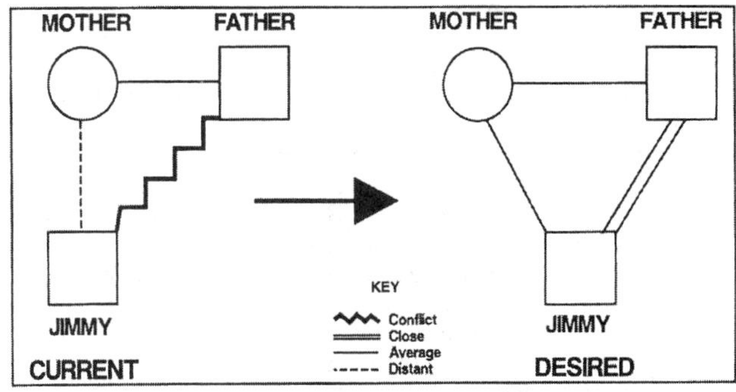

Figure 7.2. Jimmy's family: current and desired situations.

Jimmy (e.g., has Jimmy bring him a snack or clean up the house). In the ensuing discussion, the clinician discovers that the father also criticizes Jimmy for not making better grades and for spending so much time with his friends. When Jimmy argues back, the father points to his chest and threatens him by saying, *"If you keep arguing, you'll send me to my grave."* Jimmy, afraid to argue back, instead either retreats to his room or leaves the house, full of guilt and anger. The father also demands that Jimmy not reveal these arguments to the mother and threatens, *"If you do, you'll worry her to death."*

Jimmy feels neglected by his mother because *"she spends every minute with Dad."* Because she is unavailable, he withdraws; their relationship has become "distant." Jimmy is angry with his father, and they argue; but Jimmy suppresses his feelings because of his father's threats about his health and the demands to keep the arguments secret from the mother. The relationship between Jimmy and his father is one of conflict (Fig. 7.2, current situation).

Jimmy's mother is shocked to hear about this conflict and that both the father and the son have kept their conflict and feelings secret. The clinician asks the family to "talk it out at home" and to decide how they might improve the family relationships. They agree to try. He makes another appointment.

Second Family Visit

The family returns in 2 weeks. The members report that they have had a few family talks and that they are feeling a little better. The outbursts have subsided. Further questioning reveals more of the family situation, including the fact that the father is very depressed by his own situation. Compounding his depression is the fact that his own clinician has advised him not to have sexual relations with his wife during cardiac rehabilitation. He wants to resume a normal marital life. Despite urging from his clinician, he refuses to take antidepressant medication because he has heard that it "makes you lose your sex drive"; he fears that he will lose it "forever." He hadn't told his wife that he has stopped taking his medication.

The mother realizes that her memory of her father's death has intensified her concern about her husband so that she has devoted all her time to him, which in turn has isolated Jimmy from her. Jimmy, therefore, is feeling left out by both parents.

The clinician now realizes that Jimmy's anger at school is an expression of the unresolved conflict with his father and of his resentment toward his mother for neglecting him. Many stressors have converged on Jimmy and his parents and have changed their relationships with each other.

Together, the clinician and the parents develop ways to change the family interactions and to meet the family's goals of improving their relationships. The father's goal is to develop a "close" relationship with Jimmy (Fig. 7.2, desired situation). Jimmy is not as motivated, but he agrees to cooperate. The father arranges to spend some time with Jimmy each afternoon. They will take walks, play computer games, and occasionally go fishing to develop a better relationship. The father also agrees to undergo a trial of antidepressant medication with the understanding that side effects, if any occur, will not be permanent. If the medication does affect his sexual activity temporarily, his clinician will lower the dose or change the medication. Jimmy and his mother arrange to spend time together each evening. The mother will not devote all her time to her husband. Furthermore, the family plans to spend more time together in activities, such as reading and going to the library.

Third Family Visit

The family returns in a month. Jimmy and the father have done the things that they had discussed in the previous meeting, and their relationship has improved. The father feels it is close. The father is responding well to medication. His mood is brighter. His rehabilitation is going well. Jimmy and his mother have also followed through on their plans, and their relationship has resumed its "average" status. The family's new interactions are improving the relationships.

Fourth Family Visit

After another month, they return. As life returns to normal, Jimmy and his father spend less time together. Their relationship has become "average," but it is much better than it had been 5 months ago. The mother and Jimmy have maintained a good relationship. The father's health is improving, and he and his wife have resumed their sexual relationship. He continues to take his medication. The family feels it does not need any more sessions with the clinician, and everyone agrees that this will be the final family meeting.

IV. **Screening Tools**

A. **The Child and Family Evaluation (CAFÉ).** The Child and Family Evaluation (CAFÉ) is a single evaluation form used to gather and record information about family history, the family life cycle, the brief family genogram, and the family stressors and strengths. It provides a quick family profile and is easily updated (Table 7.3).

B. **Family genogram.** The genogram is a way to record medical and psychosocial information and to map out the family relationships and intergenerational processes (how patterns of behavior are maintained from generation to generation). The genogram helps the clinician understand the family structure and function. In turn, the clinician can use the genogram to help the family understand its own issues (Fig. 7.3).

Additional ways to record pertinent information are shown in Table 7.4.

C. **Screening for family–psychosocial problems.**

Whether and When to Use a Screening Tool

The clinician must make this decision because the topics, which are sensitive (e.g., marital distress), may dismay the parent. The parents may also see the screening tool as intrusive and inappropriate, or they may not understand its purpose. Furthermore, the clinician–parent relationship may not be well established, thus complicating the use of the screening tool even further. If the clinician decides to use a screening tool, he or she should do so when the clinician–parent relationship is comfortable, confidentiality is assured, and the reason for the questioning is carefully explained.

Screening questions provide invaluable information about family function, especially about family–psychosocial problems, including parental depression, substance abuse (alcohol and drugs), domestic violence, and lack of social support, all of which impact children and families. Screening, though brief and effective, should only be used in the broader context of the clinician's understanding of the family. Screening should never be substituted for comprehensive diagnostic assessments. Families may worry about the confidentiality of the screening.

Clinicians can screen in several ways. They can ask the questions themselves, or they can assign the task to someone else in the office. Optionally, self-administered questionnaires can be mailed to families prior to the visit or can be filled out in the office. Screening tools provide clinicians with specific

Table 7.3. Child and family evaluation (CAFÉ)[a]

The Family Life Cycle: The clinician can use this table to help the family members understand the expectations and challenges facing them at this particular point in their own family life cycle.

Stage		Expectations, Issues, and Challenges
1. The new couple	_____	Relationship commitment
	_____	Marriage/living together
	_____	Formation of extended family
2. The birth of children	_____	Being both parents and spouses
	_____	Sharing tasks
	_____	Using extended family supports (e.g., grandparents)
3. Families with school-age children	_____	More demands on children (school, peers)
	_____	More demands on adults (parents, spouses, careers/jobs)
4. Families with adolescents	_____	Renegotiation of parent-adolescent relationship (roles and expectations)
	_____	Parents support aging relatives (grandparents, others)
5. Midlife years (parents) Young adulthood (children)		
a. Parents	_____	Empty nest; reassess and refocus on marriage, self, and career
	_____	Increased support of aging and dying parents/grandparents
	_____	Coming to terms with own aging and physiologic decline
	_____	Accommodating new in-laws and grandchildren
b. Young adults	_____	Focus on own identity; intimate relationships; marriage
	_____	Career development
6. Later life of parents; loss, grieving, and death	_____	Generational roles change
	_____	Adult children care for aging parents
	_____	Loss of spouse, siblings, friends; life review; preparation for own death

Comments:

[a]This form may be reproduced for clinical use.

questions they want to ask and/or issues they want to explore in the general interview. However, clinicians should not use the screening tool itself to elicit answers to such specific questions; it merely serves as a guide for the clinician of areas that require more exploration.

Using a Screening Tool

The clinician can use a screening tool in two ways. He or she can administer it by asking the questions or by requesting that the parents complete the form themselves. The clinician can use a screening tool as a reminder to inquire about family psychosocial problems. He or she can also select (and modify) any questions that seem relevant (e.g., "In the past year, have you or anyone else in the family had a problem with drinking?" or "Are you satisfied with the way you and your family share time together?").

Seven brief screening tools are described in Table 7.5. The first four screen for the family psychosocial problems of parental depression, substance abuse, domestic violence, and marital distress. The next two screen for the availability of support systems and the adequacy of family functioning; the last is a general composite of overall family psychosocial functioning.

1. *Parental depression.* Rates of depression in mothers of young children range from 12% in private practices to 24% in urban teaching clinics or military pediatric clinics. For working mothers with toddlers seen in an urban training clinic, depression occurs in as high as 42% of them. Up to 50% of poor, single mothers who have not completed high school struggle with depression (Kemper & Babonis, 1992). Depression arises more often in mothers who are divorced or who have never been married.

    Children of depressed mothers and fathers are at risk for abuse, neglect, witnessing or experiencing domestic violence, and developmental/behavioral/emotional problems.

    The three-item screen for depression described here is brief yet reliable (Rost et al., 1993). Two or three positive answers, which are considered a positive screen for depression, should be followed up by further questions about changes in eating or sleeping habits, crying episodes, energy or activity levels, and concentration and about thoughts or plans about suicide. Clinicians should reassure parents with the information that many parents experience depression and that qualified mental health professionals can treat it (Table 7.6).

(*text continues on page 140*)

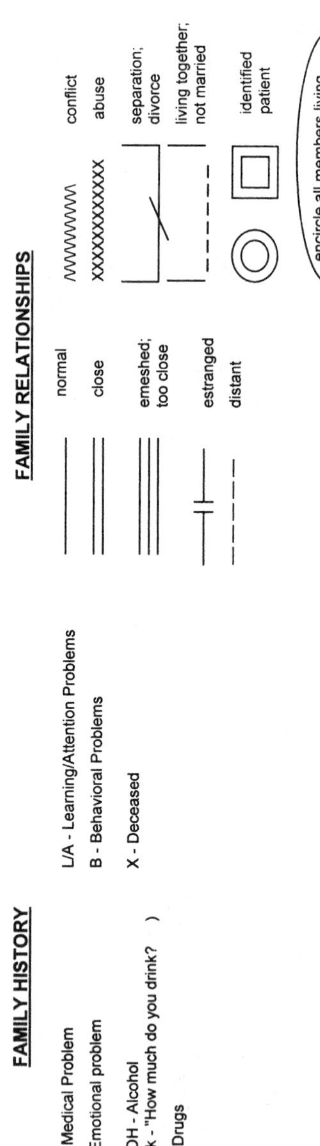
FAMILY HISTORY
M - Medical Problem
E- Emotional problem
ETOH - Alcohol
(Ask - "How much do you drink?)
D - Drugs
L/A - Learning/Attention Problems
B - Behavioral Problems
X - Deceased
FAMILY RELATIONSHIPS
normal
close
emeshed; too close
estranged
distant
conflict
abuse
separation; divorce
living together; not married
identified patient
encircle all members living in the house

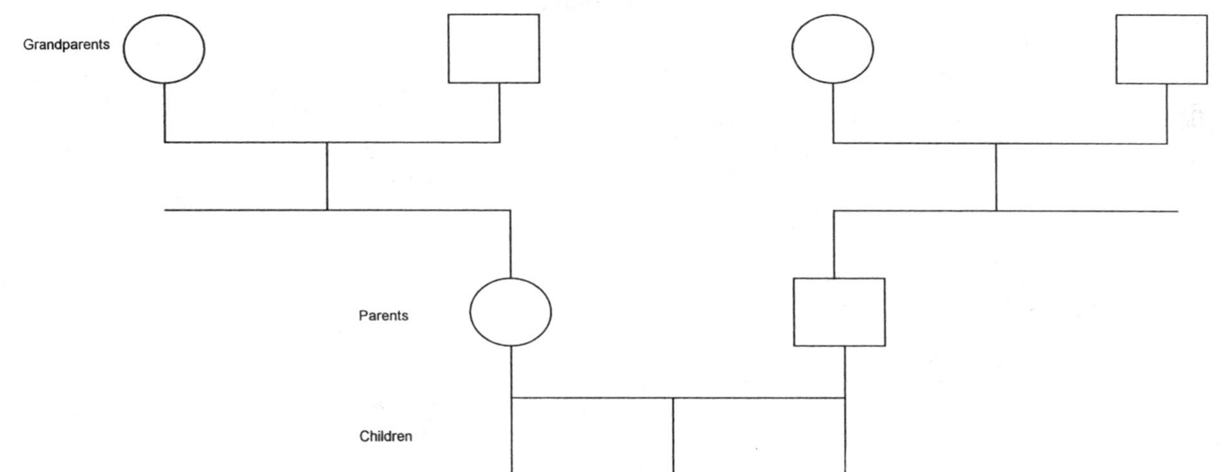

Figure 7.3. Family genogram.

Table 7.4. Additional ways to record information

Stressors and Supports

Stressors (risk factors) are negative influences on the family. Supports (protective factors) are positive influences on the family. Stressors and supports may be either internal or external. Clinicians can enhance their understanding of the family members and can better help them if they describe these factors.

Directions: Use "–" if a stressor and "+" if a strength. The absence of a support may be considered a stressor.

Extended family_____	Housing_____	Income_____
Friends_____	Schools_____	Employment/ career_____
Neighborhood_____	Transportation_____	Social services_____
Cultural system_____	Recreational resources_____	Health care_____ (physical and mental)
Religion_____		

Family goals and plans

The clinician can use this list to record the family's goals and plans.

Goals	Plans

Summary

The clinician can summarize the child-family situation: family life cycle, genogram, stressors, and supports.

Table 7.4. *Continued*

Strengths and Supports	Stressors and Risk Factors
1.	1.
2.	2.
3.	3.
4.	4.

Comments: ______________________________

____

____

Table 7.5. Seven family psychosocial screening questionnaires

1. Parental depression
2. Parental substance abuse
3. Domestic violence (spousal or partner)
4. Marital distress
5. Availability of social support
6. Family functioning (family APGAR)*
7. Child and family intake form (family psychosocial questionnaire)

*Virginia Apgar is the physician who developed a neonatal assessment tool.

Table 7.6. Screen for Parental Depression

Circle the answer given.

1. How often in the last week have you felt depressed? (*Note:* any answer other than 0 is a positive answer.)	0	1–2	3–4	5–7 days
2. In the past year have you had 2 weeks or more during which you felt sad, blue, or depressed or lost pleasure in the things you usually cared about or enjoyed?			Yes	No
3. Have you ever had 2 or more years in your life when you felt depressed or sad most days even if you felt okay sometimes?			Yes	No

2. *Parental substance abuse (alcohol and/or drugs).* Parental substance abuse is the most prevalent psychosocial problem affecting children. Approximately 10 million American children are being raised by alcoholic or drug-addicted parents. Up to 10% of American adults meet the diagnostic criteria for substance abuse, but few are identified by clinicians. If the mother exposes her children to drugs or alcohol during pregnancy, they are likely to suffer the effects. Children of parents with substance abuse problems are at higher risk for injuries and accidents, behavioral problems, depression, suicide attempts, low self-esteem, delinquent behavior, abuse and neglect, learning problems, and alcoholism and drug use (Kemper & Kelleher, 1996a). Table 7.7 shows a seven-item screening tool for family psychosocial problems (Kemper & Kelleher, 1996b).

3. *Domestic violence (spousal or partner abuse).* Domestic violence is common. During the course of a year, up to 14% of couples experience domestic violence (Domestic Violence and Children, 1999). It occurs in all racial and socioeconomic

Table 7.7. Screen for parental substance abuse

Circle the answer given.			
1. In the past year, have you had a problem with drinking?		Yes	No
2. In the past year, have you tried to cut down on your drinking?		Yes	No
3. How many drinks does it take for you to get high or feel a buzz? (*Note:* More than two drinks to feel the effects is a positive screen indicating tolerance to alcohol.)	0 1 2 3 4 5 more		
4. Do you ever have five or more drinks at a time?		Yes	No
5. In the past year, have you had a problem with drugs?		Yes	No
6. In the past 24 hours have you used any of the following drugs: marijuana, cocaine, crack, heroin, methadone, speed, LSD, amphetamines, or other drugs?		Yes	No
7. Would you like to talk with other parents who are dealing with alcohol or drug problems? Would you like more information about alcohol or drug treatment programs in our area?		Yes	No

classes but is most frequent among unmarried white couples who live in poverty and experience social isolation. Victims may have physical evidence of abuse (e.g., bruises, fractures) or behavioral/emotional suggestions of abuse (e.g., repeated visits to emergency rooms, depression, helplessness ["I can't do any more," "Nothing works," or "I've given up"]). Children living in homes with domestic violence are at risk for experiencing physical abuse themselves, developing behavioral–emotional and learning problems, and demonstrating violent behavior later in life. Currently no validated screening tools for identifying domestic violence in the pediatric clinical setting exist, but the screening tool presented in Table 7.8 (Kemper & Kelleher, 1996b) provides four questions that are useful in initiating a pertinent discussion with the parent. One positive answer equals a positive screen for spousal abuse. Present federal law does not mandate reporting spousal abuse, but further questioning (including discussion of the child's safety) and counseling are needed. Victims should be provided with information (e.g., hotlines, shelters, and police protection) and should be urged both to seek help for themselves and to assure their child's safety. Follow-up visits, continued support for the victim, and monitoring the child's status are crucial for the clinician.

4. *Marital distress.* Marital-partner distress is a common family psychosocial stress. The brief screening questionnaire shown in Table 7.9 should be used when the clinician senses a strain in the marital-partner relationship. Two or more questions that are checked "yes" equal a positive screen. If marital distress is indicated, if question number 5 is answered "no" (i.e., marital distress is *not* a main concern), or if the interview reveals that other personal problems probably stem from the marital distress

Table 7.8. Screening for domestic violence

Circle the answer given.

1. In the past year, have you ever felt emotionally or physically abused by your partner or someone important to you?	Yes	No
2. In the past year, have you been hit, slapped, kicked, or otherwise physically hurt by someone?	Yes	No
If yes, by whom? (Circle all that apply) Spouse / Ex-spouse Boyfriend/Girlfriend / Stranger		
3. Within the past year, has anyone forced you to participate in sexual activities?	Yes	No
4. Are you afraid of your partner or anyone else listed above?	Yes	No

Table 7.9. Marital distress screen[a]

Circle the answer given.		
1. Do you sometimes worry about how you and your spouse (or partner) are getting along?	Yes	No
2. Is there a lack of closeness in your relationship?	Yes	No
3. Is there too much conflict?	Yes	No
4. Have you recently thought about divorce or separation?	Yes	No
5. Is your marriage (or partnership) your biggest personal concern right now?	Yes	No

[a] Developed by William J. Doherty, Ph.D., University of Minnesota, Family Science Dept., St. Paul, MN. Used with permission.

(e.g., depressive or anxiety symptoms in reaction to marital conflict), the clinician should consider suggesting a referral for marital/couples therapy. The clinician should definitely refer the couple for marital therapy if marital distress is present and question number 5 is also answered "yes" (marital distress is a main concern) unless the personal interview reveals another major disorder (e.g., alcoholism).

5. *Availability of social support.* Screening also can identify protective factors or family strengths, such as social support. Social support, which is essential for family well being, serves as a buffer to protect the family from the effects of stress. Social support can be defined in several ways. One definition is that it is a set of emotional–social–parenting supports provided by social networks in an ongoing manner. These supports include assurance, socializing, guidance, practical help, and parent training. Social support improves parenting by providing emotional support, imparting knowledge, providing respite, empowering parents, and providing role models for parenting behavior and social relationships. Social support may also be defined as positive attachments among individuals or a feeling that one is cared for, loved, and valued as a member of a group who has meaningful and satisfactory relationships within that group. Family, friends, work colleagues, parent–teacher organizations, religious organizations, community support programs, and parent support groups all constitute social supports. Table 7.10 shows a tool that can be used to screen for the availability of social support (Domestic Violence and Children, 1999).

A positive screen indicating lack of social support is interpreted as either having an average of less than two supportive persons listed for each answer or feeling less than very satisfied with the support provided by those persons. If the screen is positive, the clinician should follow

Table 7.10. Screening for availability of social support

1. Who can you count on to be dependable when you need help?* Just write their initials and relationship to you.

Note: Provide enough space for six answers

Very satisfied	Fairly satisfied	Little satisfied
Little dissatisfied	Fairly dissatisfied	Very dissatisfied

2. Who accepts you totally including your best and worst points.* Just write their initials and relationship to you.

Note: Provide enough space for six answers

Very satisfied	Fairly satisfied	Little satisfied
Little dissatisfied	Fairly dissatisfied	Very dissatisfied

3. Whom do you feel truly loves you deeply? Just write their initials and relationship to you.*

Note: Provide enough space for six answers

Very satisfied	Fairly satisfied	Little satisfied
Little dissatisfied	Fairly dissatisfied	Very dissatisfied

*Ask the parent to rate his or her level of satisfaction with these persons.

these specific guidelines in addition to the general ones suggested above.

a. ***Inquire about help in the home with childcare, babysitting, daily chores, and errands.***

b. ***Inquire about friends and extended family and whether or not the parents have sought their support or support from others.***

c. ***Refer the family to a social service agency, a family support group, or a home visitor program.***

V. **Family Functioning: The Family APGAR and the Child and Family Intake Form**

Two more screening tools are sometimes used to assess family function: the Family APGAR (Smilkstein, 1978) and the child and family intake form/family psychosocial questionnaire.

A. **The Family APGAR.** This brief screening tool is named after Dr. Virginia Apgar, who also developed the newborn assessment tool. It assesses five levels of family function: emotional support, family communication, independence/initiative, sharing feelings, and shared family time (see Appendix A).

1. *Use.* Depending on which member of the family the clinician is interviewing, he or she may substitute the word "family" for either "spouse," "significant other," "parents," or "children."

2. *Scoring.* The patient checks one of three choices, which are scored as follows: "Almost always" receives 2 points; "Some of the time" is assigned 1 point; "Hardly ever" adds 0 points. The scores for each of the five questions are then totaled. A score of 7 to 10 suggests a highly functional family; a score of 4 to 6 suggests a moderately dysfunctional family; a score of 0 to 3 suggests a high level of current dis-

satisfaction in one family member, but it is not unmistakable evidence of severe family dysfunction. The latter diagnosis will require more evidence about the family system.

B. **Child and family intake form/family psychosocial questionnaire** (Kemper, 1996b). This form, as shown in Table 7.11, provides an overview of the child and the family. The clinician should feel free to explore any topics that appear worrisome (e.g., a parent answers "yes" to "Have you ever had a drug problem?" or "Do you feel you were neglected as a child?" or "yes" to any question under "I feel depressed"). These answers and ensuing questioning may reveal that the parents want or need a referral for themselves.

1. *Scoring criteria for child and family intake form/ family psychosocial questionnaire.*

a. ***"Family Activities."*** Three items under "Family Activities" screen for parental depression. If the parent gives positive answers to two or more positive questions, the clinician should consider this a positive screen. When a positive screen is present, exploring other symptoms, such as changes in appetite, weight, sleep, activities, energy level, ability to concentrate, feelings of hopelessness, and thoughts and plans about suicide, may be helpful. Reassuring the parent about the frequency of depression often helps them as does noting the availability of various treatment options, such as psychologists, psychiatrists, family doctors, internists, and support groups.

b. ***"Drinking and Drugs."*** Seven questions under "Drinking and Drugs" screen for parental substance abuse. A positive response to any one of the first six is considered a positive screen. The clinician should follow-up any positive answer with further questions about frequency of use, the impact on the family, and the parent's impression of the effects of parental drinking on the children's emotional–social health. Advice from physicians to quit smoking is often highly effective, but the elimination of the abuse of other substances is rarely as easy. Therefore, the clinician should make referrals for further assessment and treatment.

c. ***"Family Health Habits."*** Four questions under "Family Health Habits" assess domestic violence. Parents who respond positively to any of these questions should receive further counseling, and the clinician should explore the extent of and patterns of violence and should discuss safety issues for children (including gun storage). Parents subjected to domestic violence may need assistance for making escape plans and should be referred to hotlines or shelters. Clinicians should inform these parents that domestic violence is wrong but not uncommon. The victims need follow-up visits and ongoing support even if they return to the batterer. Forming a therapeutic relationship around the

(*text continues on page 149*)

Table 7.11. Child and family intake form (family psychosocial screening)

Child and Family Intake Form

In order for us to serve you and your child better, please take a few minutes to answer the following questions. Your answers will be kept strictly confidential as part of your child's medical record.

Child's name: ____________________ Today's date: __________

Circle either the word or the letter for your answer where appropriate. Fill in answers where space is provided.

Are you the child's
A. Mother B. Father C. Grandparent
D. Foster parent E. Other relative F. Other
G. Self (Are you the patient?)

How many times have you moved in the last year? _________ times

Where is the child living now?
A. House or apartment with family
B. House or apartment with relative or friends
C. Shelter
D. Other

What is your current monthly income, including public assistance? $____________

Besides you, does anyone else take care of your child? If yes, who? ____________________ Yes No

Has your child received health care elsewhere? If yes, what type? ____________________ Yes No

Does your child have any allergies to any medications? If yes, what medications? ______________ Yes No

Has your child received any immunizations? Yes No
Which ones? ______________________________
Where? ______________________________

Has your child ever been hospitalized? Yes No
When? ______________________________
Where? ______________________________
Why? ______________________________

How would you rate your child's health in general?
A. Excellent B. Good C. Fair D. Poor

Do you have any concerns about your child's behavior or development? If yes, what? Yes No

____

____

What are your main concerns about your child?

____

____

(continued)

Table 7.11. *Continued*

How old are you? __________ years old

Are you?

A. Single B. Married C. Separated D. Divorced E. Other

What is the highest grade you have completed?

1 2 3 4 5 6 7 8 9 10 11 12 (High School/GED)

13 14 15 16 17 18 19

Some college or vocational school College Graduate Postgraduate

Family medical history

Does your child's mother, father, or grandparents have any of the following? If yes, please write down which relative.

Yes	No	High blood pressure	__________
Yes	No	Diabetes	__________
Yes	No	Lung problems (asthma)	__________
Yes	No	Heart problems	__________
Yes	No	Miscarriages	__________
Yes	No	Learning problems	__________
Yes	No	Nerve problems	__________
Yes	No	Mental illness (depression)	__________
Yes	No	Drinking problems	__________
Yes	No	Drug problems	__________
Yes	No	Other	__________

Family health habits

How often does your child use a seat belt (car seat)?

A. Never B. Rarely C. Sometimes

D. Often E. Always

Does your child ride a bicycle? Yes No

If yes, how often does he/she use a helmet?

A. Never B. Rarely C. Sometimes

D. Often E. Always

Do you feel that you live in a safe place? Yes No

In the past year, have you ever felt threatened in your home? Yes No

In the past year, has your partner or other family member pushed you, punched you, kicked you, hit you, or threatened to hurt you? Yes No

What kind of gun(s) are in your home?

A. Handgun B. Shotgun C. Rifle

D. Other ______________ E. None

If you have a gun at home, is it locked up? N/A Yes No

Does anyone in your household smoke? Yes No

Do you currently smoke cigarettes? If yes, how many cigarettes do you smoke per day? Yes No

_____ cigarettes/day

Table 7.11. *Continued*

Drinking and drugs

In the past year have you ever had a drinking problem?	Yes	No
Have you tried to cut down on alcohol in the past year?	Yes	No
How many drinks does it take for you to get high or get a buzz? 1 2 3 4 5 6 7 or more		
Do you ever have five or more drinks at one time?	Yes	No
Have you ever had a drug problem?	Yes	No
Have you used any drugs in the last 24 hours?	Yes	No

If yes, which ones?

Cocaine Heroin Methadone Speed Marijuana

Other: ______________________

Are you in a drug or alcohol recovery program now?	Yes	No
Would you like to talk with other parents who are dealing with alcohol or drug problems?	Yes	No

When you were a child

Did either parent have a drug or alcohol problem?	Yes	No
Were you raised part or all of the time by foster parents or relatives (other than your parents)	Yes	No

How often did your parents ground you or put you on time out?

A. Frequently B. Often C. Occasionally D. Rarely E. Never

How often did your parents ridicule you in front of friends or family?

A. Frequently B. Often C. Occasionally D. Rarely E. Never

How often were you hit with an object such as a belt, board, hairbrush, stick, or cord?

A. Frequently B. Often C. Occasionally D. Rarely E. Never

How often were you thrown against walls or down stairs?

A. Frequently B. Often C. Occasionally D. Rarely E. Never

Do you feel you were physically abused?	Yes	No
Do you feel you were neglected?	Yes	No
Do you feel you were hurt in a sexual way?	Yes	No
Did your parents ever hurt you when they were out of control?	Yes	No
Are you ever afraid you might lose control and hurt your child?	Yes	No
Would you like more information about free parenting programs, parent hot lines, or respite care?	Yes	No
Would you like information about birth control or family planning?	Yes	No

Family activities

How strong are your family's religious beliefs or practices?

A. Very strong B. Moderately strong C. Not strong D. N/A

What religion/church/temple?

(continued)

Table 7.11. *Continued*

How often do you read bedtime stories to your child?
A. Frequently B. Often C. Occasionally D. Rarely E. Never

How often does your family eat meals together?
A. Frequently B. Often C. Occasionally D. Rarely E. Never

What does your family do together for fun?

Depression

How often in the last week have you felt depressed?
0 1–2 3–4 5–7 days

In the past year, have you had 2 weeks or more during which you felt sad, blue, or depressed; or have you lost pleasure in things that you usually care about or enjoyed? Yes No

Have you had 2 or more years in your life when you felt depressed or sad most days, even if you felt okay sometimes? Yes No

Help and support

Whom can you count on to be dependable when you need help? (Just write their initials and their relationship to you.)

A. No one	B. ______	C. ______
D. ______	E. ______	F. ______
G. ______	H. ______	I. ______

How satisfied are you with their support?

A. Very satisfied	B. Fairly satisfied	C. A little satisfied
D. A little dissatisfied	E. Fairly dissatisfied	F. Very dissatisfied

Who accepts you totally, including both your best and worst parts?

A. No one	B. ______	C. ______
D. ______	E. ______	F. ______
G. ______	H. ______	I. ______

How satisfied are you with their support?

A. Very satisfied	B. Fairly satisfied	C. A little satisfied
D. A little dissatisfied	E. Fairly dissatisfied	F. Very dissatisfied

Who do you feel truly loves you deeply?

A. No one	B. ______	C. ______
D. ______	E. ______	F. ______
G. ______	H. ______	I. ______

How satisfied are you with their support?

A. Very satisfied	B. Fairly satisfied	C. A little satisfied
D. A little dissatisfied	E. Fairly dissatisfied	F. Very dissatisfied

issue of the child's safety and well being is recommended because children are at risk for experiencing physical abuse in homes where domestic violence occurs.

d. ***"When You Were a Child."*** Eight questions under "When You Were a Child" assess the parents' history of abuse. Such backgrounds predispose parents to disciplinary practices that either are too harsh and abusive or are too permissive. Responding positively to one of the first four questions is considered a positive screen. The last four questions gather additional information about disciplinary techniques and the parents' need for counseling and training.

e. ***"Help and Support."*** Six questions under "Help and Support" assess social support, a strong factor in reducing overall life and parenting stresses. Adequate social support helps ensure appropriate models for parenting practices and provides social control for disciplinary techniques. A screen is considered positive when answers to the first three questions demonstrate that the parents have an average of fewer than two supportive persons or that parents appear less than very satisfied with their support. Referrals to parenting groups, social work services, home visitor programs, or community family support services are warranted.

f. ***The Child and Family Intake form.*** The "child and family intake" form has twenty questions that also assess a number of social risk factors for developmental and behavioral problems. These factors include frequent household moves, single parenting, three or more children in the home, parent(s) with less than a high school education, and unemployment. Four or more such risk factors, which also include mental health problems and an authoritarian parenting style (observed by the clinician when parents use commands excessively or when they are negative and/or minimally responsive to child-initiated interests), are associated with a substantial drop in children's intelligence levels and subsequent school achievement. In such cases, children should also be referred for early stimulation programs, such as Head Start, or a quality day care or preschool program.

2. *When the screen is positive*. When the screen for family/psychosocial problems is positive, the clinician can ask the parents more detailed questions about the problem to facilitate a discussion about a possible referral (Table 7.12). See Chapter 14, "Making a Mental Health Referral," for further discussion.

V. Summary

Assessing family functioning is one of the major tasks of family counseling. The clinician has many sources of information and strategies to assess the family. These include observing assigned activities in the meeting; gathering additional informa-

Table 7.12. When the screen is positive: questions to facilitate a discussion about a possible referral

1. **About the parents' level of concern about the problem:** "Are you concerned about the problem?"
2. **About their understanding of the impact on the child:** "How do you think the problem is affecting your child?"
3. **About help in the past; if yes, what happened:** "Have you sought help in the past? What was the result?"
4. **About getting help now:** "Would you consider getting help now?"

tion with questioning and the use of tools (family history, presence of stressors, family life cycle, and genograms); and the use of screening tools for family–psychosocial problems. A complete family assessment may not be necessary; it cannot be and should not be attempted in the first family meeting. Assessing family functioning is an ongoing process with the clinician learning more about the family with each subsequent visit.

REFERENCES

Doherty WJ. Unpublished manuscript. Family Science Department, University of Minnesota, St. Paul, 1998.

Domestic Violence and Children. *The future of children*. Los Altos, CA: The David and Lucille Packard Foundation, 1999;9(3).

Kahn RS, Wise PH, Finkelstein JA, et al. The scope of unmet maternal health needs in a pediatric setting. *Pediatrics* 1999; 103(3):576–581.

Kemper KJ, Babonis TR. Screening for maternal depression in pediatric clinics. *AJDC* 1992;146:876–878.

Kemper KJ, Kelleher KJ. Rationale for family psychosocial screening. *Ambulatory Child Health* 1996a;1:311–324.

Kemper KJ, Kelleher KJ. Family psychosocial screening: instruments and techniques. *Ambulatory Child Health* 1996b;1:325–339.

Rost K, Burnam MA, Smith GR. Development of screeners for depressive disorders and substance abuse history. *Med Care* 1993;31: 189–200.

Smilkstein G. The family APGAR: a proposal for a family function test and its use by clinicians. *J Fam Pract* 1978;6:1231–1239.

ADDITIONAL READING

American Academy of Pediatrics Committee on Child Abuse and Neglect. The role of the pediatrician in recognizing and intervening on behalf of abused women (RE9748). *Pediatrics* 1998;101: 1091–1092.

Bauman LJ. Social support. In: Green M, Haggerty RJ, Weitzman ML, eds. *Ambulatory Pediatrics*, 5th ed. Philadelphia: WB Saunders, 1999.

Bing E. The conjoint family drawing. *Fam Process* 1970;9:173.

Carter B, McGoldrick M. *The changing family life cycle*. Needham Heights, MA: Allyn and Bacon, 1989.

Coleman WL, Howard BJ. Family-focused behavioral pediatrics: clinical techniques for primary care. *Pediatr Rev* 1995;16(12):448–455.

DiLeo JH. *Children's drawings as diagnostic aids*. New York: Brunner/Mazel, 1973.

Mayfield D, McLeod G, Hall P. The CAGE questionnaire: validation of a new alcoholism screening questionnaire. *Am J Psychiatry* 1974; 131:1121–1123.

Ross Roundtable. *Family violence*. Columbus, OH: Ross Laboratories, 1993.

Rubin J, Magnussen M. Family art evaluation. *Fam Process* 1974; 13:185.

Taylor EH. Understanding and helping families with neurodevelopmental and neuropsychiatric special needs. In: Coleman WL, Taylor EH, eds. *Family focused pediatrics. Pediatr Clin N Am* 1995; 42(1):143–153.

Welsh JB, Instone SL. Use of drawings by children in the pediatric office. In: Dixon SD, Stein MT, eds. *Encounters with children*, 3rd ed. St. Louis: Mosby-Year Book, 2000.

Zuckerman B. Family history: a special opportunity for psychosocial intervention. *Pediatrics* 1991;87:740–745.

8 Three Models of Brief Family Interviews

I. Purpose

Many models of family interviews and many ways to conduct family interviews exist. This chapter describes three models for brief family interviews: Problem-oriented, Solution-oriented, and the ABC (Antecedent, Behavior, Consequence). Even though each of these models has its unique approach, they all incorporate family counseling skills, which are a combination of family systems principles, methods to help families develop their own solutions, and clinician-directed advice and interventions.

Each model described in this chapter follows the "four steps" sequence of a family interview and includes case studies that illustrate its individual aspects. (Previously in Chapter 6, "The Four Steps of a Family Interview," the problem-oriented interview was the prototype used for describing the four steps of a family meeting because it is the model with which most clinicians are familiar.) All three of these models are geared toward:

- family counseling;
- level 2 problems; and
- clinicians working at level 3 of involvement with the family.

II. The Problem-Oriented Family Interview

The problem-oriented interview incorporates many techniques of the biomedical model. Problems are like puzzles for the clinician, who gathers all the pieces, fits them together, makes a diagnosis, and then solves the problem by offering interventions and advice. In family interviews the clinician not only offers advice to the family but also helps it develop ways to change its behaviors and come up with its own solutions (Table 8.1).

Indications for Use of the Problem-Oriented Family Interview

The problem-oriented interview provides a detailed description of the problem. It is useful for clinicians who are more comfortable and skilled with the biomedical model and for families who want and need to talk about the problem before they can work on solutions. All families expect to talk about the problem initially. Beginning with a problem description fits the family's expectations and meets its needs, but the clinician must determine how much time should be devoted to the description.

CASE 1: THE FAMILY WITH A SON WITH ATTENTION-DEFICIT/HYPERACTIVITY DISORDER WHO "WON'T TAKE HIS MEDICATION AFTER SCHOOL"

The Phone Call from the Parent

The mother of a 14-year-old boy (Bobby) called because he *"won't take his medication after school."* The clinician knew Bobby

Table 8.1. The problem-oriented family interview: steps and questions

1. **Engaging the family** (time: 3 to 5 minutes).[a]
   Greet the family.
   Social conversation/Join with the family.
   State the purpose of the meeting.
2. **Understanding the family** (time: 15 to 20 minutes).[a]
   Explore the problem: gather a description of the problem.
   Assess behaviors that maintain the problem and its impact on the family.
   Identify family changes that affect the problem.
   Discuss past attempts and advice that the family has received to resolve the problem.
   Discuss a goal.
   The clinician can end the first visit. See step 4.
   Start of second visit.
3. **Working with the family** (time: 15 to 20 minutes).[a]
   Identify family strengths and resources.
   Engage the family in developing a plan of action.
   Offer advice.
   Assign homework tasks.
4. **Concluding the meeting** (time: 3 to 5 minutes).[a]
   Summarize the meeting.
   Invite the family to ask questions or share thoughts.
   Schedule the next visit.
   Compliment and thank the family.

[a] These times are approximations based on the number of questions and complexity of the case.

but really did not know the family well. He had diagnosed Bobby with attention deficit/hyperactivity disorder (ADHD) and was treating him with stimulant medication. The school had provided accommodations for his attention problems. The clinician remembered the boy as being well adjusted both socially and emotionally. The mother added that *"his behavior is concerning all of us."*

Clinician (determining who is involved, who is affected): *Who do you mean by "all of us?"*

Mother: *All of us. Me, my husband, Bobby, and his brother, Randy. Everyone is stressed out. We don't know what to do.*

After a few more minutes of conversation in which the mother kept referring to the stress on the family, the clinician suggested a family meeting.

Clinician: *I'd like to suggest that we have a few family meetings. That means I'd like your husband and Randy to come in, too.*

The clinician scheduled three meetings. Before the first meeting, he reviewed Bobby's chart.

The First Family Meeting

Engaging the Family

1. *Greeting the family.* The clinician greets the family and asks the family members to seat themselves as they wished in a semicircular pattern. He notices that Bobby uses this opportunity to distance himself from his parents.
2. *Social conversation.* Previously, the clinician had not met the father. He converses with him for a few minutes to establish an alliance with him. He hasn't seen Randy (17-year-old brother) for a year and inquires about how he is doing. He speaks with the mother and Bobby.
3. *Stating the purpose of the family meeting.* The clinician wants to be sure that everyone is clear about the purpose of the meeting and is in agreement. He addresses each member, not just the mother, and does his best to make sure that Bobby does not feel like he is "the problem."

Clinician: *Let's be sure we all agree on why we are meeting. We're here because you all want to resolve a problem that is affecting the whole family. Would anyone like to comment?* (alternatively, "Is this right?" or "Do you agree?")

Mother: *The problem is that Bobby has ADHD and won't take his after school medication.*

The clinician scans the other members for their responses.

Father: *Whatever she says is right.*

IDENTIFYING THE LEADER The clinician identifies the mother as the family leader.

Bobby (adamantly disagreeing): *That's not right! I'm here because they made me come.*

Bobby is the "identified patient" and the clinician wants to acknowledge his feelings.

Clinician: *"I appreciate you being here. I realize you didn't want to attend the meeting."*

The clinician wants the family to understand the purposes of the meeting and the shifts in focus (a) from the adolescent–patient to the family context and (b) from parents "reporting" the problem to the clinician to a family conversation.

Clinician: *I want to point out that these family meetings are to help all of you understand that the concern is really a family issue. No one person is to blame, and no one person has to do all the work. Everyone is affected, but together as a family you are the best resource for solving this issue.*

By the looks on the family member's faces, the clinician can tell that all of the family members seem a little surprised by this statement.

Clinician (permitting 10 to 15 scconds of silence as they considered his explanation): *You seem a little surprised. Do you understand the purpose of our meetings?*

One by one, he asks each member; each nods—they are surprised, but the purpose is clear. **The family must understand the purpose before the clinician can proceed.**

AVOIDING COALITIONS If the clinician had agreed with the mother and father, the family might perceive his action as forming a coalition with the parents against Bobby. By taking sides and acting like another parent, he would certainly have lost Bobby's trust and cooperation.

Clinician (giving Bobby a chance to respond): *Is there something you'd like to discuss at this meeting?*

Bobby: *They treat me like a baby. I'm doing fine. I don't need it.*

Clinician (acknowledging Bobby): *You're going to have the opportunity to share your thoughts and to speak your mind. Can you tell us all what you want?*

Bobby: *To have them get off my back about the meds.*

Clinician (getting Randy involved): *Randy, what do you want?*

Randy: *It seems like the medication thing is a stress in our house. They're always yelling about it.*

Clinician (instilling some hope): *The fact that you all are here, sitting in one place and willing to talk, means that you have taken the first step to improving things.* (Attempts to see if the family can agree on its stated concern as a starting point for the problem discussion) *It sounds like the decision about whether or not to take the medication is the problem that is causing so much stress in the family. Is that right?*

He asks each member to answer. One by one they agree.

Managing the Family's Expectations for the First Visit

To ease the family's urgency to "get to the bottom of this" in one meeting and to relieve pressure on the clinician to "fix the problem," the clinician should tell the family early in the first visit that a first visit is meant to gather information and understand the family. A second visit will be used to develop ways to help the family work together and to offer advice.

Understanding the Family and Their Concern

EXPLORING THE PROBLEM: GATHERING A DESCRIPTION OF THE PROBLEM Families usually expect to talk about the problem, and the clinician needs to understand the problem within the family context.

Clinician (encouraging everyone to participate and using the word "concern" more than "problem" because it carries less stigmatization): *I'd like to hear more about the concern from all of you.*

Mother (talking to the clinician): *He just refuses to take his medication and to study at home, and I end up nagging him because high school grades are so important for college.*

Clinician (discouraging the mother from 'reporting' to the clinician about Bobby and encouraging family communication): *Look at Bobby and tell him how you feel.*

The mother voices her concerns to Bobby.

Clinician (continuing to promote family communication): *Bobby, would you like to say anything?*

Bobby: *I feel upset, too.*

The clinician looks at the father and Randy to offer them the opportunity to respond. They both look glum and nod.

Clinician (acknowledging the family's mutual feelings): *It seems like everyone is upset.* (to the father who has been quiet so far) *How do you see things? Can you give us an example?*

Father: *When Bobby arrives home after school he wants to "hang out," but I know he will not study in the evening. His mother tells him to take his medication and study. He won't take his medication. That starts a big argument between them. That's the problem.*

Clinician (gently challenging the father's statement): *How do you know he won't study in the evening?*

Father: *I assume he can't without medication.*

Bobby (looking at the clinician): *They think I need my medication all the time and that I can't do anything on my own. I can study better after dinner when I've had a chance to relax, play some music, and talk to my friends. I'm doing fine in school, but they don't believe me.*

PRACTICING A DESIRED BEHAVIOR IN THE OFFICE If the clinician wants to improve family communication, he must help the members practice communication in the meeting. If they cannot carry out a desired behavior (goal) in the office, they probably will not be able or willing to do it at home.

Clinician (promoting family communication): *Tell your parents, not me.*

Bobby: *Mom, I can do my work better after dinner. Just give me a chance to show you. I am doing fine in school.*

Mother: *We haven't seen a report card yet.*

Assessing Behaviors that Maintain the Problem and Its Impact on the Family

Clinician: *How has the problem affected the family?*

Father: *Sometimes Bobby skips the family dinner.*

Bobby: *I'd come downstairs to dinner if Mom didn't always get so intense.*

Mother (looking at the clinician): *I worry about Bobby.*

Clinician (again encouraging family communication): *Does Bobby know how you feel? Tell him how you feel.*

The mother looks at Bobby and tells him. Bobby meets her gaze but remains silent.

Clinician: *Have you told Bobby what you worry about?*

Mother: *No.*
Clinician: *Do you want to now?*
Mother: *Not right now.*
Randy: *I don't even want to come home when they're arguing. I hang out with my friends.*
Mother (her eyes filling with tears): *I've tried so hard.*
The clinician pauses and allows 10 to 20 seconds of silence. He waits for a family member to break the silence. No one does, so he speaks.
Clinician: *It must be hard for you. You seem saddened by this situation.*
The mother nods quietly. The father reaches out and holds her hand. Bobby looks away, still angry. Randy looks at the clinician.
Clinician: *Tell me how you've responded to this problem.*
Mother: *We're not really working together. We are all so busy with other things.*
Father: *We don't really have a plan. It's kind of chaotic. Every day I just hope things will get better, but they don't. The yelling just keeps getting louder.*
Randy: *Like I said, I just hang out with my friends. I don't know what to do.*
Mother (still hoping the clinician will "fix" Bobby's "problem"): *We're here for you to talk some sense into Bobby.*
The clinician avoids playing the expert role, so he repeats that this is a family issue.
Clinician (guiding the family): *Remember I am not the expert. You all are. You have the answers. Bobby, we promised you'd have an opportunity to speak. Let's hear from you.*
Bobby (still angry): *I don't want to be treated like a baby. I told you that.*
Mother (still looking to the clinician for advice): *But you are the expert. That's why we're here.*
Clinician (maintaining the family systems approach): *I can help, but this meeting is to help you become the expert.*

Identifying Family Changes that Affect the Problem

Clinician: *Were there any other things going on about the time the problem began?*
Father: *I was under pressure at work. I put in longer hours.*
Mother: *We never see each other. We don't have a moment together.*

When parents express or hint at a need to feel supported as parents or spouses, the clinician should simply acknowledge their need, even briefly, but should not get distracted and ignore their presenting complaint. The clinician can discuss another issue later on in the meeting or in the next meeting.

Clinician: *That must be hard.*
Father: *We haven't gone out in months.*
Mother: *We're too worried.*

Clinician (noting the mother has twice mentioned being worried): *You've mentioned your worrying a couple of times. Now can you tell Bobby what worries you? Look at him and tell him.*

Mother: *I worry that you won't study, won't get good grades, won't get into college, won't get a good job, and won't have a good life, like you have now.*

Bobby (softening a bit): *Mom, you're worrying about everything. You tell me what to do all the time and even remind me to brush my teeth.*

The family is silent.

The clinician feels that the mother is overly involved with Bobby, is "micromanaging" his activities, and is stressing the family in the process.

Clinician (identifying adolescence as a challenge in the family life cycle, and reminding them of a past success): *Do you remember when Randy was Bobby's age?*

We had a talk about his need to separate and become an individual. He wanted a little more independence. You gave him some room, and he did fine.

Mother: *But Bobby has ADHD. Randy didn't.*

Bobby looks hurt.

The clinician considers the idea that the mother feels Bobby's ADHD makes him "vulnerable." Does this make her overly involved in his activities? Cause her worry?

Clinician (probing gently): *Do you think that Bobby needs more supervision because of his ADHD?*

The mother nods.

The clinician wants to respond to the mother's unfavorable comparison of Bobby to Randy and to her negative perception of Bobby and his ADHD.

Clinician (beginning to reframe Bobby and to change the mother's perception): *Later in the interview, I'd like to explore how well Bobby is coping with ADHD.*

The parents look at each other and nod.

Clinician (to Bobby): *How does that sound?*

Bobby (looking a bit less tense): *Fine by me.*

The clinician also wants to acknowledge this normal phase/stress of the family life cycle.

Clinician: *Bobby is going through the same stage of adolescence as Randy did, and he has the same developmental needs to separate and be independent. It can be a stressful transition for families each time it happens."*

Father: *It sure is.*

Discussing Past Attempts and Advice to Resolve the Problem

Clinician (seeking useful school information): *As there is a focus on medication and studying, it would help to get some information from the school and to know what they might be doing to help Bobby. I will give you a teacher questionnaire, and you can bring it to our next meeting. What have you tried in the past?*

Bobby: *I did try medication in the afternoon, but I just wasn't ready to study then and it took away my appetite for dinner.*

Clinician: *Anything else?*

Bobby: *My parents had me see the school counselor a couple of times. He was okay. He told me I was doing fine.*

Father: *I used to help Bobby with homework after dinner. That worked for a few weeks, but then demands of the job stopped that.*

Clinician (acknowledging a past success): *So something did work, even if for just a while.*

Father (remembering his own success): *I suppose.*

Clinician (exploring other attempts and advice): *Has anyone offered you any advice?*

Mother: *A friend of mine who has a boy the same age as Bobby said I should find something else to do in the afternoon instead of nagging Bobby. I haven't done it.*

Clinician: *Would you like to try?*

Mother: *I'm not sure.*

Clinician (keeping Randy involved): *Randy, do you want to add something?*

Randy: *Nope.*

Discussing a Goal

A brief goal discussion helps the family clarify its goals and expectations. It is also an effective way to end a problem discussion that has gone on too long, become repetitive, and/or turned the interview into an angry, blaming session. This tactic can be used at any point in the interview. In the problem-oriented interview, the goal discussion is brief.

Clinician (shifting the interview focus from the problem to a goal): *We've talked about the problem. Now I'd like to ask each of you what you'd like to achieve in these meetings. If the problem were gone, what would you want instead?* (Recognizing Bobby's need for autonomy and separation) *Let's hear from you first, Bobby.*

Bobby: *I want to have afternoons free and to study at night.*

Randy: *I want things to be easier at home.*

Father: *I just want Bobby and his mother to settle down.*

Clinician (seeking clarification): *Can you both be a little more specific?*

The father and Randy mention having a pleasant dinner, maybe watching TV after dinner, and letting each member have time alone.

Mother: *My goal is for Bobby to take his medication and study.*

Clinician (attempting to get agreement on a goal by showing how the goals were all connected): *It sounds like you all want pretty much the same thing . . . that is to have pleasant evenings and have your own time. Working out this medication–study issue is kind of a step toward the goals.* (The clinician now exerts some leadership by offering a suggestion.) *If Bobby studies at night and shows that he could do well, would that help the family get along?*

The family nods in agreement. Bobby and his mother both appear a bit relaxed for the first time in the visit.

In the short office visit, this is a good point to end the first meeting.

Concluding the First Meeting

The conclusion should summarize the meeting in a way that emphasizes the family's effort and achievements.

Clinician: *In this first meeting, we talked about your concern as a family issue and you all talked and helped us understand the issues. Resolving the medication issue will make family life more pleasant. It seems like you want the same goal. There are things going on that affect everyone, like Dad's job changes, Mom and Dad not having time for themselves, and two teenagers who are going through adolescence. It's obvious you care for each other and are willing to work for your goals.* (Inviting the family to ask questions or share thoughts) *Do you have any final thoughts or questions?*

The clinician allows a period of silence to let the family gather its thoughts.

Mother: *What do we do now?*

Clinician (encouraging the family to try something on its own and avoiding the expert-parent role): *What do you think you would like to do?*

Father (taking the lead): *Maybe Bobby and his mother can compromise. He'll take his medication after school for 3 days and after dinner for 3 days.*

Mother: *For the sake of peace, I will try it.*

Bobby (reluctantly): *Just this week.*

Families sometimes suggest a strategy at the end of a meeting when they don't have time to discuss it in detail. The clinician can support it or can ask them to postpone it until the next meeting.

In this case, the clinician isn't sure if the father's suggested strategy will work. It is the father's idea for the mother and Bobby to change their behaviors, not theirs. Because the mother and Bobby don't have time to discuss it and make their own decisions, the clinician isn't sure it will work. However, he does not want to squelch a spontaneous attempt from the father, who is obviously trying to assert some family leadership. Time has run out, so he makes no objection.

Scheduling the Next Meeting

Clinician: *I'd like to schedule our next meeting in one week. Can you all attend?*

Complimenting and Thanking the Family

Clinician: *I want to tell you how impressed I am with your commitment to each other.* (Pauses for a few moments to let the positive message sink in) *In our next visit, we will discuss both your plan and some other ways for you to work together. Work on your plan this week. Please call me anytime with any questions or concerns. Thank you for coming in.*

The Post-Interview Phase (First Visit)

After the family leaves, the clinician reviews the first meeting. He feels that the family is satisfied with the family meeting and is willing to come back. He is pleased with how he conducted the meeting, and he likes the family. He realizes that much of the conflict originates from the parents' perception that Bobby can't work without medication and that he needs to study in the afternoon. The mother seems very worried that Bobby's ADHD will cause him to underachieve. She projects her worries into the future and worries that he won't have a "good life." Bobby needs and wants more autonomy. The parents need to be assured that Bobby can behave responsibly. The family wants more harmony. Several issues need attention: family patterns of interactions; beliefs about Bobby, ADHD, and the developmental needs of adolescents; the unfavorable comparison between Bobby and Randy; and inadequate time for the parents' own spousal life. The clinician determines that he will help the family prioritize the issues and address them over the next few meetings. He mails a letter to the family that briefly summarizes the issues and compliments it for its efforts and then uses the letter as a chart note. (See Chapter 9, "After the Interview," for more discussion.)

The Second Family Meeting

He can tell immediately by the family members' facial expressions that they aren't pleased. They look disappointed and avoid eye contact with each other as though they have "failed." The clinician inquires about the past week. The compromise worked for only 2 days. The father reports that Bobby wanted all his afternoons medication-free, so the arguments started again.

Clinician (acknowledging their feelings): *I am sorry things didn't work out. I sense you might be feeling a bit discouraged. Does anyone else want to comment?*

The clinician looks at each member. Everyone is silent.

Clinician (reminding them of a strength and that they aren't failures, keeping them hopeful): *Last week you showed a family strength. You were willing to try something new. Even though it didn't work out, let's begin with these strengths.*

Sometimes starting with positives when the family is feeling discouraged is much more helpful than rehashing the problem at the risk of making it feel even worse or having the members start "blaming the patient" again. Using the phrase "didn't work out" is better than "failed" for a family that feels that it is failing.

Working with the Family

IDENTIFYING FAMILY STRENGTHS AND RESOURCES

Clinician (to the father, reminding him of a past success): *At our last visit you mentioned that you used to help Bobby with his homework and that it was helpful.*

The father and Bobby agree that it was.

The clinician asks for the teacher questionnaire in the hope that he might find a strength/success at school. He quickly glances at it. It contains some very positive comments.

Clinician (to both parents, exploring Bobby's strengths as a way to demonstrate his capabilities and to elicit an indirect compliment): *At the last visit, I mentioned we'd explore some of Bobby's strengths. Have you shared these comments with Bobby?*

The parents had picked up the form on the way to the meeting and had just glanced at it in the waiting room. The clinician asks them to share the comments with Bobby. They read them. Bobby is doing grade level work and is well behaved. His ADHD is "not a problem."

Clinician: *How does that make you all feel?*

The parents state that they are "a bit surprised" and "very pleased."

Clinician: *Would you tell Bobby?*

The parents look at Bobby and compliment him.

Clinician: *How does that make you feel, Bobby?*

Bobby (smiling): *Proud.*

Clinician (exploring other strengths): *Bobby, what else do you do that makes you proud?*

Bobby states that he has a part-time job and that he had just gotten a raise, which brings more praise from the clinician and the parents.

Clinician (complimenting the parents): *You've done a good job of being parents. Look at how well Bobby and Randy are doing. Can you give Bobby a chance to show you how responsible he is?*

Father: *I'm willing.*

Mother: *How can we do that?*

Engaging the Family in Developing a Plan of Action

The clinician decides to answer the mother's question by pointing out the father's support.

Clinician: (reviving a past success to create a plan): *Bobby has said that he can study at night and that Dad's support was very helpful. Could that happen again?*

Bobby nods, and the father states that he can help out when he comes home early.

CHANGING ROLES

Mother (still doubtful): *I'm not sure about this. My husband could help maybe one night. That leaves me doing most of the supervision. That's not really a change.*

One of the most effective ways for families to change their interactions is to change roles. One member "steps out" of an interaction, and another "steps in." Alternatively, a member needs to find something else to do to replace his or her former role. In this family, the mother will not give up her role of supervising Bobby unless someone else steps in. She is not yet ready to give Bobby the amount of independence he wants and needs—Bobby wants to feel trusted and responsible.

Clinician (facilitating discussion on how to remove the mother from her role): *Remember, Bobby has shown that he is responsible. Who else could we find? Maybe a tutor?*

Father: *They are expensive.*

Clinician (scanning the family, hoping Randy might "step in"): *It is a family effort. Does anyone have another suggestion?*

Randy (responding to the "family effort"): *Maybe I could help out a couple days a week. If things are calmer at home, I wouldn't mind coming home.*

This offer represents a significant change in the family's pattern of behavior. The clinician wants to emphasize that Randy himself would benefit from this effort.

Clinician (complimenting Randy): *That's really generous of you. So you get to enjoy a calm house and wouldn't have to stay away. How does that sound to all of you?*

Bobby: *I'd like that.*

They all agree that it was worth a try. The mother asks the father and Randy "to set a schedule now, so there would be no slip ups." They did that.

Clinician (to all): *Well done.*

OFFERING ADVICE Although the family has developed a plan, the presenting complaint (from the family leader) has not yet been addressed. The mother will not be satisfied until her specific concerns are addressed.

Clinician: *Have we settled the after school medication issue?*

Mother: *Shouldn't he take medication after dinner?*

Bobby: *I tried it once and it kept me awake.*

Clinician (offering a specific directive): *Bobby, how about this? When you have a lot of studying to do, it might help to take the medication an hour before dinner. That would help you, and it shouldn't interfere with your appetite or sleep.*

The family now realizes this fits with moving the homework to the evening.

Bobby (indicating his willingness to take medication after the positive family discussion): *I could try it.*

Clinician (offering more advice): *Sometimes, studying with a classmate can be helpful. Bobby, do you have a friend who you could study with, if Randy and Dad can't make it?*

Bobby: *I could study with Mel. He's a good friend and a good student. We could try that.*

Mother (still wanting to help, to be involved, to have some control): *I could help out with the driving.*

Clinician (recalling the parents' concern that as spouses they had little time for each other): *Maybe now you could find some time for yourselves. The boys are doing well. Go out on a date. You deserve some fun, too.*

Both parents: *That would be nice.*

CHANGING PERCEPTIONS AND PROVIDING REASSURANCE The clinician quickly reviews the psychosocial need of adolescents to be more autonomous. He reminds the parents of the boys' individual strengths (removing the unfavorable comparison) and once again lists the teachers' positive comments about Bobby: his ADHD is well managed and he is doing well in school. The clinician also briefly reviews Bobby's responsible behavior with his job as a reminder to the parents. He gently urges the mother to focus on the next semester instead of the next decade. Finally, he also reminds the parents that they had trusted Randy with more independence. Could they do that with Bobby?

ASSIGNING HOMEWORK TASKS (OPTIONAL) Sometimes the family benefits from a task that makes it "practice" its new behaviors. The task emphasizes the desired behaviors and each member's specific roles. The purpose of the task is to have them record and remember the family successes.

In this case the clinician doesn't want the family members to "forget" the changes or to take each other's improved behavior for granted.

Clinician: *I'd like to assign the family a homework task. How does that sound?*

Mother: *Will it take lots of work?*

Clinician: *Some work.*

Bobby: *Is it like school work?*

Clinician (laughing good naturedly and helping them relax): *Nope, and it will help you all remember the good things you've worked on here.*

Mother: *Tell us what you have in mind.*

Clinician: *I'd like you to get a notebook and call it "Good things I see and do." Put it in the kitchen or family room. Whenever anyone does something good or when you see someone doing something good, write it in the notebook. Share the notebook together every week. Do you think you can do that?*

Randy: *Maybe we'll mention the pleasant dinners we haven't had for a while.*

Concluding the Second Meeting

Clinician (pausing and then looking at each member to signal the conclusion): *I'd like to take a moment just to summarize all you have done today. Your concern was the afternoon homework, Bobby's medication, and the family stress. You agreed on a goal and developed some specific solutions: Dad and Randy working with Bobby, using a study buddy, Mom doing the driving, and Bobby taking the medication when needed before dinnertime. The family cooperation is very impressive.*

The clinician pauses for 10 seconds to let the family reflect on his words and to consider any responses the members might have.

Clinician: *Do you have any comments or questions?*

The parents say that they feel better. Bobby and Randy nod in agreement.

Clinician: *You've made some great strides. These were good visits. Congratulations to you all. Thank you for coming in. I'd* *like to see you all for a short visit in 3 weeks. Please call if I can be of any help before our next appointment.*

The Post-Interview Phase (Second Visit)

The clinician reviews the meeting. He feels that the family is caring and competent. The members appear willing to change their behaviors. The mother's perception of Bobby has improved. The clinician dictates a chart note and sends a copy to the parents. He has helped the family in several ways.

1. *He clarified the purpose of the meeting—using a family orientation to resolve the problem.*
2. *He encouraged the family to find its own solutions with a family systems approach.*
   a. ***The father offered to help out again.***
   b. ***The mother's perception of Bobby and his ADHD became more positive, and this changed her behavior.*** She "backed off," trusted Bobby, and, in effect, trusted her own good parenting.
   c. ***The clinician reminded the parents of Bobby's needs as an adolescent.***
   d. ***The clinician helped them change the family roles in the homework situation with both the father and Randy agreeing to help Bobby.***
   e. ***The mother offered to drive Bobby to his study buddy's house, thus removing herself from the homework situation.***
   f. ***The clinician supported the spousal relationship.***
3. *The clinician offered advice/teaching/reassurance.*
   a. ***He suggested the notebook task.***
   b. ***He supported Bobby's choice to study in the evening and to take his medication before dinner, when needed.***
   c. ***He suggested a study buddy.***
   d. ***He reminded the family of its past successes and strengths.***

IV. The Solution-Oriented Interview

The solution-oriented interview differs from the problem-oriented interview because it focuses less on problem description and more on solution building. It shifts the focus of the interview to solution talk to shorten the problem talk and assumes that repeating preexisting successful behavioral patterns is easier than stopping or changing existing problematic behaviors. It views past and present strengths and successes of the family as the basis for future solutions.

Solution-oriented interviewing avoids generic ways of viewing and diagnosing family problems and generic therapeutic approaches ("one size fits all"), which often unintentionally deny creative possibilities to the clinician and the family.

Solution-oriented interviewing encourages co-constructing solutions with both the family and the clinician viewed as "experts." The clinician conveys his or her need to know more about the family instead of merely testing preconceived values and notions.

In this way, the clinician receives constant information about the family's values, traditions, and explanations so that he or she can better understand the family.

Indications for Use of the Solution-Oriented Interview

The solution-oriented interview is useful in the following situations:

- The clinician is familiar with the problem.
- Problem talk is counterproductive.
- Families want solutions that fit their individual and cultural values.

Table 8.2 lists the steps and questions in an example of a solution-oriented interview.

CASE 2: A 10-YEAR-OLD BOY WHO "ACTS RUDELY ALL THE TIME"

The mother calls the clinician, stating, *"My husband asked me to call you for an appointment. Our boy is acting rudely, and we can't stop it."*

Table 8.2. The solution-oriented interview: steps and questions

1. **Engaging the family** (time: 3 to 5 minutes)[a]
   Social conversation
   Explain the purpose of a *family* meeting.
2. **Understanding the family** (time: 7 to 10 minutes)[a]
   Brief problem description
   Parenting history (optional)[b]
   Behaviors that maintain the problem
3. **Working with the family** (time: 15 to 20 minutes)[a]
   Three questions (two may suffice):
   - Goal discussion
   - Exception questions
   - Scaling questions
4. **Concluding the meeting** (time: 3 to 5 minutes)[a]
   Summarize the meeting
   Invite the family to ask questions or share thoughts.
   Schedule a follow-up visit.
   Compliment and thank the family.

[a] These times are approximations based on the number of questions and complexity of the case.
[b] The clinician can ask any questions that he or she feels are necessary. See Chapter 6, "The Four Steps of a Family Interview."

The clinician inquires about past interventions (family-initiated or professional). The parents have tried to be "stricter," but that has failed. They have not sought professional help.

The mother says, *"We come from a culture that says families should take care of their own problems. We have tried everything we know, but now we need help. As our son's pediatrician, we thought you could help."*

The pediatrician makes an appointment for a family meeting.

Engaging the Family

Social Conversation

The clinician hasn't seen Ricky and his mother in a year. She has not met the father until now. She starts the session by stating that it is good to see both Ricky and the mother again and that she is happy to meet the father finally. She notes that Ricky sits closer to his mother and looks worried. He doesn't smile and keeps glancing sideways at his parents. The clinician asks about the father about his job, and she asks Ricky about school and other activities. Ricky pauses, and the mother answers for him, stating that he is doing well in school and has lots of friends.

Clinician (deliberately writing this good news on his notepad and complimenting Ricky): *Well done, Ricky!*

Father (angrily): *But that's not the whole story.*

Clinician (acknowledging his anger): *We're going to let you share your side in just a minute.*

Explaining the Purpose of the Family Meeting

Clinician: *First, let me explain what I would like us to accomplish in this visit. This meeting is different from what happens when you bring a child in with a medical problem. Instead of focusing just on Ricky, we can address your concerns best by understanding the problem and the whole family together. As a family, you are an invaluable source of knowledge; and you have many strengths and resources. I'd like to learn more about both Ricky and the family so that we can develop solutions that fit your values. How does that sound to you?*

Father: *But I need to tell you about Ricky's bad behavior.*

Clinician (easing the pressure to do it all in one visit and adding a positive "spin" to the concern): *You will. That's where we'll start. First, we will briefly discuss your concern; then we'll discuss your goal and other issues that may affect the problem, and finally I'll help you all develop some solutions. If we can't do all of this today, we will schedule another meeting. Then we'll have a few more visits after that. I know you and Ricky have some family strengths. I need to hear about those, too.*

Father (speaking for the family): *I thought we only had this one visit. That makes me feel better. It's too much for one visit.*

The offer to schedule another meeting to complete the interview takes pressure off both the family and the clinician.

Understanding the Family

The clinician has reviewed Ricky's chart. He is healthy, and his immunizations are up to date. The only prior visits have been for well-child care and minor acute illnesses. She has noted that both parents were born and raised in Cambodia. They married there and came to the United States about 12 years ago.

Understanding the Hierarchy

Clinician: *Whose idea was it to bring Ricky in?*

Father: *Mine. In my country, we handle these problems at home. Or we get advice from relatives. We don't have relatives here. I've tried a few things, but the problem is getting worse. I told my wife to call you.*

The clinician identifies the father as the leader.

Brief Problem Description

The problem description should be brief.

Clinician: *Now I'd like to ask each of you to describe very briefly your concern.*

Father: *He acts rudely all the time.*

Clinician: *Can you give us an example?*

Father: *When he is at the table, he talks loudly and often in a disrespectful manner.*

Mother: *Ricky wants to talk and talk. My husband likes a quiet dinner. He tells him to be quiet. Ricky doesn't listen and keeps talking, raising his voice, and acting rudely. Then my husband yells at him to stop or tells him to leave the table. The dinner ends on a bad note.*

Father (angrily): *He's a rude child.*

Clinician (reframing the issue): *It seems like the talking at the table is the rude issue.*

Ricky: *I just like to talk.*

Father (angrily): *Loud and nonstop.*

Clinician: *How long has this been happening?*

Mother: *It has been going on for several months.*

The clinician notes the father's negative comments and angry mood. She has enough information about the problem. She wants to end the nonproductive problem talk and also to stop the father's negative, angry comments.

Clinician (signaling the end of the problem discussion): *Is there anything else you'd like to add?*

Father: *We're tired of talking and yelling. Nothing gets better. That's why we're here.*

Clinician (acknowledging that they may need to "revisit" the problem): *If we need to discuss the problem again, we can do so. This information was helpful.*

Parenting History (Optional)

Clinician (exploring influences in the parents' behavior and expectations): *Sometimes it helps to know how you* (the mother and father) *were parented and how you were raised. For example, what were family meals like? How did your parents expect you to behave? Were there certain rules?*

The mother's parents had encouraged conversation at the table and insisted that everyone participate but would not allow them to interrupt one another.

The father's family dinners were "very quiet." His father was "very strict." He explained that, in Cambodia, the father is the leader of the family and expects complete obedience. His father had been a "traditional Cambodian father."

The clinician senses that the father's childhood experiences are influencing his own parenting behavior. His rigidity may be part of the problem.

Father: *We had a rule that you only spoke when spoken to. If you broke the rule, you were sent to your room.*

The clinician attempts to point out the connection to the father between his father's style and his own style. If the father makes this connection, he might develop some empathy for Ricky.

Clinician: *Did you enjoy the family dinners?*

Father: *Not especially. Dinner was the only time we were together, but I didn't get enough attention from my father.*

Clinician (following up on the father's own feelings): *Do you think Ricky is seeking your attention?*

Father: *Yes, but there are better ways to do it.*

The father has offered the possibility of a solution with this statement. The clinician responds to this "offer."

Clinician: *What are those ways?*

Father: *We're not sure. Nothing seems to work. That's why we're here.*

The clinician feels that she is still missing something. She doesn't understand the family interactions as well as she needs to, so she needs more information.

Behaviors That Maintain the Problem

Clinician: *I'd like to hear an example of a specific incident at the table. I'd like to hear from all of you.*

The father states that Ricky will start talking about something that happened at school. After a few minutes the father asks him to stop. Ricky stops only momentarily and then will continue. The father again asks him to stop. Ricky persists. Soon the father and Ricky are both speaking loudly. The father then either raises his voice, which silences Ricky, or sends him to his room.

Mother: *Just like his father did to him.*

Clinician (seeking confirmation from the father and developing empathy for Ricky): *Is that right?*

Father: *Yes. I don't like doing it, but it seems to work.*

Clinician: *But the problem is still there. Does this happen a lot?*

Mother: *Over and over. I don't interfere because I do not want to disagree with him in front of Ricky. I get upset with him in private later, but it doesn't change things.*

Clinician (to Ricky): *What would you like to say?*

Ricky: *I hate it when Daddy sends me to my room.*

The clinician points out that the family is repeating the same behaviors "over and over" with increasing intensity. All the family members are affected. The interactions have worsened despite their efforts.

She feels that this is a good point to shift to a goal discussion.

Discussing Goals

Goal discussion creates an atmosphere of hope, energy, and action that moves the family from the past into the present and future. The family engages in a discussion, which is often hopeful and optimistic, of what it wants to achieve. Several ways to initiate a goal discussion are listed in Table 8.3. Because families are usually unfamiliar with the solution-oriented questions, introducing them as "another kind of question" often helps.

Clinician (introducing a new kind of question): *Now I'd like to ask another kind of question. What do you think you'd like to achieve with these meetings?*

Father: *I want the rude behavior to stop.*

Mother: *No more unhappy meals.*

Ricky: *I don't understand.*

The clinician opens a drawer, takes out a magic wand, and hands it to Ricky. (See Chapter 7, "Assessing Family Functioning," for further discussion.)

Clinician (using a simpler question geared to Ricky's level): *Wave this magic wand, and make a wish about dinner. What is your wish?*

Ricky: *No more yelling.*

Table 8.3. Ways to initiate a goal discussion

1. "What would you like to see happen as a result of coming here?"
2. "Pretend you could fast forward a video of your life 6 months into the future. What would you see?"
3. "Imagine you woke up one morning and things were better? What would you first notice?"
4. "What would tell you, after a few visits, that you wouldn't need to come here anymore?"
5. Two questions for younger or less verbal children:
   a "Wave this magic wand and make a wish. What would it be?"
   b. "Pretend you have a magic crystal ball. Look into it and make believe that something good happened. What would you see?"

The family still hasn't defined the goal as a positive, specific behavior that the members want to see more of. The clinician needs to help them do that.

Qualities of Well-Formed Goals

Families' goals, which are often too vague, are usually stated as desires for less of or absence of undesirable behaviors instead of as a hope for certain desirable behaviors. Clinicians must help the family state its goals as specific, positive behaviors members can visualize. Qualities of well-formed goals include the following:

- *The goal is meaningful and important to the family.* The goal must arise from the family's frame of reference and its own value system.
- *The goal is realistic and achievable.* The goal should be small rather than large because achievement is more likely, which gives the family a sense of satisfaction and a feeling that the work is worthwhile. The clinician can provide an appropriate developmental perspective on the child (i.e., goals that are appropriate for the child's abilities).
- *The goal has contextual, situational features.* The goal is a behavior that occurs in familiar, daily, or near daily situations (e.g., doing chores, doing homework, obeying parents, playing with siblings, demonstrating affection, and communicating).
- *The goal is described in specific, concrete, behavioral, and interactional terms.* Observable, specific behaviors are more likely to be recognized and achieved. Families usually need guided discussion to attain this. A term like *"be good"* is vague and subjective; in contrast, a specific goal is *"When I ask you to put your toys away, I would like you to put them in the toy box within 2 minutes."*
- *The goal is described as a positive past behavior or the start of something new.* The absence or end of a negative behavior or less display of a certain behavior (e.g., "I want no more fighting," "I want this arguing to end," or "There will be less swearing in this house") is not a goal. The above examples are not adequate goals because they do not define or specify the desirable behaviors that would replace undesirable behavior. Families often have a hard time stating goals as positive behaviors because they have become so accustomed to discussing the problems and because they perceive the clinician as the problem solver. The clinician can ask, "What do you want to see happen instead of 'less swearing'?" or "What would happen if there was 'no more fighting'?"
- *Families must perceive that achieving goals requires commitment and real work.* The clinician must tell the family that goals will be achieved only if the family is committed and willing to work. He or she must keep the family's expectations at a realistic level and should caution it with the reminder that disappointments or setbacks occur. Families usually improve their behaviors for a short time after each meeting because they are motivated to work on the behaviors. However, they often revert to their old ways because they don't remember or

practice; they forget that achieving their goals requires consistent motivation and work.

Clinician (asking Ricky to state a positive goal): *You wished for no more yelling. What would be happening instead if there was no more yelling?*

Ricky: *Talking.*

Clinician (eliciting a more specific goal): *Tell Mom and Dad what you mean by talking.*

Ricky: *Just talking about school and things.*

The clinician wants to encourage a family conversation, a family interaction that the members could practice and continue at home. He asks them to role play an interaction. (See Chapter 7, "Assessing Family Function," for further discussion.)

Clinician: *Pretend you are at home. I'd like you to have a family conversation. Would you tell each other what you'd like to see happening if there were "no more unhappy meals?"*

Mother (to Ricky): *Hearing your goal helps me understand things better. I would like to hear more about your school day.* (To the father) *I'd like it if you would let Ricky talk more. He wants to talk to you.*

Clinician (to the father): *Can you tell Ricky what you mean by "wanting the rude behavior to stop?"*

Father (to Ricky): *I'd like you to be quiet when I ask you.*

Clinician (helping them negotiate a goal): *It sounds like you all pretty much want the same thing—a pleasant, polite family conversation. How could you make that happen? Tell each other.*

Father (to Ricky): *I suppose I could let you talk more without raising my voice. I do like to hear about your school activities.*

Clinician: *Can you be more specific when you say "have quiet conversation?"*

Mother: *We could let Ricky talk first. He and I could begin a conversation, and my husband could join in if he wanted to.*

Clinician (to mother): *Would you look at Ricky and say that again?*

The mother's voice and expression soften as she speaks to Ricky.

Father: *I would like Ricky to be quiet when I ask him.*

Clinician: *Tell Ricky that.*

The father does. Ricky looks at him but doesn't respond.

Clinician (bringing out the interactive aspect of behavior): *How could you help make that happen?*

Mother: *If Ricky had some time to talk and share his day, I think he could then obey his dad when asked.*

Father (in a softer voice and with a pleasant expression): *What do you think, son?*

Ricky (looking back and forth between mother and father): *I'll try.*

Clinician (helping them understand Ricky's behavior): *What else do you think Ricky wants?*

Mother (looking at her husband): *Our attention, especially his dad's.*

Father (remembering what he missed from his childhood dinners): *Like I wanted.*

Giving a Family Hope and Motivation

A brief problem discussion and a detailed goal discussion may constitute one meeting. More talk about where the family wants to go (goal) and less about where it has been (problem) leaves the family members feeling hopeful and motivated.

Exception Questions

The purpose of exception questions is to reveal those times when the problem does not happen, is not so bad, is corrected, or is unnoticed. Their function is to uncover, identify, and explore those behaviors, feelings, thoughts, and perceptions that are exceptions to the problem because exception behaviors are the family's own real life solutions. Therefore, discussing exception questions is the pathway from problem talk to solution talk.

Exceptions are those behaviors that have occurred in place of the problem behaviors. By asking about them, the clinician aims to elicit what is working, what is going right, and what has worked in the past that the family might try again. They often also reveal goals. *The clinician can ask exception questions instead of or in addition to goal questions.*

Exception Questions

Exception questions shift the focus of the interview from problem talk to solution talk. This initiates a search for past successes. Three examples of these types of questions include the following:

1. "If things were better, what would be different?"
2. "Surely there must have been times when things were a little better. Tell us about one of those times."
3. "When the problem is not happening, what's happening instead?"

Clinician: *Tell me about a recent dinner when things were just a little bit better. What was happening instead?*

Father (after a long pause): *A few weeks ago, Ricky and I talked about a pro football game we had watched on TV.*

Clinician (acknowledging an exception): *So you do have pleasant family conversations. Tell us more.*

The father and Ricky describe their behavior in more detail.

Clinician (looking for more exceptions): *What else has helped?*

Mother: *Last week, I asked Ricky to help fix dinner. As we worked, he told me all about school. At dinner, he didn't feel the need to talk as much.*

Clinician: (pointing out their successes): *You've described two family behaviors that help you all have a pleasant dinner: when Ricky and his father talk about sports and when Ricky talks with his mother while they prepare dinner together.*

Purpose of Goal Discussion and Questions

The goal discussion and the exception and scaling questions help the clinician to understand the family and its concern and to work with the family. It is not necessary to ask all three types of questions. One or two will suffice.

Assigning a Homework Task (Optional)

Exception questions can yield homework tasks for the family. In this case, the clinician reviews her perceptions of the family's problem. She can share these perceptions with the family or keep them to herself. This choice depends on whether she thinks that the family will benefit from an insight orientation. In this case, she does, so she says that Ricky, like all children, needs attention from his parents. The dinner routine didn't seem to give him the attention he needed, but his "rude" behavior did gain their attention. Being sent to his room does temporarily stop the conflict but it doesn't get at the root of the problem, his need for attention.

Clinician (referring to what was revealed by the exception questions): *Do you think you can do these things at home again—the sports talk and the pre-dinner talk?*

The family agrees.

Clinician: *Between now and our next meeting, I'd like you to practice each of those behaviors several times: Dad talking sports at the table, and Ricky helping Mom with dinner and sharing his school day with her or at the table.*

The clinician and the family review the specific behaviors in these interactions.

Scaling Question

Scaling questions serve three purposes: (a) they encourage each family member to "rate" his or her own sense of competence and hopefulness; (b) they help each member develop or improve behaviors and problem-solving strategies that move the family toward its goal; and (c) they promote family communication and cooperation because the family responds to each member's "rating" and knows it needs to work together to achieve its goal. The clinician may use scaling questions alone or with goal or exception questions.

Scaling Questions

Children especially like the scaling questions because they are like playing a game. The clinician might ask children these questions first so they won't be influenced by the parents' replies. If the child cannot grasp the concept or is uncooperative, the parent should go first.

Examples of scaling questions are listed in Table 8.4.

Clinician (preparing the family for a scaling question and measuring their feelings of hope): *I'd like to ask you all a different kind of question. On a scale of 1 to 10 with 1 being how hopeless you felt a few weeks ago when you called for the appointment and 10 being how you'd feel if you were to achieve your goal, where are you right now? Ricky, why don't you go first?*

Table 8.4. Scaling questions

Measuring the problem
"On a scale of 1 to 10, with 1 being the worst the problem has been and 10 being the best things could be (if the problem were solved), how would you rate things right now?"

Measuring feelings
"On a scale of 1 to 10, with 1 being how you felt (happy, hopeful, sad, angry) when we first met 2 months ago and 10 being how you'd feel when you wouldn't need to come here anymore, how are you feeling now?"

Describing one's change in behavior
"So you went from 5 to a 6. How did you do that? What did you do?"

Developing a new behavior
"You said you are a 4. What would you need to do to go from a 4 to a 5? How would you do it?"

Describing interactive patterns of behavior
"How would mom know that you have gone from a 4 to a 5?"
"What could you do to help your son go from a 7 to an 8?"
"How would your mother act when she sees you at an 8?"

Describing interactive emotions
"How do you think you would feel when your mother is at 6?"
"How would your sister feel when you share your toys with her (when you're at a 7)?"
"How would you know she felt happier? What would you notice?"

Ricky: *I'd say about 5.*

Mother: *I'm at 7.*

Father: *Sounds like we're all doing better. I am 6.*

Clinician (complimenting them and eliciting specific behaviors that helped them): *That's very impressive. What's helped you all get there?*

Ricky (smiling and "brightening" up): *Dad and I will talk about football.*

Father (demonstrating his insight and understanding): *I realize that Ricky wants attention just like I did when I was a kid. That helped.*

Mother: *I enjoy my time alone with Ricky.*

Scaling questions can yield homework tasks to help the family develop new patterns of interactions or revive past successful interactions.

Clinician (assigning homework tasks: helping each member practice a new behavior): *I am impressed by what you all have done. Let me ask another question. What would each of you have to do to move ahead on the scale by one number? For example, Ricky, what can you do to go from a 5 to a 6?*

Ricky: *I could quiz dad on some sports trivia.*

Mother: *I liked Ricky helping me at dinner.*

Clinician (helping the family appreciate the interactive context of achieving a new behavior): *Ricky, how could your mom help you go from a 5 to a 6?*

Ricky: *Letting me help her with dinner.*

Clinician (to father): *Is there some way you could help Ricky? Tell Ricky.*

Father: *I could bring the sports page to the table as a reminder for us to talk about sports together.*

If the family can't readily think of other behaviors, the clinician can suggest some that fit the family's style and coping abilities.

Concluding the Meeting

The clinician summarizes the meeting, emphasizing the family's effort and achievements.

Clinician: *I'd like to take a minute and summarize all you've done—it's quite impressive. You were concerned about Ricky's rude behavior at the dinner table. You realized that several factors contributed to the problem. It wasn't just Ricky. You defined a family goal and developed some good solutions.*

The family was insightful, and the clinician did help the family members understand how their upbringings and ineffective responses influenced their dinnertime practices and affected their family relationships. She pointed out that Ricky did want attention and interactions through dinnertime conversation but that the "quiet" dinners thwarted this need and caused conflict. Sending him to his room isolated him and only intensified his need for attention.

The clinician helped the family remember its strengths by recalling past behaviors that had been successful. The clinician utilized the family's insight to point out the interactive nature of the solution.

Clinician: *If Ricky can talk at the table, even for a short time, share his day, and get your attention and approval, then he's capable and willing to quiet down when asked. Ricky can change his behavior, but changing your behavior must also happen.*

Inviting the Family to Ask Questions or Share Thoughts

Clinician: *Do you have any questions or final thoughts you'd like to share with me or with the family?*

Mother: *It felt good to sit here and talk instead of arguing, but I hope we don't forget what we did here.*

Clinician (using the homework tasks derived from the exception and scaling questions): *It is easy to forget. That's why I suggested you choose and practice a behavior at home; they're like reminders.*

Father: *I think we can do it.*

Clinician (reminding them of the family relationship aspect of changing their behavior): *But don't forget that you are not working alone. Everyone is working together and helping each other.*

Scheduling a Follow-Up Visit

The clinician makes a follow-up appointment for 2 weeks.

Complimenting and Thanking the Family

Clinician: *Once again, congratulations on all you've done. Each of you contributed a lot. Thank you for coming in. I will see you soon.*

The Post-Interview Phase

The clinician reviews the meeting. She feels satisfied with this first meeting because she had helped the family in these ways:

1. *At the outset, she clearly stated that meeting was family-oriented, not child-oriented.*
2. *The clinician encouraged the family to discover and develop its own solutions.*
   a. ***Goal questions helped the family define and negotiate its own goals.***
   b. ***Exception questions helped the members rediscover past successes and reframe Ricky's behavior.***
   c. ***Scaling questions helped members measure their hope and competence and define new behaviors.***
3. *She used family systems techniques.*
   a. ***The parenting history helped the parents understand how their past experiences influenced their present parenting practices.***

b. ***She used insight-oriented questions and statements to help the family understand how repeating patterns of behavior maintained the problem and affected the family relationships.***

c. ***The clinician helped the family develop specific behaviors to change the repeated patterns of interactions.***

d. ***The clinician identified the father as the leader of the family and established an alliance with him.***

e. ***The clinician reframed Ricky's behavior and helped the father change his perception of Ricky as a "rude child" to one of Ricky wanting to be a "considerate child."***

4. *The clinician offered advice/teaching/reassurance in these ways:*

a. ***He assigned homework tasks so the family could practice the new behaviors at home.***

b. ***He explained Ricky's need for attention. The parents needed to help Ricky develop positive, not negative behaviors, to get their attention.***

c. ***He set a follow-up date, dictated a brief chart note, and sent a letter to the parents.***

IV. The ABC Interview

The ABC interview (Antecedent, Behavior, Consequence) highlights the "interactional context" of a parent–child behavioral problem. Invariably, child noncompliance, the most common parent complaint, is characterized by circular dynamics: the parent makes a request; the child responds/does not respond; the parent responds; the child responds; and so on. This pattern, which the ABC interview illustrates, can be repeated many times in a single incident (e.g., *"I've told him six times to go to bed."*). These repetitive interactions rapidly become increasingly intense, maintain patterns of behavior, and leave both the child and parent feeling "stuck" (*"Nothing works"*) and frustrated (*"I've had it!"*).

A. **The "A" in ABC stands for the *Antecedent.*** The antecedent is the "trigger" or situation that initiates child noncompliance. The trigger is part of the parent's communication and behavior—proximity to the child, parent's mood, actions, body language, word choice, eye contact, and/or facial expression. For example, the parent, with her hands on her hips, bends over the child while the child is reading a book and says impatiently, *"Come in the kitchen right now and do the dishes."*

B. **The "B" in ABC represents the Behavior.** Behavior is the child's response to the trigger, which is the parent's request or command. It can be expressed by mood, actions, body language, word choice, eye contact, and/or facial expression. This is the identified "behavior problem." For example, the child could pause and initially pretend not to hear. Then he rolls his eyes, turns away from the mother, and answers in a sarcastic manner, *"Who do you think I am? Your slave? I don't want to."*

C. **The "C" in ABC signifies the Consequence.** The consequence is the parent's reaction in response to the child's conduct. For example, the mother's demeanor is angry: her face reddens; her eyes narrow; her mouth tightens; and her lips are pursed. She reaches down, pulls the child up by his shirt, gets in his face, and responds in a shrill, strident voice, saying, *"How dare you talk to me like that. I work so hard and you treat me like a slave."* The parent's reaction affects the child, who responds to the mother more defiantly. She responds again with even more anger and attempts to drag him into the kitchen. This downward spiral can go on and on.

Once the clinician has an initial understanding of the problematic interactions, he or she can make suggestions and/or can help the family develop its own solutions. Fig. 8.1 illustrates the ABC interview.

ABC Interview For Interactive Behaviors

A: **Antecedent Event**--Parent's Request or Command: Communication Style and Affect

B: **Behavior**--Child's Response to Parent: Behavior and Affect

C: **Consequence**--Parent's Response to Child: Behavior and Affect

BC: The Circular Dynamics Are Repeated and Form Parent-Child Interactive Patterns

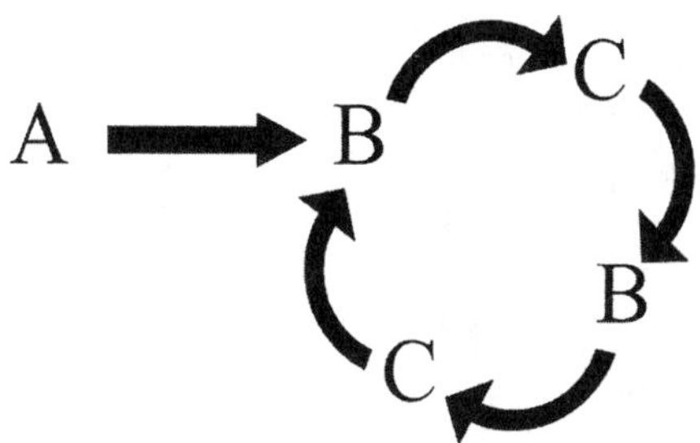

Figure 8.1. ABC interview for interactive behaviors. ©1999, William L. Coleman, M.D.

Indications for Using the ABC Interview

The ABC interview is useful as an initial interview for child noncompliance. Its use does not preclude exploration of the family context.

The ABC interview follows the same sequence of steps as the other models outlined in this chapter. Initially however, it focuses on the ABC interactions. More information (e.g., a family history or recent family stresses) is gathered, as necessary, in subsequent interviews. An example of an ABC interview with both the steps and the questions is listed in Table 8.5.

CASE 3: THE FAMILY WHO IS "HAVING PROBLEMS" WITH THEIR 8-YEAR-OLD DAUGHTER

Mrs. Greenwood calls to make an appointment because *"we're having problems with Pam."* The mother sounds very tense and says she wants "a few minutes" on the phone "to explain the situation." She makes so many references to "we" (the entire family) that the clinician suggests a family meeting. Mrs. Greenwood says that she will ask her husband. She calls back to agree to a meeting.

Table 8.5. The ABC—antecedent, behavior, consequence—interview: steps and questions

1. **Engaging the family** (time: 3 to 5 minutes)[a]
   Greet the family.
   Explain the purpose of the meeting.
2. **Understanding the family** (time: 10 to 15 minutes)[a]
   Define the problem.
   Use the ABC model.
   Understand the hierarchy.
   Identify family behaviors that maintain the problem.
3. **Working with the family** (time: 10 to 15 minutes)[a]
   Help the family cooperate in developing their own solutions.
   Offer advice when something unexpected happens.
4. **Concluding the meeting** (time: 3 to 5 minutes)[a]
   Summarize the meeting and answer questions.
   Ask the family for feedback.
   Schedule a follow-up visit.
   Compliment the family.

[a] These times are approximations based on the number of questions and complexity of the case.

Engaging the Family

Greeting the Family

The clinician reviews Pam's chart before the meeting. He has known her since she was a baby. The mother called her daughter "strong willed" when she was a toddler. Otherwise, the chart contains nothing remarkable. The clinician knows little about the parents except that they seemed to be good and caring parents. The father owns a hardware store, and the mother is a hospital lab technician. After a cordial greeting and brief social conversation, the clinician explains the purpose of the meeting.

Explaining the Purpose of the Meeting

Clinician: *Mr. and Mrs. Greenwood, have you explained to Pam why we are meeting?*

Father: *Not really.*

Clinician: *Pam, do you know why we are meeting?*

Pam: *My problem.*

Clinician: *What does "my problem" mean?*

Pam: *That's what Mommy said.*

Clinician (removing the blame focus from Pam and emphasizing the family context): *Pam, we're not here to discuss your problem. No one is blaming you. We're meeting to talk about a family problem and, most of all, to help you and Mom and Dad get along better. Everyone is going to work together.*

Pam does not look up or respond. The clinician allows a silence of about 10 seconds and then speaks.

Clinician: *How does that sound to you?*

Pam: *All right, I guess.*

The clinician isn't sure if Pam understands or agrees with this shift to a family orientation. She tries again.

Clinician (deciding to avoid the word "problem"): *Sometimes families are not happy and need help. We are here to make your family happy . . . you, Mom, Dad, and I need the whole family to talk and work together to make that happen. Would you like to try?*

Pam: *I think so.*

Clinician (to parents): *How about you?*

The parents nod vigorously.

Clinician (to Pam): *Can you talk with us and help us?*

Pam: *I'll try.*

Clinician: *Good for you.*

The clinician has explained the purposes carefully, and Pam is willing to try. When the clinician compliments Pam, he looks at the parents, hoping they will respond. They get the hint and compliment Pam too. The clinician did this because he wanted to bring out a positive quality in Pam and to lessen the "problem" focus of the meeting.

Understanding the Family and Its Concern

Defining the Problem

Clinician: *I know we spoke on the phone, Mrs. Greenwood, but let's review your concern again to be sure that it's clear to everyone and that you all agree.*

To reduce any feelings of blame, the clinician avoids the buzzword "problem."

Mother: *Everyday I call her for breakfast, and she dawdles until the morning is ruined.*

Clinician (seeking clarification and also confronting): *Ruined?*

Father: *We are upset. We eat in 2 minutes. We rush to work and school. It's a helluva way to start the day.*

Clinician (getting Pam's input so the interview is not dominated by the parents' problem-talk): *Pam, what do you want to say?*

Pam: *They yell at me. I don't like that.*

Clinician: *It sounds like arriving late for breakfast and then having everyone get "upset" are the problems. Is that right?*

Father: *That's right.*

Mother: *If Pam could just get ready. . .*

Clinician (intentionally preventing the mother from resuming problem-talk): *Let's find out what the family is doing in the morning.*

Using the ABC Model

Antecedent

The next step for the clinician is to obtain a very clear, specific description of the antecedent, or "A" aspect of the ABC model.

Clinician (to parents): *I'd like you to think of the specific situation in which the problem occurs. Give us an example of how you ask Pam to come, including your words, tone of voice and your location when you are asking Pam.*

Mother: *"Pam, come down for breakfast." My tone of voice is pleasant. Of course, she can't see me because I am in the kitchen and she's upstairs in her bedroom, so I do have to raise my voice.*

Clinician (determining the father's involvement): *Mr. Greenwood, where are you and what are you doing at this time?*

Father: *I'm usually in our bedroom watching the morning news. I just have a bagel and coffee for breakfast so I get downstairs a few minutes later. I do step into the hallway to tell Pam, "You heard what your mother said." That's my routine.*

Clinician: *Pam, what are you doing?*

Pam: *I'm watching TV in my room.*

Clinician: *How are you all feeling when this part happens?*

The report that they are all feeling "okay."

Behavior

Next, the clinician explores the parents' complaint, which is usually the child's problematic behavior (the "B" aspect of the ABC model). He wants to know the child's response to the parent's request or command, which is the behavior that the parents want to change. The clinician asks Pam and her parents to describe her behavior briefly (actions, words, and emotions) and to establish a baseline measure (e.g., frequency [number of incidents daily or weekly] and/or duration [how long a single incident lasts]). The measure will allow them to negotiate a reasonable goal (e.g., 10% improvement in several weeks).

Clinician: *Pam, when Mom calls you, what do you do?*

Pam: *I don't hear Mom.*

Clinician: *Do you hear Dad?*

Pam: *Sometimes.*

Clinician: *What do you do?*

Pam: *I keep watching TV.*

Clinician (to parents): *Is that the problem?*

Mother: *That's it. She doesn't answer me and doesn't come to breakfast.*

Father: *I know she hears me, but she stays in her room.*

Clinician: *How often does this happen, and how long does one incident last?*

The parents state that it happens "every school day" and lasts about 5 minutes "until we blow up."

Consequence

The clinician should next explore the consequence (the "C" in the ABC model) or the parental response to the child's initial behavior (B). The clinician would ask the parent(s) to describes his or her (their) actions, words, and emotions. For example, the parent's response might include repeating the requests, threatening ("I'll tell your father"), giving up ("Oh well, it doesn't really matter"), postponing ("We'll talk about this tomorrow"), doing the task alone ("It's easier to do it myself"), or scolding the child ("You are being so rude").

Clinician (to mother): *Tell us how you respond when Pam stays in her room.*

Mother: *I raise my voice and repeat the command several times in short succession. I yell at my husband to bring her down.*

Clinician (to parents): *How does each of you feel when Pam stays in her room?*

Mother: *I am angry with both of them because I'm trying to fix breakfast and get ready for work and Pam doesn't come when I call her. I yell at him to bring her to breakfast.*

Father: *I raise my voice too and tell Pam to get downstairs. I'm losing patience with her, but I'm trying to see the end of the news report. I also don't like my wife yelling at me. So I'm upset at both of them.*

The clinician realized how each member's behaviors contribute to the problem. The mother is now trying both to get Pam to breakfast and to enlist her husband's support, and both parents are getting upset at Pam and at each other.

The clinician explores the next cycle of the child–parent interaction, another cycle of B and C.

Clinician: *Pam, do you hear Mom and Dad now? What do you do?*

Pam: *I hear Mom and Dad, and I start to get ready.*

Clinician (seeking clarification): *Ready?*

Pam: *I still watch TV because I know Mom or Dad will come and get me.*

Clinician: *How are you feeling at this time?*
Pam: *Okay.*
Clinician (to parents): *What happens next?*
Mother: *I am exasperated by now. I stomp upstairs to Pam's room, turn off the TV, and tell her "Now!" I know I have a "mean" expression on my face.*
Pam: *Mom's face is red.*
Father: *When I hear her coming up the stairs, I turn off my TV and go to Pam's room. I try to help out by calming my wife, but she's fussing at me and at Pam. I'm upset with Pam too, but also with my wife for losing her temper again.*
Clinician: *Pam, now how do you feel?*
Pam: *Sometimes I feel scared.*

At this point, Pam begins to cry. Her mother takes her on her lap and comforts her.

Father: *It gets pretty intense some days, especially if we are running late for the school bus and work. But sometimes Pam gets kind of mad, yells back at her mother or me, and says she doesn't want breakfast. Then one of us brings her downstairs. Once at the table, she usually eats something although she's pouting.*
Clinician: *Do you spank her or grab her?*
Mother: *Never. Neither one of us. But sometimes, I do feel like giving her a "pop" on her rear end.*
Clinician: *Thank you for telling this story. It helped me understand the family behavior.*

Understanding the Hierarchy

The clinician still is not sure who was in charge of getting Pam downstairs.

Clinician: *Who's in charge of the morning routine?*
Mother: *I am, but I can't do it all.*
Father: *Sometimes I feel like Pam is in control. She makes it happen.*
Clinician (attempting to remove the blame from Pam and to change the father's perception): *It seems like there is a lot going on. Everyone is affected. It's not just Pam.*

The clinician wonders who is in charge. The mother is taking on too much. She is making breakfast, packing Pam's lunch, and trying to get Pam and her father down for breakfast. Maybe the father could be in charge of Pam. The clinician decides to raise that issue later in the interview (see "Working with the Family" below).

Identifying Family Patterns That Maintain the Problem

Now that the family has described the problematic interactions, the clinician reviews the series of behaviors, hoping the family members might better understand how each of their behaviors maintain the problem. However, the clinician must realize that this insight-oriented task will not work with all families.

Clinician: *Can you see how the family's interactions tend to prolong the problem? Everyone is stuck in the same pattern, and it's very hard to break out and try something new.*
Mother: *It seems like we're all caught up in this together. I used to think she was just being stubborn, but it's not that simple.*

Father: *We just go round and round and get nowhere.*

The family's responses are insightful and indicate that the members are ready to make changes in their morning routine.

Clinician: *Again, let me emphasize that no one is to blame. It's just that your responses, which are to work harder, louder, and longer, just aren't working. You need to find another way. And one of you needs to be in charge.*

Working with the Family

The clinician helps the family cooperate to develop its own solutions.

Clinician (helping the family change the situation and its behavior in the Antecedent): *How can you work together to improve things? For example, how could the first situation, when Mom first calls Pam to the table, be improved?*

Mother: *It's probably true that she can't hear me. Maybe I should go to her room.*

Father: *That's fine. I could help out by turning off my TV and getting Pam when I hear you call.*

Mother: *Maybe Pam's door could stay open, so she would hear me.*

Clinician (helping the family change its interactions in the next phase): *Pam, is there anything you could do to get down to breakfast on time?*

Pam: *I don't know.*

Father: *I could bring Pam downstairs with me.*

The clinician had hoped that the father would "volunteer" to be in charge of Pam. This change of role removes the mother from her repetitive patterns with Pam and lessens the burden on her. The father's offer signals a very important and positive change that clearly demonstrates his support for his wife. This change alone, if carried out successfully, will improve the family functioning.

> **The Family's Own Ideas Work Best**
>
> When families come up with their own ideas and solutions, they are more likely to work than if the clinician suggests them.

Clinician: *Are you saying you will be in charge of Pam? That would let your wife be in charge of making breakfast and lunch only. Tell her.*

Father (looking at his wife): *I'm willing to try.*

Clinician (acknowledging the mother as leader and gauging whether she will agree): *Can you go along with that? Tell him.*

Mother (holding on to her power and reluctant to try this): *I'm not sure if you can come through.*

Clinician (gently persuading mother to try): *Do you think you could let go a bit and allow your husband and Pam try it together? Tell them what you think.*

Mother (looking at the family): *If it would make things easier, let's try it.*

Father (stepping up to his new role and asking Pam to consider how she might change her behavior): *Pam, how can you help out?*

Pam: *By coming downstairs with you when Mom calls.*

Sometimes, families have unrealistic expectations or want to "change things" too fast. In this case, the mother is realistic.

Clinician (helping the family set a realistic goal): *How much improvement would you like to see in the next 2 weeks?*

Mother (looking at her husband and Pam): *We all need to improve our behavior, but let's be realistic. If Pam and her dad came down together twice a week, that would be a good start. If I have to call out again, which I probably will at times, I will walk upstairs and tell him. I will try to remember not to yell.*

Clinician (to Pam and the father): *Does that sound like a workable plan?*

Offering Advice/Support When Something Unexpected Happens

Mother: *I have a last thought. I think we might remove the TV from Pam's room. It is such a distraction, and she watches silly cartoons.*

Father: *I don't agree.*

At this point, Pam breaks into tears, hops off her mother's lap, and sits in her own chair.

For a parent to suddenly "add on" another problem or request at the end of a visit is not unusual. The clinician should politely postpone this agenda and offer to address it in the next meeting.

Clinician (respecting this new concern, but wanting to preserve the family's sense of accomplishment, and knowing this was not the time to address another issue, says the following): *With all due respect, I'd like to suggest that you not try anything else at this time. You've done lots of work here and have a lot to practice at home. This is obviously an emotional topic. I am not dismissing it, but I think we can address it at our next meeting.*

Concluding the Meeting

Summarizing the Meeting and Answering Questions

Clinician: *This has been a very productive meeting. Through your open and honest conversation, you have seen how everyone can keep a problem going and how everyone can help end it by changing roles and behaviors. You've come up with a realistic goal and a good plan.*

Mother: *I'm not convinced that it's going to work. Can we call you if we have problems?*

Clinician: *Certainly. Do you have any questions or comments you would like to share with one another ?*

Pam: *Does that mean I can still have my TV?*

Mother: *For the time being.*

Asking the Family for Feedback

Clinician: *I'd like to ask you how the meeting went for you. Did it help you address your concerns?*

The family feels it has been a "good start."

Clinician: *Do you feel more hopeful than when you came in?*

Father: *A litle bit.*

Pam: *What do you mean?*

Clinician: *Do you feel better now than before?*

Pam: *I think so.*

Mother: *I'm not sure. I'll tell you at the next meeting.*

Scheduling a Follow-Up Visit

The clinician schedules a follow-up appointment in 2 weeks.

Complimenting the Family

Clinician: *I want to tell you how well you worked together. It's apparent you really want to change the morning routine. Each of you came up with a behavior that working together on should help make a change. I hope you can practice at home what you discussed here. Thank you for coming in.*

The Post-Interview Phase

The clinician reviews the meeting. He had done several different things.

1. He *explained the purpose of a family meeting.*
2. *He helped the family develop its own solutions.* Most importantly, ***the father had "volunteered" to take on a new role/behavior and to support his wife.*** This is a key change.
3. *The clinician used several family systems techniques.*
   a. ***He illustrated the interactive context/ relationship aspects of the problem.***
   b. ***He identified family interactions that maintain the problem.***
   c. ***He explored the hierarchy and identified the mother as the leader.***
   d. ***He helped the family discuss ways to change its behaviors/interactive patterns.***
4. *The clinician offered advice /support.*
   a. ***He gently urged the mother to relinquish some power, to drop one responsibility, and to agree with her husband's desire to assume some power/ leadership.*** This agreement is a major change.
   b. ***He raised the issue of setting realistic expectations, and the mother responded with a realistic goal.***

c. ***He postponed the discussion of removing the TV from Pam's room because it would probably have "undone" all the good work the family had accomplished.*** He did this respectfully and did acknowledge its importance to the family by promising to discuss it later.

d. ***He complimented the family and reminded it of its homework assignments.***

e. ***He dictated a summary letter to the family and used a copy as his chart note.***

V. **Summary**

Many models of family interviewing exist, leaving no one right way to conduct the family interview. This chapter describes three brief interview models: the problem-oriented model, the solution-oriented model, and the ABC model. The problem-oriented model, which is based on the medical model, emphasizes a detailed description of the problem. The solution-oriented model emphasizes solution building by using goal discussion, exception questions, and scaling questions. The ABC model, which is very brief, is especially suited for specific child noncompliance. All of these models follow the four steps described in Chapter 6, "The Four Steps of a Family Interview." Each model incorporates family systems techniques and clinician directives. These models are aimed at level 2 problems and are intended for clinicians at level 3 of family involvement. Clinicians are encouraged to modify these interviewing models or to create their own models to fit their skills and personal style, the family, and the problem.

ADDITIONAL READING

Baker B, Brightman A, Heifetz L, et al. *Behavior problems.* Champaign IL: Research Press, 1976.

Barker P. *Basic family therapy*, 3rd ed. New York: Oxford University Press, 1992.

Berg IK. *Family-based services.* New York: Norton, 1994.

Coleman WL. Family focused pediatrics: solution-oriented techniques for behavioral problems. *Contemp Pediatr* 1997;14:121.

DeShazer S. *Keys to solution in brief therapy.* New York: WW Norton, 1985.

Doherty WJ. *Take back your kids.* Notre Dame, IN: Sorin Books, 2000.

Gottman J. *The heart of parenting.* New York: Simon & Schuster, 1997.

Harkness S, Keefer CH, Super CM. Culture and ethnicity. In: Levine MD, Carey WB, Crocker AC, eds. *Developmental–behavioral pediatrics,* 3rd ed. Philadelphia: WB Saunders, 1999.

Jacobs EH. *Fathering the ADHD child: a book for fathers, mothers, and professionals.* Northvale, NJ: Jason Aronson, 1998.

Johnson S. *The one minute father.* New York: William Morrow, 1983.

Klar H, Coleman WL. Brief solution-focused strategies for behavioral pediatrics. In: Coleman WL, Taylor EH, eds. *Family focused pediatrics. Pediatr Clin N Am* 1995;42(1).

Nichols MP, Schwartz RC. *Family therapy: concepts and methods,* 2nd ed. New York: Allyn and Bacon, 1991.

Robin AL, Foster SL. *Negotiating parent–adolescent conflict.* New York: Guilford Press, 1989.
Sameroff AJ, Emde RN. *Relationship disturbances in early childhood.* New York: Basic Books, 1989.
Selekman MD. *Solution-focused therapy with children.* New York: Guilford Press, 1997.
Walsh F. *Strengthening family resilience.* New York: Guilford Press, 1998.
Walter JL, Peller JE. *Becoming solution-focused in brief therapy.* New York: Brunner/Mazel, 1992.
Webster-Stratton C, Herbert M. *Troubled families–troubled children.* New York: John Wiley and Sons, 1994.

9 After the Initial Interview: The Post-Interview Phase, Follow-Up, and Choosing a Termination Point for the Meetings

I. **Purpose**

After the interview, the clinician has several tasks in the post-interview phase, the time the clinician uses (a) to review the quality of the meeting, (b) to assess his or her own feelings, and (c) to prepare for the next meeting. Subsequently, follow-up visits represent the only way for the clinician to measure the success of the meetings and to ascertain the family's status. Finally, at some point in the clinician–family relationship, the clinician and the family must terminate the meetings when either they are no longer needed or they cease to be helpful. This chapter describes the clinician's tasks in the post-interview phase, offers suggestions for carrying out follow-up meetings, and recommends guidelines for making decisions on timing the termination of the family meetings.

II. **The Post-Interview Phase**

In the post-interview phase, the clinician reviews the quality of the meeting. Questions the clinician can ask himself or herself are listed below. In general, the clinician wants to know the following: Was the meeting a success or failure? What worked? What failed? If something failed, how can it be fixed? The clinician does need some input from the family to obtain the best answers to these questions.

A. **Assessing the quality of the meeting and the family's satisfaction.**

1. *Did the clinician respect the presenting concern and stay focused on it, or did he or she change the focus without the family's "invitation," "consent," or awareness?* For example, a family complains that the son's attention-deficit/hyperactivity disorder (ADHD) problem is causing family conflict; however, the clinician presumes that the family conflict is really caused by the parents' marital tension and chooses to focus on that instead. The family understandably will feel disrespected and dissatisfied by this shift. If marital tension is present, it will usually be revealed in a later visit as the clinician gains the family's trust and explores the family context.

2. *Were the family's goals specific and realistic?* If not, did the clinician help them define and negotiate more specific and realistic goals? For example, the family's goal may be "We want to be a happy family," which is vague and unrealistic. The clinician must then help the family define and negotiate a more specific and realistic goal (e.g., "We'd

like to have two pleasant evenings each week doing something together, such as talking, playing board games and cards, or watching TV.")

3. *Did the clinician explain the purpose of the family meeting?* Does the family understand? Did the family members "accept" the idea of a family meeting?

4. *Was everyone involved in the session?* Did the clinician form an alliance with each member of the family ("touch" each member) and encourage his or her participation?

5. *Did the clinician identify the hierarchy and family structure (e.g., leadership, coalitions, and boundaries)?*

6. *Did the clinician help the members develop new interactions?* Did the clinician engage the family in a cooperative effort? Was he or she too directive?

7. *Was the session comfortable and orderly?* Did the clinician make it "safe" for all family members to express themselves without fear of ridicule or disapproval? Was the meeting time-efficient?

8. *Was it necessary to impose rules for the session or to change the seating?* Did the clinician demonstrate appropriate leadership?

9. *Does the family appear satisfied?* Do the members feel some progress has been made? How does the clinician know? Did he or she ask them?

10. *Does the family seem willing to return?* Gauging its willingness can be difficult. Even a statement, such as, "Yes, we'll come back" does not guarantee its return.

B. **Assessing the clinician's own feelings.** The clinician should ask himself or herself some questions about his or her own emotional response to the family.

1. *How does the clinician feel about the family?* What were his or her positive or negative feelings about it?

2. *Did the clinician convey these feelings to the family, either intentionally or unintentionally? How?*

3. *What would the clinician do differently in the next meeting?*

4. *Did the clinician identify too closely with either the family or an individual member? Did he or she thus lose objectivity or effectiveness?* Did he or she form a coalition with a parent or child?

5 *Does the clinician have a "rescue fantasy," a wish to "save" the family, that caused him or her to rush in too fast with advice or to make impossible promises?*

6. *Does the clinician want to see the family again?*

7. *Would the clinician prefer that this family not return?* If not, what should he or she do?

C. **Preparing for the next meeting.** The clinician prepares for the next meeting by asking more questions of himself or herself.

1. *Does the clinician think that his or her initial impression/hypothesis needs to be revised?*

2. *What other information does the clinician think is still needed?*
3. *Should the clinician invite other members?*
4. *Should the clinician consider making a referral?*

D. **Reviewing for the next meeting.**

Several helpful tasks that assist the clinician's preparation for the next meeting are given below.

1. *The clinician can revise* the original hypothesis after the first meeting when more is learned about the family. For example, what might first appear as a parenting disagreement about discipline now seems to be the symptom of alcoholism instead. The parents avoid confronting the drinking problem by maintaining their parenting disagreements. The symptom (parents arguing) operates as a way to maintain the family balance and function.
2. *With the family's consent, the clinician can obtain copies of past individual or family evaluations, school records, or any other information that might prove helpful in understanding the family.* A record of attempted interventions and outcomes often proves very helpful.
3. *The clinician can speak with a consultant or a colleague to get a second opinion or to seek guidance for the next meeting.*
4. *The clinician should dictate or write a chart note. He or she must document the visit for both medical–legal and billing purposes; to record confidential, important information; and to summarize the visit.* The family should then be sent a copy of this summary. Reviewing the notes before the next meeting helps the clinician remember the pertinent points and organize his or her approach.
5. *The clinician should make a plan for the next visit* (e.g., invite another member, add more structure and order, encourage more communication between certain members, or direct the family focus to a particular issue).

III. **Follow-Up Meetings**

In the busy practice setting, the clinician may need two meetings to carry out a complete initial interview. The first visit entails engaging and understanding the family, and the second entails working with the family. See Chapter 6, "The Four Steps of a Family Interview," for more discussion. Then, shorter follow-up visits are used to gauge the success of the meetings and to show support for the family efforts.

A. **Purposes of follow-up meetings.**

1. *They provide the clinician with a better understanding of the family's functioning.* Every meeting reveals more information about the family's communication patterns and adaptability.
2. *They reveal the efficacy of the clinician and the treatment plan.* Follow-up visits give the clinician his or her only way to measure the success of the meeting. They provide feedback about the clinician's abilities.

Follow-up Visits and the Family's Progress

Follow-up visits are the only way the clinician can measure a family's progress and gauge his or her own skills.

B. **Steps of follow-up meetings**. Follow-up meetings are usually shorter than the initial meeting, but follow a similar sequence of steps: (a) engaging the family; (b) understanding the family; (c) working with the family; and (d) concluding the session.

1. *Engaging the family.* Follow-up visits start with a welcoming, friendly greeting to put the family at ease (e.g., *"It's good to see you all again. Thank you for making the effort to get together again."*). If a family member is attending for the first time, the clinician needs to introduce himself or herself, welcome the new member, and determine this individual's relationship to and role in the family. Question for assessing this include, *"What is your relationship to Timmy (the child)?" "Do you live with the family?"* and *"What is your role in the family (e.g., caretaking responsibilities, decision making)?"*
2. *Understanding the family and its concern.* This phase should begin with open-ended questions (e.g., *"Tell me how things have been going since our last visit."*). The follow-up visit provides more information about the family in several ways.
   a. ***Family meetings stir up feelings that remind the family of other issues; in the follow-up visit the family may wish to focus on these feelings or issues instead of on the initial complaint.*** When this happens, the clinician should respect the family's wish and should explore the new issue for a short time. Then the clinician must help the family determine what is more important at this time—the initial complaint or this present issue. For example, a family's original complaint might be poor family communication *("We yell and scream all the time")*, but at the follow-up visit its new issue might be the family's disappointment about the child's recent report card (*"He's failed math"*). The clinician needs to provide some leadership and help the family decide which to discuss. The other issue can also be addressed at another meeting.
   b. ***In a follow-up visit, the family may feel more comfortable and thus may talk more openly.*** Beginning with an open-ended question allows the members to reveal new information, if they wish. The family also may want to review or clarify certain aspects of the previous meeting.

c. ***During the interval between visits, the family may have experienced an unexpected event—either negative or positive—that it may want to discuss at the meeting.*** If the family's reply is, *"We're not doing so well,"* the clinician should first acknowledge those feelings. He or she might say, *"I'm sorry to hear that. Let's take a few minutes and review what happened. Were you all clear about or in agreement with what happened at the last meeting? What do you think has been difficult since the last meeting?"*

d. ***When things don't go well for the family and/or it doesn't make progress, the clinician must also consider whether the suggestions that he or she made were accurate, timely, or clear.*** The clinician can convey this by saying, *"Maybe I suggested something before I really understood the situation;"* or *"Maybe I didn't make myself clear in our last meeting."* The clinician should not label the family as "noncompliant," "resistant," or "difficult." Instead, the reasons for the family's reluctance to comply should be explored.

Is the Family is Doing Better?

If the family reports *"We are doing better,"* the clinician should ask the members to elaborate with specifics. Good news and progress should never be taken for granted or minimized. These are the "victories" that the family wants, needs, and is working for. The clinician can ask the following questions:

- "What is better?"
- "What are you doing now?"
- "How did you do it?"
- "Did the family cooperate?"
- "Does everyone share this feeling?

3. *Working with the family.* In this part of the interview, the clinician helps the family develop or refine solutions. If the family is "doing better" (changing the interactions, expectations, roles, or perceptions), it might be content to "rest" at this point. The clinician can help the family members decide if they want to "work" or to "rest" and should support their decision. If the family wants to work, the clinician could use the scaling question to direct the meeting. *("So, let me ask you a question. At the last meeting you said you all felt you were at a 6 in terms of doing well. What would you have to do to go from 6 to a 7?")* Together the family can devise a few strategies. See Chapter 8, "Three

Models of Brief Family Interviews," The Solution-oriented Interview, for examples.

If this visit is planned to be the last, the clinician should remind the family so that they can prepare to say goodbye.

4. *Concluding the meeting.* The clinician should leave 3 to 5 minutes for the conclusion in the plan for the meeting. The clinician concludes the meeting by providing a brief summary to help the family remember its accomplishments and the tasks ahead *("Let me review what we've done here today.")*. This synopsis is especially helpful for the discouraged family or one that has difficulty following through and accomplishing its goals. The clinician should also ask the family members how they feel about the session and should give them time to respond *("What are your thoughts about the meeting? Did it help?")*. See Chapter 6, "The Four Steps of a Family Interview," for more discussion.

C. **Scheduling the follow-up visits.** The clinician should give the family an idea of how many follow-up visits he or she thinks are necessary (*"Let's plan on three or four visits. We can schedule more visits if necessary."*).

As a general guide, if the complete initial interval requires two sessions, those should be scheduled as close to one another as possible and should take place no more than 1 to 2 weeks apart. The first actual follow-up visit should be scheduled 1 to 3 weeks after the completed initial interview(s). Subsequent follow-up visits should be scheduled at increasingly longer intervals—up to 2 to 3 months apart—depending on the family's progress and the clinician's judgment.

Finally, the clinician should end the follow-up meeting by complimenting and thanking the family (*"You've done good work in these meetings. Thank you for all your hard work."*).

IV. **Choosing a Termination Point for the Meetings**

The number of family meetings is finite as their ultimate goal is to make the family competent enough so it does not need the clinician's help. At some point, the clinician and family will realize that the family is not dependent on the clinician any more; it is capable of problem solving on its own. The family members have achieved their goal. When the family and the clinician make this realization, they should choose a time together for terminating the meetings. Although this phenomenon is known as "terminating the relationship," this term often sounds too harsh or too final to the family. Families often find the term "terminating the meetings" easier to accept. Ideally, the clinician should schedule a final meeting because this meeting allows time for the clinician and the family to express their final feelings and thoughts and to say good-bye.

Below are listed a few different situations that signal that the time to terminate the meetings has arrived.

A. **In the course of a routine follow-up session, the clinician and/or the family sense that the family is**

competent and that it doesn't need to come back. Suddenly, this routine session becomes the final one. In this case, the clinician should voice this idea and should let the family respond (unless they have already voiced it). If the members agree, the clinician should provide enough time in that meeting for all family members to share their final thoughts.

B. **The clinician and the family have agreed to a specific number of meetings.** If the family members have agreed to three meetings, the clinician should remind them at the end of the second meeting that the next visit (the third) is their last scheduled meeting. When the third visit begins, the clinician can remind them that this visit is the final meeting (*"Before we begin, let me remind you that this is our last scheduled visit."*). The clinician should always allow a few minutes at the end of the meeting for both the family and the clinician to answer questions, to share final thoughts, and to say good-bye. The clinician should always offer the option of more visits if the family feels it needs or wants more. It should feel welcome to return in the future as necessary. The clinician can suggest more meetings if he or she feels that the family has not yet achieved its goal.

C. **Sometimes in the final meeting, the clinician senses the family wants and needs more meetings; or the family indicates a continued need or desire to continue them.** In this situation, the clinician might say, *"Although this is our last scheduled visit, we can schedule more if you would like."* or *"I think that one or two more visits would be very helpful."*

D. **The family's goal is achieved before the final scheduled visit.** For example, the clinician and the family initially scheduled four visits; but by the end of the third visit, the family has demonstrated so much adaptability and growth that the fourth visit appears unnecessary. The clinician might raise the issue, while still offering the family the full number of agreed upon visits. He or she might say, *"You seem to be doing so well that the fourth visit may not be necessary. I still will be very happy to see you at the next scheduled visit, or we can schedule it at a later date. But I need to hear what you think."*

E. **Sometimes the family raises the issue of a final meeting.** A family member may say, *"Doctor, we feel we have made progress in these three meetings and don't need a fourth visit."* The clinician should agree with the family, if he or she thinks the family has made sufficient progress, by saying, *"I agree. We don't need the fourth meeting. But I am always available if you want to return."*

If the clinician feels the family needs the fourth visit, he or she should be frank yet supportive. He or she could say, *"I agree that you've made real progress, but I think that one more visit would be helpful. We can schedule it for a longer interval. Is that okay with you?"*

V. Summary

What happens after the initial meeting carries as much importance as the initial meeting itself. The clinician has several tasks. In the post-interview phase, he or she reviews the quality of the meeting, assesses his or her personal feelings, and plans for the next meeting. Follow-up visits are essential as they are the only way for the clinician to measure the success of the meetings and the family's status. Finally, as the family–clinician relationship must come to an end, the clinician must know when to terminate the meetings.

Family meetings are not always successful. Therefore, the clinician must be aware of the pitfalls and disappointments of family counseling. See Chapter 13, "Dealing with Disappointment and Failure: Avoiding Pitfalls and Working with Difficult Families," for further discussion.

ADDITIONAL READING

Allmond BW, Tanner JL. *The family is the patient*, 2nd ed. Baltimore: Lippincott, Williams & Wilkins, 1998.

Coleman WL. The first interview with a family. In: Coleman WL, Taylor EH, eds. *Family focused pediatrics. Pediatr Clin N Am* 1995;42(1):119–130.

Coleman WL. The interview. In: Levine MD, Carey WB, Crocker AC, eds. *Developmental–behavioral pediatrics*, 3rd ed. Philadelphia: WB Saunders, 1999.

Doherty WJ, Baird MA. *Family therapy and family medicine*. New York: Guilford Press, 1983.

Lichstein PR. Terminating the doctor/patient relationship. In: Lipkin M, Putman SM, Lazare, eds. *The medical interview*. New York: Springer-Verlag, 1995.

McDaniel S, Campbell TL, Seaburn DB. *Family-oriented primary care*. New York: Springer-Verlag, 1990.

Napier AY, Whitaker CA. *The family crucible*. New York: Harper and Row, 1978.

Stuart M, Lieberman JA. *The fifteen-minute hour: applied psychotherapy for the primary care physician*, 2nd ed. Westport, CT: Praeger Press, 1993:14.

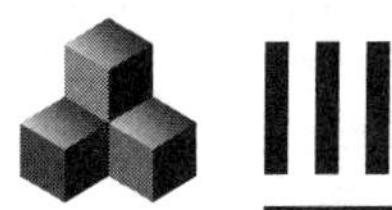

III

Clinical Issues and Strategies

10 Family Communication Problems

I. Purpose

Family communication is one of the biggest challenges families face. One of the most frequent complaints from families is *"We can't communicate."* Parents complain that children "don't listen," and children complain that parents "don't listen." Everyone wants to be heard, yet nobody seems to listen (e.g., the failure to accept another's position). Communication is a dynamic, interactive process that entails both listening and speaking. The most difficult aspect of family communication is the inability of family members to communicate their feelings effectively, especially love/affection, anger, or sadness. When family communication is problematic, strained relationships result.

This chapter describes family communication problems and offers solutions, which, though directive in nature, should be offered as suggestions. They are not family systems techniques.

The major communication problems include the following:

- ineffective listening skills;
- family rules;
- children who don't appear to listen;
- threats, commands, and requests;
- invalidation by other family members; and
- ineffective communication.

When a Family Responds Negatively

When offering advice, the clinician should be prepared to accept a "No" from the family. In this case, he or she should offer to help the family develop its own solutions. For example, he or she could say, *"What do you think would help?"*

II. Ineffective Listening Skills: How to Teach Listening Skills

Listening and speaking are learned behaviors. The clinician can help parents improve family communication by teaching and modeling listening and speaking skills. Twelve ways to teach these skills follow.

A. Parents can teach listening skills early with these techniques.

1. *As children grow more verbal, parents can block out "listening times" when both child and parent are free from distractions,* such as sitting quietly in a room (with the TV off and telephone answering machine turned on) or sharing a snack at bedtime. Car rides also provide excellent opportunities. The parent(s) can engage the child in

a conversation about a topic of the child's choosing and then let the child do most of the talking.

2. *Reading to children enhances listening.* Parents should encourage children to comment and to ask questions about the material.

B. **Parents can model listening to children like they themselves want their children to listen to them.**

1. *Parents can use active listening.* Children will listen to parents in the same way. Active listening means actively responding with discernable verbal and nonverbal reactions to the speaker's thoughts and feelings (as represented by tone of voice, facial expression, and words). These listening skills include facial expressions that match the speaker's moods, eye contact, body posture, and one or two word responses ("Uh-huh," "I see," or "It sounds like you were feeling pretty good.") or short summaries of what the child just said. Sitting at the child's level and making eye contact can help parents better detect the meanings and feelings portrayed by the child's words and facial expressions.

2. *Let children complete what they are saying.* Sometimes parents react too quickly, interrupt, or say things that they don't really mean. Parents need to remember that children are just learning how to express themselves, a complex skill requiring time and practice, and that parental patience is crucial.

C. **Parents should listen to children when they talk about their interests.** Children love to talk about their adventures, fantasies, discoveries, and successes. They eagerly await the parent's response or feedback. Parents can do the following to encourage this interaction:

1. *Provide the time and encourage their children to talk about these things.*

2. *Learn about the children's accomplishments in school, their after school activities, their friends, and the popular culture (music, sports, fashions).* This knowledge will provide much subject matter for discussion.

3. *Develop and discuss common interests with their children, which in turn motivates children to listen.* For example, parents and children can discuss their favorite movies, meals, TV shows, or activities.

4. *Tell their children about what they do at work.* Children are interested in their parents' jobs and activities.

5. *If possible, take their children to work for a few hours.*

D. **Parents can appreciate the child's perspective.**

1. *Initially, parents should listen without judging or moralizing.* A child communicates better when he or she feels that the parents respect his or her actions or viewpoints. Some parents find this difficult.

2. *Parents must learn when to talk and when to remain silent.* For instance, if a child has a bad day at school, he or she may need time to settle down. Parents should wait until the child is ready to talk about the problem.

3. *Parents must understand the child's stage of language and social development so that the parent can help him or her learn to express himself or herself effectively and to use common courtesy* (e.g., "May I?", "Excuse me," "Please," and "Thank you").

E. **Parents can recognize, acknowledge, and reward good listening habits.** Like other learned behaviors, listening is reinforced by positive feedback. *"I like the way you are looking at me and listening quietly."* Feedback is most effective when it is immediate, specific, and frequent (e.g., at the end of a conversation, not hours or days later).

F. **Parents can use paraphrasing and clarifying statements when listening.**

1. *Paraphrasing statements do the following:*

a. ***Enhance the parents' understanding of what the child is saying.***

b. ***Tell the child that he or she is heard.***

c. ***Reduce the escalation of the child's anger*** (e.g., "So, what you are saying is that when no one plays with you, you feel upset.").

d. ***Help children remember what they are saying.***

2. *Parents can use clarifying statements for the following reasons:*

a. ***Enhance their own understanding.*** (e.g.,"I'm not sure I understand.")

b. ***Indicate that the parent is interested.*** (e.g., "I want to know what you feel, but I need a little help.")

c. ***Help the child improve his or her expressive language.*** (e.g., "Do I understand that you mean . . .?")

G. **Parents can teach empathy by listening with empathy.** Parents need to figure out the feelings that lie behind the child's words and that "drive" their behavior. Children feel strong emotions but have little experience expressing them or skills that are inadequate.

Child: *Are there big kids in school?*

The parent should make a supportive statement instead of a question, and the child can confirm, deny, or ignore it. This at least gives the child the chance to share feelings.

Parent: *Maybe you feel afraid there will be bullies at school, or maybe you're worried about being left out.*

H. **Parents can use "I" messages instead of "You" messages.**

1. *The "I" message allows parents to express themselves in a nonthreatening, nonjudgmental manner* that makes the listener more open and more likely to accept the message. For example, the following statements exemplify times when "I" messages should be used:

- "I feel worried when you do your homework so fast."
- "I can't clean the house with all the toys out."
- "I feel angry when you swear."

The "I" message communicates the effect of the child's behavior on the parent instead of suggesting that the child is inherently bad because of his or her behavior. When "I" messages are used, the child is more likely to assume responsibility for the behavior.

2. *Conversely, the "You" message sounds like a personal attack and conveys a put-down.* The following statements are generic examples of "you" statements:

- "You are just trying to get me mad."
- "You do your homework too fast."
- "You leave your toys out, and I can't clean up."

The child often reacts defensively (with denial, resistance, anger, or ending the conversation) to "You" messages.

I. **Parents can substitute "Yes" for "No" when stating a condition for participating in some activity.** "Yes" should be the first word the child hears when a parent attaches a condition to a child's request. Doing so acknowledges the child's need or desire and reduces conflict. For example, a child might say, "Can we play ball?" The parent's response should be, "Yes, when you have finished your chores," instead of "No, we can't because you have not finished your chores."

J. **Parents can explain their reason for saying "No."** Children are more receptive to a "No" when the parent briefly explains the reason why. A parent can briefly elaborate by saying, "We need to leave in 5 minutes" instead of "No, you can not play now."

K. **Parents should acknowledge the child's point of view.** When parents acknowledge their child's point of view, the child feels validated because his or her feelings have been recognized (e.g., "I know it's hard to leave the party during the middle of it.").

L. **Parents and children can learn to apologize to one another.** Parents and children often say hurtful things to each other. Therefore, both parties need to be able to apologize by saying, "I'm sorry." Both also must be willing to forgive and to accept a sincere apology when it is offered. Effective communication may not be possible until the hurt feelings are addressed. For example, if a parent gets angry and says something hurtful, he or she should apologize to the child by saying, "I'm sorry for hurting your feelings. I didn't mean to do it. I was angry." If a child swears at a parent or says something insulting, the child likewise should be encouraged to apologize.

Teaching Children to Apologize

Parents need to teach children to say "I'm sorry" when necessary. When parents say *"I'm sorry,"* they should not expect or ask the child to forgive them right away. Hurt feelings take time to mend.

III. Family Rules

The unspoken, unconscious rules of communication of families often inhibit self-expression. These rules, which determine what members can or cannot ask for, talk about, think, and feel, can put each member at risk for a variety of social and psychological problems (e.g., inhibiting the expression of feelings and needs may lead to low self-esteem, externalizing behaviors, or acting out). Children unconsciously follow these rules, which are reinforced by disapproval, withdrawal of affection, or fear of punishment. For example, if the father becomes angry or disapproving when a child is fearful or needy, the child learns to repress those feelings. Children learn these rules and patterns from parents who learned them from their parents. Thus, this style is passed on from generation to generation. Spouses often adopt each other's rules in order to maintain their relationship (e.g., don't ask for emotional support). Some examples are listed in Table 10.1.

CASE 1: FAMILY RULES

First Child Visit

The father of a 10-year-old girl makes an appointment because his daughter Fran has been *"kicked off the school bus."*

The bus driver's report states that Fran suddenly pushed a girl off the seat. A fight ensued, after which Fran was warned and her parents were notified. The very next day, Fran threw a boy's backpack out the window. The result was that she lost bus privileges for a week. The parents are concerned about the behavior but also are very stressed because they now have to drive Fran to and from school, causing problems at work. Fran is generally "quiet and well behaved." She earns good grades and has good health. The parents deny any recent stresses on Fran. Fran herself is cooperative, and her affect is appropriate. She cannot explain these fights, and the parents cannot understand her behavior. The clinician suggests that "a few family discussions at

Table 10.1. Examples of family rules

- Don't ask for attention.
- Don't ask for help.
- Don't admit feelings of loneliness, sadness, hurt, or disappointment.
- Don't show anger toward parents and relatives or disagree openly.
- Don't seek positive feedback and praise for your work.
- Don't ask for emotional support or show affection.
- Don't talk about or ask about sexual feelings or orientation.
- Don't talk about your own or others' problems (e.g., alcoholism, depression, abuse, affairs, hostility, or alienation in family relationships).
- Don't express uncertainty and doubt, especially within the family.

home would help her talk things out." He explains how to carry out the meetings and schedules a follow-up visit in 2 weeks. (See Chapter 12, "Strategies to Enhance Family Functioning," for more discussion.)

Second Child Visit

At the next visit, Fran's parents report that she has been ordered to sit by herself behind the driver on the bus, so she "feels embarrassed." Another problem has come up—the teacher suspects her of stealing her classmates' pencils. Fran denies it, but her parents have removed TV privileges for 2 weeks. The parents have not tried conducting family meetings because they are "too busy and tired" in the evenings. The clinician speaks with the parents alone and then with Fran. He thinks that Fran might have an attention-deficit/hyperactivity disorder (ADHD) or a kind of behavioral impulsivity or perhaps that she might be suffering from depression. He mentions conducting a more formal evaluation and the possibility of medication, but the parents are hesitant. The clinician suggests family meetings again, saying *"I am sure you all have lots of feelings that a few good talks will help."*

Third Child Visit

A meeting is set for 2 weeks later, but the mother calls after 5 days. The teacher has reported that Fran is "cheating on tests and is being isolated by friends." The clinician, at a loss, feels that a family meeting is warranted. He explains the purpose to the mother, who agrees to it.

First Family Meeting

Understanding the Family

During the family meeting, the clinician first reviews the past interventions. The family has not used family talks because "they don't feel right," but they are unable or unwilling to elaborate on the reason why. The family history is negative for medical or psychosocial problems. He again inquires about recent stresses, defining this as "any change that affects the family." The mother states that she and her husband are both busier with work and explains how that leaves less time and energy for home life. Also, a maternal aunt is going through a "nasty divorce," so the mother visits or calls her frequently, which takes even more time away from the family. When asked why they hadn't revealed this in the first meeting, the mother replies, *"You just asked about Fran."*

The clinician, trying to understand the family's communication habits, asks if they have much time for conversation. The father responds with, *"We talk about work and home activities."* Watching TV is the major family activity. When he asks the parents if they talked to Fran about how she feels, they give him a quizzical look and say, *"Not really."*

The clinician explores the teacher's concern about Fran being "isolated." With some gentle prodding, Fran begins to tell how she has been "pushed out" of her group of friends and that she doesn't know why. When the clinician asks her how she feels, she hesitates and then says, *"Mad and sad."* The parents had not heard about the problem with the friends until the teacher mentioned it. They hadn't realized how upset Fran was. *"We didn't ask. I wish she had told us. We never know her feelings."* Therein lay the problem, the unspoken rule: **No one asked. No one told.**

Fran's eyes fill with tears, and her body shakes with crying. The mother puts her on her lap.

Working with the Family

The clinician considers all the factors influencing the parenting practices, home life, and Fran's behavior. He knows that sharing his own "explanation" of the family dynamics to a family with unconscious rules would not be productive. But he does feel that he can share other information: the family is experiencing stress at work; the aunt's divorce drains the mother's energy and time; and, as a result, the family has less time together. Fran has good reason to feel upset, but she hadn't told anyone. The clinician explains, *"Sometimes kids express their feelings with these behaviors."* He points out that Fran has many strengths, including loving and supportive parents.

During three meetings the clinician and the family develop some plans together.

1. The parents agree to let the clinician help Fran express herself—*"To help her do more talking and less fighting."* The focus is on Fran, which the parents are comfortable with.
2. The clinician wants to monitor Fran for possible depression. The outcome is that she is not depressed.
3. The parents take turns arriving home about the same time as Fran does.
4. The mother tells Fran's aunt that she cannot see her as often.
5. The teacher investigates the problem with friends but can find no obvious reasons for their behavior.
6. Fran finds another group of friends.

As a result of these changes, Fran's behavior improves. The parents' communication style stays the same, but their efforts to modify their work and home behaviors conveys a feeling of love and support.

Because family "rules" are unspoken and unconscious, the clinician should not challenge them or try to "explain" them unless the family seems open and receptive. The clinician can help the family in other ways, as this case illustrates.

IV. **Why Children Don't Appear to Listen**

Parents often complain that children "tune out," don't listen, or don't appear to listen. Children usually don't consciously decide to "tune out," but other explanations exist which clarify their difficulty in listening to their parents.

- Parents communicate at a level above the child's receptive language ability.

- Parents don't state their expectations clearly.

Clinicians can help parents appreciate their children's level of language development in many ways, eleven of which are listed below. Of course, normal variation must be considered, and the clinician and parents should remember that boys tend to develop speech and language more slowly than girls (Table 10.2).

CASE 2: MOTHER TALKING ABOVE THE CHILD'S LISTENING ABILITY

Well-Child Visit

A mother brings her 5-year-old daughter Lynn in for a regular well-child visit. As the visit is concluding, the mother lists several things she wants Lynn to do.

"Lynn, put on your shoes and get your book."
"Then we are going shopping and I expect you to behave."
"When we get home, you can help me with dinner."

Lynn suddenly turns to her and yells, *"I won't and you can't make me!"* The mother, embarrassed, takes Lynn by the arm, raises her voice and tells her, *"You do what I say!"* Lynn then begins to cry and throws herself on the floor. The clinician asks if this happens at home, and the mother replies, *"She yells at me whenever I ask her do something, and I would like some help."* The meeting is almost over, so the clinician offers two suggestions: that the mother makes only one request at a time and that she try to not yell at Lynn.

Second Visit

Understanding the Family

During the follow-up meeting, Lynn plays quietly with toy cars and trucks while the clinician takes a more detailed history. The mother is 25 and single, and the father has "disappeared." Her parents, who live in town, enjoy baby-sitting Lynn and are supportive. The mother drinks socially and denies drug use or affective problems. She is in good health and states that *"I love Lynn. She's all I have, but sometimes I just lose my temper with her."*

Lynn is in kindergarten all day and attends a day care program after school until 6 P.M. Both mother and daughter come home tired. Shortly after arriving home, the mother usually begins issuing commands. The clinician asks the mother to recount an example of a communication problem with specifics about actual words that were used, the tone of voice, and the facial expression.

"Lynn, clean your room and when you finish, put your toys away, then wash your hands, and come help me in the kitchen, okay?" The mother's tone of voice and facial expression are stern, not friendly, and she expects Lynn to comply right away. When Lynn dawdles, the mother repeats the command in a louder voice and with a very stern look. Lynn's response is to yell back, so the mother threatens to spank her (which she never does) or to send her to her room (which she does do).

Table 10.2. Expressive and receptive language development

Age	Expressive Language	Receptive Language
18–24 months Tantrums begin	Knows 20–100 words; uses short sentences, two words ("Me cookie"), with two exchanges	Points to objects when pointed out; recognizes names of familiar people, objects, body parts; follows simple instructions
Age 2–3 years (greatest variation in this phase) Tantrums and mood swings common; is "selfish" and self-centered normally; little control over emotional and behavioral impulses; curious and active	Knows 200–300 words; uses three-word sentences ("Where is doggie?"); says name, age, gender; recognizes most common objects; begins to express affection	Follows two-sequence command; understands most simple sentences; understands concept of "two"; confuses reality and fantasy (may cause worry); beginning to understand "mine", "his or hers"
Age 3–4 years Views self as whole person: body, thoughts, feelings	Knows 300–1000 words; uses four-word sentences; begins to express thoughts and feelings; speaks clearly so that most is understood; begins to negotiate solutions to conflicts; "No" is a common word; responds to where, what, who	Can listen to and repeat grammatically correct sentences; listens to stories; recalls part of stories; follows three-step simple command
Age 4–5 years	Knows 1500 words, which will increase by another 1000 by age 6; uses five- to six-word sentences; tells longer stories; can act/sound bossy (often repeating commands he or she has heard); may use swear words (often repeating what he or she has heard)	Recalls much of a story; can distinguish fantasy from reality; follows a 3- to 4-step simple command

The clinician recognizes two problems: the mother's talking exceeds Lynn's language abilities, and her general demeanor is negative so it hinders effective communication. These communication problems contribute to the disturbance in their relationship. (See Chapter 8, "Three Models of Brief Family Interviews," ABC Interview, page 178.)

Working with the Family

The clinician asks Lynn, *"Do you want to say something?"* Lynn shakes her head. She gives her paper and crayons and asks her to draw a picture of "you and Mommy doing something." While Lynn draws, the clinician explains the issues. She knows Lynn well and feels that she has a normal level of language development (Table 10.2). The mother's commands are vague ("Clean up your room") and overly long (four sequences) and are delivered with a negative emotional intensity that discourages listening. Together, these factors overwhelm Lynn's abilities, so she responds in a negative emotional manner. The mother in turn responds emotionally, and soon they are both caught up in a problematic interactive pattern that often leaves them in tears.

The clinician asks the mother what she thinks she could do.

She replies, *"Talk in shorter sentences and sound friendly?"*

The clinician suggests that the mother make only two requests initially, using a maximum of six to ten words and maintaining a neutral facial expression, while sitting at Lynn's level and making eye contact. The clinician discourages yelling and threats. Goals for Lynn are to make eye contact, listen, and comply.

Then she asks the mother and Lynn to role play an interaction in the office.

When assigning a task or new behavior, the family should practice it in the office if feasible.

Lynn agrees, and the mother promises to give her a sticker.

Mother (using the suggestions): *Lynn, look at me. Let's pretend it's bedtime. I need you to do two things. I will ask you just once. Change into your pajamas; then bring me your storybook.*

Clinician (to mother): *Now tell her to repeat what you said.*

The mother does.

Lynn: *Put on my PJs and get my bedtime book.*

Mother: *That's close enough. I like the way you listened and answered.*

The mother gives Lynn the sticker.

Clinician: *Can you do this at home?*

The mother nods. The clinician tells her that, at times, she will make progress but will also have relapses.

Third Visit

At the follow-up visit 2 weeks later, the mother reports that she and Lynn have had about a 20% success rate, which she feels is a definite improvement. They have three more visits over the next

2 months. At the last visit, the mother reports a 50% improvement. She is satisfied and feels she does not need to return.

Together, the clinician and the mother had developed some of the following strategies:

1. The mother understood Lynn's language abilities.
2. The mother adjusted her instructions to fit Lynn's abilities.
3. The mother adopted a positive demeanor.
4. The mother asked Lynn to make eye contact when she is listening to the mother.
5. The mother rewarded Lynn.

Below is a list of specific problems and solutions that are often applicable to children who do not appear to listen:

A. **Parents' communications exceed the child's short attention span.**

1. *Problem:* A child's optimal attention span is about 3 to 4 minutes per year of life (up to about 20 minutes), which is shorter than most parents realize.
2. *Solution:* The clinician should explain normal attention spans to the parents (e.g., a 4-year-old child has an optimum attention span of 12 to 16 minutes in a calm and distraction-free environment and when engaged in a motivating task). But if the child is tired, anxious, or distracted, the attention span is greatly reduced. Therefore, the parent should reduce the time of sustained listening appropriately.

B. **Parents talk over children's heads.**

1. *Problems:*

- Sometimes parents deliver too much information or speak too rapidly, exceeding the child's memory and processing abilities (e.g., *"First, I want you to brush your teeth. Then lay out clothes for tomorrow and start your homework. Then finish your chores."*). The child may remember "finishing chores" but will remember nothing else.
- Parents use "big words" that children can't understand because they surpass the child's developmental–cognitive ability (e.g., use of "democracy" with a 5-year-old child).

2. *Solutions.* Parents can:

- Use smaller "chunks" of information (e.g., one, two, or three short sentences).
- Slow the rate down and speak slowly.
- Use simple, familiar words that children have in their vocabulary.

C. **Parents are not clear about what they want or expect from the child.**

1. *Problem:* Parents often issue commands that are too general and vague (e.g., "Be good," "Behave," "Do better," or "Stop misbehaving.").

2. *Solutions.* Parents can:

- State their expectations clearly (e.g., *"I want you to do your homework. That means you must finish the ten math problems on page 23."*).
- Pause and calmly ask the child if he or she understands what the parent expects (e.g., *"Do you understand?"*).
- Ask the child to repeat or paraphrase what the parent said (e.g., *"Would you repeat what I said?"*).
- Encourage the child to indicate if he or she needs clarification (e.g., *"Mommy, I don't understand."*).
- Use concrete, specific examples (e.g., *"Remember how you cleaned up your room yesterday? You picked up the clothes, put them in a drawer, and then made your bed."*).
- Demonstrate what is being asked of the child (e.g., *"Let me show you how to do it first."*)

D. **Parents expect children to respond quickly to a request, even if the child is involved in an activity.**

1. *Problems:*

- Parents do not give the child an advance warning that allows the child to finish one task and then prepare to listen to a request from the parent.
- Children often feel that parents don't appreciate their needs to pursue their own activities and that sometimes they are not ready to respond suddenly to a parent.

2. *Solutions.* Parents can:

- Let the child finish a task, such as playing a game or watching a TV show, before making the request.
- Give the child a signal or warning (e.g., *"In 3 minutes, we need to stop the game, and then we will speak."*).
- Adjust their schedule or priorities so that it fits better with that of the child's activities and interests (e.g., *"I can wait until after dinner to discuss this."*).
- Set a convenient, regular time to converse with the child.

E. **Parents' "emotional" message (e.g., anger, frustration) often interferes with the child's understanding or willingness to respond to the verbal message.**

1. *Problem:* Anger, frustration, and irritability are "heard" first by children, and the other message (directive, request, explanation) is "lost" in the emotional message.

2. *Solutions.* Parents can.

- Self-monitor their emotions, body language, facial expression, and tone of voice (e.g., *"I'm feeling pretty upset."*).
- Step back, take a deep breath, count to 20, or take a "time out" to calm down (e.g., *"I need 3 minutes for myself before we talk."*).
- Ask the spouse/partner (if available) to take over and/or to be primarily involved in a particular task

(e.g., directing the child to do homework or getting the child ready for bed).

- Acknowledge the child's emotions (e.g., *"I can tell that you are pretty upset about what I said."*).
- Avoid humiliating the child (e.g., *"Are you crying again?"*).
- Apologize (e.g., *"I'm sorry. I didn't mean to be so angry or hurt your feelings."*).
- Teach children how to apologize.

F. **Parents don't detect children's feelings or understand their thoughts and perspectives.**

1. *Problems:*

- Children feel that parents have forgotten what they (parents) were like when they were children.
- Children may be worried or sad; they often express these feelings through behaviors that parents criticize. Their underlying feelings go unrecognized.

2. *Solutions.* Parents should:

- First try to understand the underlying cause of children's behavior before reacting to the behavior.
- Remember and share a similar experience from when they were children.

G. **Parents' communication is often critical, judgmental, and hurtful.**

1. *Problem:* Children feel that parents don't notice what is right and that they focus only on what is wrong.
2. *Solutions.* Parents can:

- "Catch" their children doing something right. Recognize good behavior instead of just taking it for granted and ignoring it.
- Give a new accomplishment, a good effort, or any small positive change the recognition, praise, and reinforcement that it deserves.
- Record positive efforts and changes in a notebook and share them at a family meeting. (See Chapter 12, "Strategies to Enhance Family Functioning.")
- Appreciate children's differences and respect their right to be different.
- Ignore many inconsequential negative behaviors—often they will disappear.

H. **Parents' communication often is too task-oriented and too directive.**

1. *Problems:*

- Children are always being told what, when, and how to do something.
- The communication contains too little humor, affection, playing, or just being together with no specific agenda.

2. *Solutions.* Parents can:

- Provide unstructured time together. Just being together yields the possibility of enjoyable and unexpected things.
- Find time to express affection and approval to their children.

I. **Parents are often discussing their personal matters or problems.**

1. *Problem:* Children don't necessarily want to hear the details of their parents' personal problems. Children often become anxious or confused when they hear about adults' problems, especially when the children are treated as confidantes or are expected to provide support or advice. Children don't have the emotional or cognitive abilities to respond to their parents' needs.
2. *Solutions.* Parents can:

- Avoid exposing children to their personal problems in a way that makes them anxious.
- Seek help from friends, relatives, and professionals.
- Reassure children that they are seeking help for themselves.
- Nourish and support their children's developmental needs as children. Children should not be "adultified" or "parentified."

J. **Parents' communications are often repetitive and predictable.**

1. *Problem:* Children don't bother to listen. They "tune out" because they expect to be bored by their parents' communication. For example, a child might think *"It's the same old thing"* or *"Here comes lecture number 78"* when a certain subject comes up.
2. *Solutions.* Parents can:

- Monitor the content and repetition in their communication.
- Surprise their children by saying something outrageous, funny, and unpredictable.

V. **Threats, Commands, and Requests.** Parents issue commands and make requests of their children. Sometimes parents make a request when they should make a command and vice versa. Parents also resort to threats, which elicit fear or worry in children, especially when the parents carry them out; however, empty threats cease to be effective and frustrate the parents.

CASE 3: A TIRED MOTHER SLAPS HER SON IN THE OFFICE

The Visit for a Camp Physical

A mother brings her 9-year-old son Jeremy to the clinician for a summer camp physical examination. The clinician notices that the mother is not her usual energetic, talkative self and instead looks quiet and worn out. After the examination, the mother tells Jeremy that he has to do some errands with her. Jeremy protests, stating that he wants to go the mall. The mother explains several times that they have other things to do, but every time he asks her *"Why not?"* in a whiney voice. The mother clearly becomes exasperated, and when he yells *"You're just an old bag!"* she slaps him. Jeremy begins to cry, and then the mother cries.

The clinician sits down with them both. He acknowledges their feelings and asks what is going on. The mother states that she has never slapped Jeremy before but that he always *"argues and makes me explain myself over and over. It's gotten so bad that I just let him do whatever he wants most of the time. My husband tells me to be strict, but I can't; so things just get worse."*

The clinician tells the mother that he thinks a family meeting with her husband present would be very helpful and that he would like to schedule two meetings.

The Family Meeting

Engaging the Family

The clinician explains how the events of the past visit resulted in this meeting and that this family meeting is not just aimed at Jeremy. Its intention is to help all of them understand the problem and work together to resolve it.

The clinician asks the family members what they would like to achieve. The mother's goal is to have Jeremy do what she asks. The father says that she is "too weak." Jeremy pouts and refuses to answer. The clinician assures him that he is not being blamed and encourages him to speak up.

The clinician realizes that the mother's authority has been eroded because the father's criticism has undermined her parental power. Therefore, the mother–child hierarchy has been altered; and the father needs to support the mother.

Understanding the Family

Jeremy sits by his father and away from his mother. The clinician wonders if a father–son coalition exists and works against the mother to undermine her authority. The father feels his wife needs to be more "strict." When Jeremy hears this, he states, *"I can always get my way."* He is proud of his ability to "win arguments."

The clinician decides to use the ABC approach, so he asks the family to describe a specific problematic situation. (See Chapter 8, "Three Models of Brief Family Interviews," The ABC Interview, page 178.)

ANTECEDENT Getting Jeremy to do homework is predictably difficult. When he gets home from school, he speeds off to watch TV, which is a daily source of conflict.

BEHAVIOR As Jeremy continues to watch TV, the mother asks in a polite manner, *"Jeremy would you turn off the TV and start your homework? Okay?"*

CONSEQUENCE Jeremy, without taking his eyes from the TV, answers, *"No, not now. Later, I promise."* He also states a few reasons why he needs to relax and rest before doing his homework.

The mother returns to the kitchen, comes back in 20 minutes, and makes the same request. This time Jeremy usually answers that he doesn't need to do homework now because *"I can do it all in 20 minutes."* Again he gives his mother several reasons why he doesn't really need to do the homework now. The mother then requests that he show her his homework assignments. Again Jeremy explains that he will show it to her later. Then the mother asks Jeremy if he would like her help with his homework. When he refuses her offer, she loses her temper and tells him that she will have his father speak with him when he comes home. Lately however, she has *"given up because it's easier than arguing."*

The clinician realizes that the mother's repeated requests give Jeremy several options for getting his way: ignore, refuse, procrastinate, and argue. Eventually, he will wear his mother down. The boy needs a clear, firm command, not a polite request followed by much persuasion. Their communication pattern is not working for the mother and disrupts the mother–son relationship.

Working with the Family

The clinician asks the father what he means by "strict." The father explains that it means "giving orders when you have to." The clinician asks him to demonstrate. The father faces his son at eye level. He puts his face about 12 inches from his son, assumes a stern expression, and orders in a slow, deliberate manner, *"Jeremy, I want you to turn off the TV, go right to your room, and start your homework. Do it* ***now****."*

The mother asks Jeremy if that would make him obey her. With a somewhat startled expression on his face, he says that it would. The mother says that she could make such a command but that she needs the father's support, and she asks him to *"back me up, but don't criticize me."* He agrees to help out. With his support, she becomes more confident and uses commands, not requests with Jeremy. Jeremy responds positively.

Below are six examples of threats, commands, and requests.

A. **Interrupted commands.**

1. *Problem:* The parent continues talking beyond the initial command or makes irrelevant requests, which confuse, distract, and delay the child. For example, a mother might say, *"Please go and clean up your room and then do your math homework. Before you do that, help me put away these dishes. Remember the last time I asked you to clean your room? You really argued with me. I hope that doesn't happen again."*
2. *Solutions.* Parents can:

- Keep the message short and simple so that the focus is on the major request.
- Make a mental note to wait to introduce other topics until after the first task has been completed.

B. **"Let's" requests.**

1. *Problem:* The "let's" requests may imply a lack of parental authority or parent–child differentiation in situations when differentiation is appropriate (e.g., *"Let's go clean up your room."*).

2. *Solutions.* Parents can:

- Change the request to a command.
- Make the requests so that they are perceived by the child as a way to spend time with a parent and to gain the parent's approval. This then provides a chance for the parent and child to cooperate and to share. In this way, the parent is modeling good behavior. For example, the parent might say, *"Let's work in the garden together. I bet that you could really help me. We'll have lemonade after we finish."*
- Avoid making the requests and then either not joining in or leaving before the task is completed. Then the requests become a form of deceit or disappointment. If the parent has been doing this, then the parent should either stop using requests or should work with the child until either the task is done or they both agree to quit.

C. **Repeated commands.**

1. *Problem:* Excessive repetition allows the child to figure out the parent's maximum number of commands or "boiling point," at which time the parent "explodes." The child "tunes out" until just before that "boiling point" is reached. Then the child finally "listens" to the parent and complies.

2. *Solutions.* Parents can:

- Understand that the child has figured out the parent's limit is.
- Use the one-two-three rule. With the one-two-three rule, the parent explains to the child that he or she will only request or command three times in 15-second intervals and specifies the consequences for both obeying and disobeying. Then, the parent gives a command in an appropriate manner (calm, firm voice, eye contact, short command) and says, *"That's one."* The parent looks at the child, waits 15 seconds, and repeats the command with *"That's two."* He or she should wait another 15 seconds and repeat, if necessary, with *"That's three."* After another 15 seconds, the parent should act according to the consequences he or she laid out. If the child complies, a suitable positive reinforcement should follow; if the child doesn't comply, an appropriate negative consequence should be immediately applied (e.g., time out or a restriction of a favorite activity). Corporal punishment is discouraged.

D. **"Nattering."**

1. *Problem:* The parent repeats commands; the child ignores them; and ultimately, the parent gives in and does

the task himself or herself, muttering, *"It's easier to do it myself rather than to tell him to do it 6 times."*

2. *Solutions.* The parent can:

- Understand how his or her behavior maintains the problem.
- Prioritize tasks for the child (e.g., "Pick your battles.").
- Allow the child to experience the logical consequences of his or her actions (e.g., "If dirty clothes are not put in the hamper, soon you will have no clean clothes to wear."). See Chapter 12, "Strategies to Enhance Family Functioning," Natural and Logical Consequences, page 248, for more discussion.

E. **Requests and questions that imply equal power.**

1. *Problem:* The parent asks a question or makes a request in a way that implies equal power (e.g., "Wouldn't you like to go to bed now?"). This gives the child the opportunity to refuse, bargain, or manipulate.

2. *Solutions.* Parents can:

- Change their request to a command (e.g., "I want you to come over here *now*!") to convey a sense of proper parental authority.
- Combine two acceptable alternatives or choices. *"You have a choice to set the table or clear the table. Which one do you choose?"*
- Recognize and reinforce the behavior with a kiss, hug, or smile.

F. **Threats.** The use of threats often causes the family to focus more on the threats than on positive behaviors and problem solving. Threats cause resentment, anxiety, and sadness; and they put pressure on the parent to carry them out. Additionally, to remain effective, threats often have to increase in severity, creating a potentially dangerous environment for the child. Moreover, if threats are not carried out, they lose their coercive power. So, in the end, threats are not effective.

1. *Problems:* (Described here are several different types of threats.)

- The parent combines a threat and a command. These commands evoke confusion and tension and possibly even negative emotions or actions, such as anger, refusal, regression, hurt, fear, resentment, or guilt. *"I want you to finish your homework and be in bed by 9 o'clock. If you don't do it, I'm really going to spank you."*
- The parent may threaten to hurt himself or herself. (e.g., *"I'm going to go crazy!"* or *"If you don't do what I say, I'm going to kill myself."*)
- The threat made by the parent is disproportional for the misdeed (e.g., *"No TV fcr a month"*), or it can imply physical harm (e.g., *"I am going to whip you."*).

- The parent may threaten to abandon the child, saying something like *"I'm going to walk out this door and never come back."*
- The parent's threat may damage the child's sense of self-worth and ability to feel loved. The parent may say, *"Sometimes, I wonder why I had you,"* or *"I wonder why you turned out so bad."*

2. *Solutions.* Parents can:

- Understand that empty threats are ineffective and may instill fear and anxiety and that real threats to harm a child may lead parents to be overly punitive or violent.
- Learn never to threaten to hurt themselves because of the child's behavior.
- Learn never to threaten to abandon the child. To develop empathy in the parents, the clinician might ask the parents to pretend they are the child and to imagine how the child might feel.

VI. **Invalidation by other Family Members.** Invalidating communication patterns diminish one's sense of self-worth and discourage communication between family members. Six ways in which communication patterns invalidate a family member are described below.

A. **Generalizing statements.**

1. *Problems:*

- Generalizing statements imply that a child can never do any good. Examples include *"You're always disobeying me"* or *"You never take responsibility for anything."* If the parent has these attitudes, then the child will always feel like he or she is a disappointment to the parent and can never measure up. This engenders in the child a sense of shame and failure.
- Whenever something goes wrong, the child is always blamed. For example, if the child brings home a poor school grade, the parent assumes the child is at fault and blames him or her without first investigating. He or she may say to the child, *"There you go again—more lousy grades. What's wrong with you?"*

2. *Solutions.* Parents can:

- Stop using generalizing terms like "always" or "never" in a negative way.
- Seek to understand first before judging or assuming.
- Learn that comparisons between siblings may cause the child to feel that he or she does not measure up. Rather than to compare, parents should help each child develop his or her unique skills and interests. The child can't do this alone.

B. **Evading statements or actions.**

1. *Problems:*

- Parents find ways to evade a discussion or avoid a meeting/interaction with the child. The parent can pretend not to hear, respond with silence, or postpone the conversation. For example, a father might say, *"Ask your mother," "I know you want to talk about the baseball game, but I am too tired right now,"* or *"Wait till this weekend."* Eventually, the child begins to feel unwelcome and unimportant and stops approaching the parent.
- A parent can avoid a child by being unavailable either physically or emotionally, such as leaving home early, coming home late, retreating to the bedroom, sitting in front of the computer or television, or appearing harried and unapproachable.

2. *Solutions.* Parents can:

- Respond to the child's needs at the moment.
- Put off some of their activities until the child is busy with homework or in bed.
- Set aside "special time" on selected evenings for activities and conversations. (See Chapter 12, "Strategies to Enhance Family Functioning," for more discussion.)
- Call or e-mail the child on evenings when the parent(s) is out of town.

C. **Disqualifying statements.**

1. *Problem:* The parent praises the child in a qualified manner. *"Congratulations on the B you earned in math! I am proud of you. But if you'd only studied like I said to, you could have made an A."* The result of such qualification is that the child feels that he or she can't ever do enough to please the parent and that he or she is a loser, not a winner.

2. *Solutions.* Parents can:

- Encourage the child and help him or her make a renewed effort.
- Recognize and reward the effort and/or success; let the child savor it.
- Appreciate the developmental level of the child and set new, appropriate expectations and goals.
- Ask the child his or her own opinion of the grade.

D. **Closing a discussion prematurely by way of verbal and nonverbal messages.**

1. *Problems:*

- Verbal messages, such as, *"I have to go," "I don't have time to listen to this,"* and *"You make me so mad I'm leaving"* make the child feel unimportant and disrespected.

- Nonverbal messages, such as rolling the eyes in disbelief, averting them from the child's gaze, turning one's back on the child, standing up, glaring at the child, yawning with feigned boredom, walking away, looking at TV, or reading the paper, discourage communication.

2. *Solutions.* Parents can:

- Permit the child to conclude the conversation.
- Set another time to talk, if necessary.
- Ask questions and show interest.

E. **Unwanted advice.**

1. *Problem:* Parents often offer advice or suggestions when the child does not want it or is not ready for it. Examples include *"Let me tell you what you ought to do," "Listen to me,"* or *"When I was your age, I did. . . ."*

2. *Solutions.* Parents can:

- Hear the emotional message behind the verbal message.
- Determine if the child might only be seeking praise and support but not advice.
- Tell the child that the parent is always available if the child wants advice.

F. **Guilt trips.**

1. *Problem:* Guilt trips happen when one family member tries to get attention by inducing guilt, often by letting others know that he or she is in pain or by using sad facial expressions, sighs, and stories of past pain. The message, either verbal or nonverbal is, *"If you cared for me you would stay home"* or *"After all I do for you, you treat me like this."* Eventually, others tire of this behavior, become exasperated, and pull away.

2. *Solutions.* Parents and the family can discuss methods of helping the person using guilt trips so that they meet his or her needs in other ways. When parents use "guilt trips," children eventually become resentful and avoid the parent. If the clinician detects this in a family meeting, he or she should first speak to the parent privately and respectfully.

VI. **Ineffective Communication Patterns**

Ineffective communication problems involve all family members. Members are often unaware of these patterns and of their own contributions to them. Three types of ineffective communication patterns and solutions for remedying them include the following:

A. **Denial.**

1. *Problems:*

- Denial occurs when a family member does not want to recognize another's feelings or need to communicate. Examples of denial statements are *"I don't care," "No problem," "Whatever you say," "It doesn't matter,"* or *"You don't really feel that way."* Associated behaviors might be slouching, shrugging, withdrawing, speaking in a monotone voice, or avoiding eye contact.

- Stonewalling is a form of denial. Stonewallers are silent, unresponsive, and nonrevealing. They often withhold love and approval and don't readily expose their own thoughts and feelings. Stonewalling affects children deeply and causes pain, self-doubt, anxiety, and distrust. Stonewallers confuse children because they don't know what to expect from the stonewaller and they don't get needed feedback. A stonewaller doesn't allow children the chance to interact, so they don't feel loved.

2. *Solutions.* The clinician can:

- Help the family understand its behaviors and how it affects individual family members.
- Help the family members acknowledge the feelings of others in the family meeting.
- Take the parenting history.

B. **Indirect expression.**

1. *Problem:* Indirect expression means a veiled way of stating one's needs or desires. The speaker does not plainly express himself or herself, so the listener does not hear the real message. For example, a family member might say, *"It's been quiet around here"* instead of *"I am lonely and would like you here."* Or the child might say, *"Boy, this homework is hard"* instead of *"I need some help and encouragement."*

2. *Solution.* The clinician should help the family members express their needs with a direct statement that starts with "I." Members can become more perceptive, sensitive, and responsive to other's expressions of need.

C. **Substitutions.**

1. *Problem:* Substitutions allow an expression of feeling in a safe way or with a safer person. For example, a father who is angry with his wife instead may get angry with his son; or a parent who feels hurt or neglected when a teenager stays in her room all the time criticizes her friends or the quality of her school work instead of telling her. Another example is an older sister who can't express her secret happiness about her brother's success at school so she worries about his eating habits instead.

2. *Solutions.* The clinician can:

- Help the family express what they want and need in a clear, calm manner (e.g., *"I would like . . ."* or *"I am feeling . . ."*).
- Help the family listen to and acknowledge the feelings and thoughts of others (e.g., *"I hear what you're saying,"* or *"I sense you are feeling . . ."*).

VII. Summary

Communication problems are one of the major challenges for all families. They form the underlying factor in many relationship problems. Communication can be defined as listening, speaking, observing, making proper choices about when to speak and when to be silent, stating thoughts and feelings in a clear, nonthreatening manner, and demonstrating empathy. The clinician observes family communication in every patient encounter. The family meeting is a very effective way to help families resolve their communication problems. This chapter described a variety of communication problems and solutions. The solutions, which are clinician-directed, are aimed at parents and give them strategies for improving family communication, often entailing that parents change and model desirable communication.

ADDITIONAL READING

Allmond BW, Tanner JL. *The family is the patient.* Baltimore: Lippincott, Williams & Wilkins, 1999.

Brazelton TB. *Touchpoints: your child's emotional and behavioral development.* Reading, MA: Addison-Wesley, 1992.

Faber A, Maylish E. *How to talk so kids will listen and listen so kids will talk.* New York: Avon Books, 1980.

Gordon T. *Parent effectiveness training.* New York: Peter Wyden Publications, 1970.

Hendrix H, Hunt H. *Giving the love that heals: a guide for parents.* New York: Pocket Books/Simon and Schuster, 1997.

Kelly DP, Sally JI. Disorders of speech and language. In: Levine MD, Carey WB, Crocker AC, eds. *Developmental–behavioral pediatrics,* 3rd ed. Philadelphia: WB Saunders, 1999.

McKay M, Davis M, Fanning P. *How to communicate.* New York: MJF Books, 1983.

Phelan TW. *1-2-3 magic: effective discipline for children.* Glen Ellyn, IL: Child Management, Inc., 1996.

Satir V. *People making.* Palo Alto, CA: Science and Behavior Books, 1972.

Satir V. *The new people making.* Mountain View, CA: Science and Behavior Books, 1983.

Senn, MJE. The psychotherapeutic role of the pediatrician. *Pediatrics* 1948;2:147–152.

Severe S. *How to behave so your children will too.* Tempe, AZ: Greentree Publishing, 1997.

Tannen D. *You just don't understand.* New York: William Morrow, 1990.

11 Supporting Parents

I. **Purpose**

In many cases, the best way of helping children is by supporting their parents. Adapting to parenthood presents multiple changes, especially for first-time parents. This chapter describes how the clinician can help the parents adapt to parenthood from the time when they are expecting a new baby through the preschool-age years. This adaptation starts with the prenatal visit; monitors issues, like the loss of marital intimacy, sibling rivalry, and postpartum blues and depression in both the mother and father; and discusses balancing parenting responsibilities and enhancing the father's role.

II. **Adapting to Parenthood**

The birth of a child ushers in a variety of changes for which most new parents are unprepared. The clinician plays a vital role in promoting optimal parenting by helping both the father and the mother (or the single parent) adjust to new roles. For couples, their relationship changes from partners to parents. The prenatal visit and the first well-baby visits provide the clinician with an excellent opportunity to offer guidance to new parents and to monitor their well-being. See Chapter 7, "Assessing Family Functioning: Additional Methods," The Family Life Cycle, page 127, for more discussion.

A. **The prenatal visit.** In the prenatal visit, the clinician can employ the following seven tips to help the soon-to-be parent(s) adapt:

1. *Understand the family composition and function.*
2. *Assess the parent's or parents' comfort and readiness for the new baby.*
3. *Help the couple or single parent express thoughts, feelings, and expectations about becoming parents.* "How are you feeling about becoming a parent?" "What are your hopes, dreams, worries, and fears about being a parent?"
4. *For a married couple or partners, ask questions about the marriage/relationship to predict the relationship satisfaction after the baby is born.* Examples of questions include "How would you describe your marital relationship?" "What activities do you enjoy together?" "How do you resolve your differences?" and "Have you ever had couples counseling or thought you might benefit from it?"
5. *Emphasize the importance of support systems and of respite for helping the couple adjust to parenthood* (e.g., the extended family and friends). The clinician should ask:

- "Who do you count on for support?"
- "Can you count on your family for support?"
- "What is your relationship with your parents and relatives, including in-laws?"
- "Do you have friends with young children?"
- "Are you members of a religious institution or other social groups?"

6. *Explore the preparation for baby and child-care issues.* Examples of questions for assessing this include "Do you

have all the things the baby will need (clothes, diapers, toys, crib, blanket)?" "Do you have a car seat, smoke alarms, and phone numbers of doctors and hospitals?" "Do you have (paid) maternity/paternity leave?" and "What are your child-care arrangements for after you return to work?"

7. *Inquire about the parents' family history, including medical and mental health and substance abuse. (Use another visit, if necessary.)* See Chapter 7, "Assessing Family Functioning: Additional Methods," for further discussion.

B. **The first well-baby visits.**

If the clinician did not have the opportunity for a prenatal visit, the above questions can be asked in the first well-baby visits. Now that the baby is born and has been brought home, the clinician should also address other important topics that affect the parents' relationship and the care of the child.

1. *Loss of marital/relationship privacy, time, and intimacy.*

The presence of a baby deprives the parents of privacy, even in their own bedroom. Parents usually have little time or energy for dialogue, sex, and intimacy. The new mother may feel that sex is a minimal duty, and the father may feel rebuffed or unappreciated. Both parents may feel that they are taken for granted and unappreciated by the other. The parents, especially the mother, are exhausted; in general, the marriage/relationship feels less fulfilling. The clinician can:

a. ***Ask questions, such as "How is the baby affecting your marriage/relationship?" "What is better?" "What is more difficult?" and "What would help?"***

b. ***Assure the new parents that these feelings are normal and temporary.***

c. ***Direct and encourage the new parents to find at least 5 minutes a day to sit and be with each other; encourage them, after a few months, to find a babysitter and to go out on a regular basis.***

d. ***Encourage the new parents to compliment and show appreciation for each other several times a day.*** The compliments can be just a few words, a thank you, a smile, a kiss, a hug, or any special way that conveys their commitment to and love for one another.

e. ***Explore the support systems and/or the parents' openness to a referral for counseling if they are stressed and before emotions get too intense and positions are too entrenched.***

f. ***Offer reassuring words and compliments.*** A clinician might say, *"You are loving and devoted parents. You have a wonderful child. This is a very challenging, yet fulfilling time for you. It's hard to do it all—parenting, maintaining your relationship, having jobs, and finding time for yourselves."*

2. *Impact of the baby on older children.* Parents worry about the impact of a new baby on older children. Four tips the clinician may suggest to these parents include:

   a. ***Parents should reassure the child/children of their continuing love*** (e.g., demonstrate it with hugs, kisses, smiles, words, and special time). (See Chapter 12, "Strategies to Enhance Family Functioning," for more discussion.)

   b. ***They should maintain routines and provide continuity*** (e.g., bedtime rituals). If changes need to be made, they should be explained to the child and should be made gradually and as early as possible.

   c. ***They should answer children's questions honestly and in a developmentally appropriate way so that their underlying concerns are addressed*** (e.g., the fear of loss of a parent's love and attention, the need to share toys).

   d. ***They should read books to older children that address their concerns about the birth of a sibling.***

3. *The single parent.* Single parents may need more attention and support from the clinician during the well-baby visits (e.g., more frequent visits, referrals to social service agencies, and aid in getting access to medical and mental health care). Single parents often look to the clinician, who is sometimes perceived as a coparent, for guidance and advice. The clinician's role is to help the parent connect with the family and community supports and to serve as a child/parent advocate. Single parents, especially young ones who may have to drop out of high school to raise their child, are at risk for poverty and related psychosocial stresses. They and their children need careful, long-term follow-up.

4. *Postpartum blues and depression.* No one is better positioned than the clinician is to detect postpartum blues and depression. This phenomenon, which can occur in both mothers and fathers, can be heightened by sleep deprivation and fatigue. Clinicians should be on the alert for any signs of postpartum blues and depression and should respond to them immediately. The clinician should arrange a meeting to understand the family context better, to attend to any issues, and to suggest a referral for the parent(s) if necessary. See Chapter 14, "Making a Mental Health Referral," for more discussion.

   a. ***The mother.*** Postpartum blues occur in approximately 50% of new mothers. Symptoms include tearfulness, irritability, and insomnia. Postpartum blues appear 3 to 7 days after delivery and may last several weeks. Postpartum depression, which is more severe, occurs in 5% to 25% of first- time mothers (Ohls & Osborn, 1988). Many women with this condition have a history of mood disorders and will experience problems well beyond the normal course of postpartum depression. The risk of recurrence in later pregnancies is high. Etiologic factors are a positive family history for mood disorders, domestic violence, hormonal changes, a difficult delivery, stressful life events, marital discord, and low maternal self-esteem. The symptoms are depressed mood, guilt, feelings of worthlessness, inability to enjoy things, lack of energy, anxiety, mood swings, and even suicidal ideation. Crying, irritability, and insomnia are more severe than in postpartum blues. For example, if a clinician sees a mother who cannot sleep even when the baby is asleep, he or she must realize that this mother may be experiencing depression. Depression tends to have a later onset than postpartum blues—about 4 to 6 weeks postpartum—and can last for 6 to 9 months. Postpartum blues and depression adversely affect the mother–baby bonding; the maternal responsiveness, which is key to a child's development of cognition, language, confidence, and social skills, is also threatened. For these reasons, the clinician should respond promptly to each situation. Table 11.1 lists seven suggestions for the clinician.

b. ***Screening for postpartum depression.*** The Edinburgh Postnatal Depression Scale (EPDS) is designed to help the clinician identify postpartum depression 4 to 8 weeks after birth (Cox et al., 1987). The mother is instructed to underline the response which best describes how she has felt in the past 7 days and to complete the scale herself. If the mother has difficulty reading the form or does not read/speak English, the items should

Table 11.1. Maternal postpartum blues and depression[a]

The clinician can:

1. Explain to all new mothers that postpartum blues and depression are common; describe the symptoms.
2. Encourage the mother (husband/partner/relative) to call the clinician or to schedule a visit within a few days if she is experiencing these symptoms.
3. Inquire about the symptoms at the well-baby visits.
4. Take a family history, and inquire about prior births and depression.
5. Show special sensitivity to mothers who are more likely to experience depression, (e.g., single mothers, mothers living in poverty, mothers with several young children, victims of domestic violence, and mothers with a past history of depression).
6. For postpartum blues, offer an explanation of the disorder and reassurance. The clinician should monitor the mother's mental health until the blues subside.
7. For postpartum depression, refer the mother to a mental health professional as soon as possible.

[a] Fathers are also subject to postpartum blues and depression. These suggestions are for both mothers and fathers. See the section "Postpartum blues and depression, The father" in this chapter.

be read to her or interpreted accordingly. Responses are scored 0, 1, 2, and 3 according to increased severity. Items marked with an asterisk (*) are reverse scored (i.e., 3, 2, 1, and 0). All ten items on the list must be completed for accurate results. The final score is the sum of the ten scores. A score greater than 13 suggests postpartum depression. In doubtful cases, the clinician can either interview the mother and/or can repeat the screening after 2 weeks have passed.

Screening should never substitute for clinical judgment. A positive screen should always be followed by further clinical assessment (see Chapter 7, "Assessing Family Functioning: Additional Methods"). The clinician may also refer the mother for further clinical assessment (Fig. 11.1) (see Chapter 14, "Making a Mental Health Referral").

c. ***The father.*** Men are also subject to postpartum blues and depression, which, like maternal depression, can affect the marriage and the child (Yogman & Kindlon). Paternal depression is especially evident in the first 6 to 8 weeks, but it may last for months. At the birth of a child, fathers initially experience "paternal engrossment" (elation at holding the newborn baby), which is followed by an emotional letdown. They experience a sense of estrangement and distance, which might increase if the mother is nursing and therefore is especially involved with the baby. Fathers typically have decreased involvement with the child; those suffering from postpartum blues or depression might become more involved in their career and job roles, which further increases marital estrangement and distress. Other symptoms of depression or the blues include more silence and less conversation at home, increased alcohol consumption, staying away from home (putting in longer hours at work, spending time with friends or in a bar), and more solitary activity like watching TV. The clinician should inquire about paternal depression and the family history and follow the same guidelines given above for maternal postpartum blues and depression.

5. *Balancing both parents' responsibilities.* Gender-based, traditional parental roles are still the norm in most American families. Despite the fact that most mothers have jobs and careers, women still are usually in charge of the in-home activities: cooking, shopping, cleaning, paying the bills, coordinating the family's social life, and most of the child care. Fathers are usually in charge of the outside-home activities: yard work, home repair, car repair, and some of the child care. Family relationships are often adversely affected when the mother feels that the father never/seldom helps out and/or when the father feels uninvolved or excluded from the child's upbringing. When the clinician detects tensions between the parents, he or she should inquire about their respective responsibilities and

Name: ______________________ Address: ______________________

Your Date of Birth: ______________________ ______________________

Baby's age: ______________________ Phone: ______________________

As you have recently had a baby, we would like to know how you are feeling. Please **underline** the answer that comes closest to how you felt in the past 7 days, not just how you feel today.

Here is a completed example:

I have felt happy:

Yes, all the time.
Yes, most of the time.
No, not very often.
No, not at all.

This would mean: "I have felt happy most of the time" during the past week. Please complete the other questions in the same way.

In the past 7 days:

1. I have been able to laugh and see the funny side of things

   As much as I always could.
   Not quite so much now.
   Definitely not so much now.
   Not at all.

2. I have looked forward with enjoyment to things

   As much as I ever did.
   Rather less than I used to.
   Definitely less than I used to.
   Hardly at all.

3. *I have blamed myself unnecessarily when things went wrong

   Yes, most of the time.
   Yes, some of the time.
   Not very often.
   No, never.

4. I have been anxious or worried for no good reason

   No, not at all.
   Hardly ever.
   Yes, sometimes.
   Yes, very often.

5. *I have felt scared or panicky for no very good reason

   Yes, quite a lot.
   Yes, sometimes.
   No, not much.
   No, not at all.

6. *Things have been getting on top of me

   Yes, most of the time I haven't been able to cope at all.
   Yes, sometimes I haven't been coping as well as usual.
   No, most of the time I have coped quite well.
   No, I have been coping as well as ever.

7. *I have been so unhappy that I have had difficulty sleeping

   Yes, most of the time.
   Yes, sometimes.
   Not very often.
   No, not at all.

8. *I have felt sad or miserable

   Yes, most of the time.
   Yes, quite often.
   Not very often.
   No, not at all.

9. *I have been so unhappy that I have been crying

   Yes, most of the time.
   Yes, quite often.
   Only occasionally.
   No, never.

10. *The thought of harming myself has occured to me.

   Yes, quite often.
   Sometimes.
   Hardly ever.
   Never.

Figure 11.1. Edinburgh Postnatal Depression Scale (EPDS).

then explain the benefits of balancing the mother's and the father's responsibilities and should specifically focus on enhancing the father's role in parenting and on redistributing the child-care responsibilities. These are clinician-directed interventions, and the clinician should help the parents make these changes if they ask for advice or if they seem open to intervention.

6. *Enhancing the father's role and the benefits to the child.* The involvement of fathers with their children improves family relationships by balancing the child-care responsibilities and by developing the fathers' empathy for mothers (getting fathers involved in child-care is a strong predictor of empathy for mothers). Furthermore, fathers have a significant influence on their children's development, as is seen below.

Infants who have a great deal of contact with their fathers are usually more comfortable with strangers, and they also vocalize more. Cognitive development of premature infants is enhanced by positive father parenting (Yogman et al., 1995). Fathers who are physically present, emotionally available, validating, supportive, and comforting in times of distress exert a positive and unique influence on their children's development, especially in the areas of peer relationships and academic achievement.

Conversely, children with fathers who criticize, humiliate, and don't validate feelings are often more aggressive toward their peers, perform poorly in school, and exhibit delinquent and violent behavior (Harris, 1998).

Table 11.2 lists ways that the clinician can help fathers enhance their role in parenting. The clinician must decide whether to state these as directives or as suggestions based on whichever appears to be most acceptable to the parents.

7. *Redistributing the child-care responsibilities.* Five common problems and their solutions are covered in this section.

a. ***Problem.*** Mothers do the majority of all the family-related chores. They have an "endless list" of tasks and often complain of feeling overwhelmed, exhausted, and unappreciated. Women may hesitate to share child-care responsibilities for several reasons:

- *Efficiency:* "It's faster and easier for me to do it."
- *Quality:* "I can do it better anyway. It's better if I do it myself."
- *Sympathy:* "He's had a long day. I don't want to stress him."
- *Admiration:* "He's a good dad. He does a lot. That's enough."
- *Cultural:* Women are raised to believe that they are the natural and best caretakers of children. As a result, many are unwilling to give up control of child-care responsibilities.

Men may also resist changes in role expectations.

Table 11.2. Enhancing the father's role in parenting

The clinician can help the father to:

Realize how important his interactions with his child are for the child's development. This improves his self-esteem and overcomes his fear of boredom and sense of inadequacy.

Request paternity leave and/or take vacation time for the first few weeks of the baby's life.

Get involved early in the baby's care (e.g., feeding, changing, bathing, and putting to sleep). Caregiving skills are mostly learned behaviors. Parenting is a hands-on, trial and error learning experience. With more confidence, the father becomes more involved.

Participate in structured situations with specific roles (e.g., rocking the baby after feeding). This makes the father feel invested and competent.

Accompany the mother on visits to the clinician and have the clinician involve him in the visit (e.g., talking to him, getting him to answer questions, encouraging him to hold and play with his child).

Bring his child in alone for a well-child or acute illness visit, and schedule appointments at a time that suits the father's schedule.

Use quiet play to allow the child to talk about feelings or to ask questions.

Rearrange his schedule and set new priorities in order to be alone with his child, especially when the child is older and more involved with outside activities and peers. A car ride to an after school activity, doing chores together, and sharing an activity or hobby are such opportunities.

Learn about his child's activities, interests, the names of his child's friends, and developmental changes. Conversation comes easier when fathers are informed.

Attend Parent Teacher Association (PTA) meetings, teacher–parent conferences, and extracurricular activities.

Volunteer to be a coach or helper on his child's team or after school activities.

Call or e-mail the child from business trips or work, especially if he is going to be late for dinner or a promised activity.

b. ***Solutions.*** The clinician can offer suggestions to the parents so that both feel they are equally involved in parenting. One way he or she can accomplish this is to suggest that each parent make a list of tasks that he or she does that are related to child-care responsibilities.

- The list should cover a specific period of time (e.g., from after school to the parents' bedtime hour) or a certain activity (e.g., getting ready for school or going to bed).
- The list should include tasks that might be overlooked, like returning videos, making phone calls to

arrange for a social or sports activity, or helping with homework.

- Neither parent should share this list with the other while they are making them. The lists should not be shared until the family meeting with the clinician. When they do share their lists, parents may feel anger, guilt, empathy, and admiration. The father may be surprised by the mother's "endless list," or he may gain an appreciation for all that she does and may develop empathy for her, a critical factor for improving their relationship. This approach is not automatic or guaranteed, but it is worth trying.

The "endless list" discussion provides a starting point for renegotiating responsibilities. In addition to the "endless list" tasks, the clinician can suggest ways that the mother and father can negotiate tasks so that the child-care responsibilities are redistributed.

Table 11.3 lists five tips for the clinician on ways to help the parents with their redistribution of child-care responsibility.

III. Summary

In many instances, the clinician is the only professional who sees an entire family during the first few years of a child's life. Clinicians can use this special position and role to help children by helping their parents. Adapting to parenthood is a joyful, yet challenging and stressful time for parents. During the first several months following the birth of a baby, parents have to contend with the loss of marital intimacy, sibling rivalry, the possible onset of

Table 11.3. Redistributing the child-care responsibilities[a]

The clinician can:

1. Ask if the father might encourage his wife to take some time off for herself (lunch or dinner with friends, exercise, business trip). This also allows the father and child to have time alone.
2. Ask the parents if there are some tasks or activities they might eliminate or that could be done less frequently in order to reduce the work (e.g., yard work, laundry, grocery shopping, cleaning the house, and volunteer activities).
3. Promote a problem-solving discussion during the visit and offer him support. The clinician could say, *"Let's take a few minutes to let you discuss a situation and a few possible solutions that you can work on."*
4. Suggest the mother ask for help (e.g., ask the father to do some of the errands that she usually does or help with the children at home).
5. Help the mother encourage the father's involvement without criticizing his abilities.

[a] Whenever the clinician offers advice to one parent or the other, he or she must be careful not to appear to be taking sides with that parent.

postpartum blues and depression in both the mother and father, and attempts to balance the parenting responsibilities. The clinician has many opportunities to help new parents address these issues during the prenatal visit and the first well-baby visits. This chapter gives a variety of ways for clinicians to help parents deal with these issues from the prenatal and well-baby visits and all the way through childhood.

REFERENCES

Cox JL, Holden JM, Sagovsky R. Detection of postnatal depression: development of the 10-item Edinburgh Depression Scale. *Br J Psychiatry* 1987;150:782–786.

Harris KM, Furstenberg FF, Marmer JK. Paternal involvement with adolescents in intact families: the influence of fathers over the life course. *Demography* 1998;35(2):201–216.

Ohls R, Osborn LM. Maternal depression: the pediatrician's role. *Contemp Pediatr* 1988;5(5):103–114.

Yogman MW, Kindlon D. Pediatric opportunities with fathers and children. *Pediatr Ann* 1998;27(1):16–22.

Yogman MW, Kindlon D, Earls F. Father involvement and cognitive/behavioral outcomes of preterm infants. *J Am Acad Child Adolesc Psychiatry* 1995;34(1):58–56.

ADDITIONAL READING

Arnstein H. *Billy and our new baby*. New York: Human Services Press, 1973.

Brazelton TB. *On becoming a family*. New York: Delacorte Press, 1981.

Cowan CP, Cowan PA. *When partners become parents: the big life change for couples.* New York: Basic Books, 1992.

Dixon SD. The prenatal visit: making an alliance with a family. In: Dixon SD, Stein MT, eds. *Encounters with children*, 3rd ed. St Louis: Mosby, 1999.

Doherty WJ. *The intentional family: simple rituals to strengthen family ties.* New York: Avon Books, 1997.

Forgatch MS, DeGarmo DS. Parenting through change: an effective prevention program for single mothers. *Journal of Consulting and Clinical Psychology* 1999;67:711–724.

Green M. Promoting parental "presence." *Contemp Pediatr* 1999; 16(2):118–138.

Kahn RS, Wise PH, Finkelstein JA, et al The scope of unmet maternal health needs in pediatric settings. *Pediatrics* 1999;103(3): 576–581.

Parke RD. *Fatherhood.* Cambridge MA: Harvard University Press, 1996.

Sachs B. *Things just haven't been the same*. New York: William Morrow, 1992.

Taffel R. *Why parents disagree*. New York: William Morrow, 1994.

Wallerstein JS, Blakeslee S. *The good marriage: how and why love lasts*. New York: Houghton Mifflin, 1995.

Walsh F. *Strengthening family resilience.* New York: Guildford Press, 1998.

Werner E, Smith R. *Overcoming the odds*. Ithica, NY: Cornell University Press, 1992.

12 Strategies to Enhance Family Functioning

I. **Purpose**

Families often come to the clinician for reassurance and guidance. As a family counselor, the clinician can facilitate the family's own efforts to change its behavior. The directive clinician can suggest specific strategies. The family can then modify the clinician's suggested strategy to fit its needs and coping abilities. This chapter describes six strategies for enhancing family functioning.

II. **Six Strategies**

Suggested strategies (e.g., advice, medication, other interventions) can help if they fit the problem and if the family accepts them. The family can modify a suggested intervention to fit its own style and level of functioning. The six strategies are given below:

- Feedback: helping parents and children give and receive it.
- Home family meetings.
- Special time.
- Resolving parental disagreements: natural and logical consequences.
- Family rituals and traditions.
- Writing assignments and the compliment box (Table 12.1).

A. **Feedback: helping parents and children both give and receive it.**

1. *Feedback makes parents more effective.* Feedback tells family members how they are doing in the eyes of another. In a behavioral context, it is a way of helping a member understand the impact of his or her behavior on others. Feedback reveals a parent's "perception" of a child ("What I hear . . ." or "I'm seeing . . ."). Children are more likely to accept feedback (and to respond appropriately) if parents voice it as their perception. Parents often act on their perceptions of a child's behavior, so feedback is important because it gives the child information on how he or she is perceived. Feedback also reveals a parent's perception of himself or herself.
2. *Feedback creates dialogue by allowing/encouraging a family member to respond to the feedback.* It gives an individual a chance to explain a behavior, to correct a wrong perception, to appreciate another's feelings, and finally to change his or her behavior if needed or desired.
3. *Feedback is the final step in the teaching and learning loop.* Feedback gives the "learner" information on how well he or she has learned, performed, or behaved. It also enlightens the "teacher" as to how effective he or she is as a teacher, parent, or clinician. Thus, the "teacher" and the "learner" both need feedback. In the family meeting, feedback is considered essential; everyone benefits from giving it, receiving it, and responding to it.

Table 12.1. Six strategies to enhance family functioning

1. Feedback: giving and receiving it
2. Home family meetings
3. Special time
4. Resolving parental disagreements: natural and logical consequences
5. Family rituals and traditions
6. Writing assignments and the compliment box

CASE 1: A TEENAGE SON NEEDS FEEDBACK FROM HIS PARENTS

The Visit for a Sports Physical

Allen, a 16-year-old adolescent, comes in with his mother for a sports physical examination. The clinician has known Allen for several years, sees him only for occasional school and sports physicals, and knows that he is a good athlete. While examining the boy alone, the clinician inquires about the sports he plays and about his athletic abilities and successes. Allen tells him about his success in baseball. The clinician replies that Allen's parents must be very proud too. Allen's expression and tone of voice suddenly sadden as he states, *"My parents never say anything. They don't come to my games. I wish I knew if they were proud of me."* The clinician asks Allen if he has ever asked his parents to go to the games or has let them know how he feels. Allen replies that he does not ask. The clinician is so impressed by Allen's sadness that he asks if he can share their conversation with Allen's mother. Allen agrees.

Clinician: *I was just talking with Allen. I asked him if I could share our conversation, and he agreed. He wishes you and his father went to his games and feels that he doesn't get recognition or feedback from you and his father about his sports. He wants to know if you're proud of him. He seems pretty sad about this.*

The clinician pauses and remains silent.

Mother: *We are so busy with work. We just started our own business. He knows we're proud. We just don't make a big deal about it.*

Clinician (gently challenging): *How does he know you're proud?*

Mother: *He just does. Besides feedback is for little kids when they need lots of help. Allen's a young man. He doesn't need it.*

Allen: *How do you know?*

Mother: *Maybe I don't know.*

Clinician (searching for other sources of feedback): *Do you let Allen know how you feel about other things?*

Mother: *If he messes up, he hears about it.*

Clinician (realizing he wasn't making progress with this line of talk, explores instead the family's perception of his sadness): *Allen seems pretty concerned.*

Mother: *You should talk with his dad.*

Clinician (using this comment to suggest a family meeting): *That's a good idea. It would be helpful for all of us to talk. Could you ask your husband?*

The First Family Meeting

Engaging the Family

Clinician (explaining the purpose of the meeting): *Thank you for coming in. I know you're busy. I'd like to explain that we're not here to talk about Allen's sadness although that is what prompted the meeting. Instead I'd like to have a few family talks to help us understand the big picture, which is the apparent reason for his sadness. Your views as parents are invaluable, and together we can find some ways to make things better. How does this sound?*

The family members nod their approval.

Understanding the Family

Mother: *I've been thinking about our last visit. I'd like to see us all tell each other how we are doing but in a way that is helpful and doesn't cause blowups.*

Father: *People need to know when they're screwing up.*

Clinician (bringing the focus back to Allen and what he's doing right): *How about when they're doing well?*

Father: *I can't be running around checking every little thing. Take pride in a job well done.*

Clinician: *Allen, would you like to say something?*

Allen: *Nope. Not now.*

Mother: *There's too much anger.*

Father: *That's right. Some things that Allen does just drive me nuts.*

The clinician looks at Allen, hoping he will engage in a dialogue with his father.

Allen: *Like what?*

Father: *Like not using my tools correctly.*

Allen: *But Dad, you never tell me what I'm doing right or doing wrong. You just blow up.*

The father sits silently.

Mother: *That is what happens. And I do it, too. We all do. We forget to tell Allen what he's doing right . . . like his sports.*

Allen: *What about the tools, Dad?*

Father: *Are you interested?*

Allen: *Sure I am.*

Father: *I always thought you just didn't care about the tools.*

This is a "breakthrough" family interaction in the meeting. The father and son are talking to one another calmly, and they realize they have a common interest. Helping them communicate about the tools could lead to more interactions and understanding that eventually might help resolve the problem that brought them here. At this point, the clinician has decided that the father is the family leader.

Working with the Family

Clinician (keeping the dialogue alive and encouraging the family to develop its own solution): *How could you two get this tool thing going?*

The father starts to address the clinician who asks him to talk to Allen.

Clinician: *Could you look at Allen and talk to him?*

Father (to Allen): *Maybe I could explain how to use the tools, then watch you use them, and let you know how you're doing.*

Allen: *You won't get mad with me?*

Father: *Not if you do okay.*

There is a silence. The clinician waits about 15 seconds and then speaks.

Clinician: *How would Allen know he's doing okay?*

Father: *I'd tell him.*

The father appears uncomfortable and unwilling to discuss Allen's feelings. The clinician does not want to alienate the father, so he asks an open-ended question to see if they would follow through with this interaction.

Clinician: *Are you going to try this during the next week?*

Father (indicating he is not totally sold on this): *It sounds good, but I'm not sure. We'll see how it goes.*

The meeting is ending, and the clinician wants to "model" giving feedback in the form of compliments.

Clinician: *Before you go, I'd like to tell you all that I thought this was a good first meeting. It's just the beginning, but the way you all got right down to business was very impressive.*

Father: *It's no big deal.*

Mother: *See you next week.*

The Second Family Meeting

The family reports that Allen and his father have worked together one time and that it went "okay."

Clinician (asking them to amplify this success): *Tell me what was okay.*

The father showed Allen how to use the table saw, and he did "pretty well."

Clinician: *Did you tell him?*

Father: *Yeah. He's pretty coordinated.*

Clinician (unable to resist using father's comment as a link to the presenting problem): *After all, he is a good athlete.*

Mother: *I came out and watched them work. It was the first time we had been together enjoyably for some time.*

Clinician (acknowledging another positive interaction): *That must have been pleasant.*

Allen: *When I was cleaning up, we talked about sports.*

Clinician (encouraging more conversation): *What did you talk about?*

Allen: *The Red Sox and my game next week.*

Clinician: *How did that feel?*

Both Allen and his father shrug their shoulders as if to say "okay." The clinician senses that apparently no more can be said about this subject. The rest of the meeting is devoted to discussing a project that Allen and his father will do together.

The Third Family Meeting

The family reports that the next session with the tools went well also. The mother joined father and son; after Allen and his father finished the tool project, Allen and his mother talked about sports. The mother declares that she is going to see Allen's next game, but the father expresses no interest. When the clinician asks if the father is letting Allen know how he is doing with the tools, the father says that he isn't telling him but that he feels that Allen is gaining skills by watching and trying.

Father (looking at the clinician): *I don't need feedback on how I am as a dad, and he doesn't need it as a young man.*

The clinician has no response. He determines that, for now, maybe it is enough for this family that they are doing an activity together.

The Fourth Family Meeting

At the next visit, the family reports that the tool project has become a regular family event. The mother and Allen have continued their sports talks after the tool project. Each parent has developed an activity, and thus, a new relationship with Allen: the father with the tool project and the mother talking about sports and attending Allen's games. The father, however, is not going to give any more feedback. The family decides that four visits are enough. The clinician asks them for feedback about the effectiveness of the visits. Allen and his mother feel that the meetings have been worthwhile and thank the clinician. The father noncommittally offers a brief "thanks." About a month later, the clinician received a newspaper clipping about Allen and his team. The father had mailed it.

The clinician can help parents and children share feedback with each other.

Feedback is more effective under the following conditions:

1. *It is specific rather than general.* To tell a child she is "too talkative" is not as effective as saying, *"When we were discussing the birthday party plans, you talked so much I gave up. I felt I couldn't get a word in."*
2. *It is descriptive rather than judgmental.* Describing one's own feeling or reaction to another's behavior allows the other person to choose whether to accept it or not and makes a positive response more likely. Sharing one's perception reduces the likelihood of the recipient either responding defensively or ignoring the feedback. Examples of descriptive feedback include, *"I feel happy when I see you sharing with your brother,"* or *"I feel angry when I have to repeat myself over and over about doing homework."*

3. *It offers the receiver an alternative or assistance with altering the behavior.* For instance, a parent could say, *"I feel very worried when I see you staying up so late. I am concerned that the lack of sleep makes you feel grumpy. I'd like to discuss how we can help you get to bed earlier."*

4. *It takes into account the needs of both the receiver and the giver.* A mother demonstrates this when she says to her son, *"I'd like to talk about getting ready for school. When we argue, you are late for school, I am late for work, and we both feel pretty upset. I'd like to help both of us get out of the house on time."*

5. *It is directed toward behavior that the receiver can affect or control.* A child's frustration increases when he or she is reminded of shortcomings over which he or she has little or no influence. Therefore, a parent might speak to her child in the following way, *"I'd like to help you get along better with your brother. I realize that when you two play sports, he usually wins, and you get upset. I suggest you play board games with him instead of sports all the time. You're good at them, and the two of you could have fun."*

6. *It is given at the earliest opportunity after the specified behavior.* Brief, immediate feedback is more effective than delayed, detailed feedback. When a child completes a chore, the parent should acknowledge the accomplishment right away with a positive statement, such as *"Thank you for cleaning your room. I really appreciate it."* Later at dinner or at a family meeting, the parent can give more specific feedback as follows: *"When you cleaned up your room, I was really proud of you. I only asked you once, and you picked up your clothes, put away your toys, and put your books in your pack. That was really great."*

7. *The giver considers the receiver's readiness to hear it and accept it.* Feedback should not be given when the giver or receiver is angry. If a child and parent argue about a chore that has not been done, the focus becomes their feelings (or the consequence/punishment) and not the behavior. The parent should wait until the child is more likely to accept the feedback, until the parent is calmer, or until another family member can offer support.

8. *It is more effective when support is available.* Feedback often entails giving support. If a child has very poor study habits, he or she usually is disorganized, which often results in losing papers and missing deadlines. The mother can give the child feedback and tell him or her what needs to be done. However, without her support (e.g., buying an organizer notebook, restricting TV, and showing the child how to manage time effectively) the child is unable to respond to her feedback even though he or she is willing. In this case, the mother might delay feedback until she is able to provide the support.

B. **Home family meetings.** The home family meeting is a method of promoting family communication, family and individual tasks, and cooperative behaviors. In the home family meeting every member is encouraged to share his or her thoughts and feelings and to take a legitimate part in family decision making as determined by the parents. The meeting also allows the family to practice or to repeat at home the behaviors, the cooperation, and the communication of thoughts and feelings that it has already demonstrated in the family meeting in the office or clinic.

When the clinician suggests that the family have a home family meeting, he or she needs to explain the purposes.

1. *Purposes of a home family meeting.*

a. ***To develop cooperative leadership, which gives every member a role—however limited—in family decision making.*** Families need a leader and a hierarchy with the parents at the top. Even though the parents have control, children still need and want to have some say in the decision-making processes. Family conflicts result when the children don't have appropriate input or when they feel they aren't "heard" or appreciated. However, the children must realize that they are not in control. If they are in control, the family hierarchy is seriously unbalanced, and conflicts result. The parents make the decision on how much power the children share. In the meeting parents share this limited and defined power with the children. Parents should realize that this sharing of power teaches children the values of responsibility and cooperation, but the children must understand and accept that the parents have the final word.

b. ***To provide a regular, scheduled time for the family members to sit down together, organize the week(s) ahead, and prioritize individual and family activities.*** This time allows limited "participatory democracy" and negotiation, prevents schedule conflicts, and safeguards family time from the often crowded schedules of children and parents.

c. ***To acknowledge and praise the efforts and achievements of the past week(s)*** (e.g., doing a chore or completing a homework assignment). The meeting can become a time for giving feedback, praising children, and passing out their weekly allowance or earned rewards. Parents also need and should receive acknowledgment and praise.

d. ***To bring up problems or disagreements that need to be discussed and solved*** (e.g., chores, morning routines, TV viewing, disrespectful behavior, sharing toys). Although consequences for behavior need to be discussed, the focus of the meeting should not be on disciplinary actions for individuals. The meetings also should not turn into "negative" feedback sessions or scolding lectures. These events should take place at another time in a private setting and on an individual basis that avoids public humiliation.

e. ***To provide a time that is pleasant and positive for the family.*** Members should feel free to discuss things that are working, improving, and going right. Everyone should feel able to talk without fear of being blamed, judged, or cut off. No family member should be scapegoated or humiliated.

f. ***To inform parents about their children's activities and interests.*** Parents often complain that children don't tell them about what they do in school or what their interests are; they feel "left out" and "in the dark." Family meetings provide children the opportunity to be more talkative and to tell parents about their interests. Parents may hear about an activity or game the child enjoys (skating, computer game) and decide to learn the game or needed skill so that they can participate with their child.

2. *Implementing a home family meeting: suggestions from the clinician.*

a. ***Introduce meetings at an early age*** (e.g., 4 or 5 years old). Even if the concept is introduced in adolescence, these meetings succeed because teenagers want to negotiate and share power.

b. ***Introduce meetings as a positive and appealing family event.*** Parents can either briefly clarify the purposes (e.g., to let everyone share thoughts and feelings, to give praise and rewards, to discuss chores, to plan weekly activities) or use an inducement that motivates the children (e.g., a favorite desert will be served or allowances will be given). All children want attention, which the family meeting provides.

c. ***Encourage parents to state that they would like the children's help and to ask them for their thoughts about the family meeting.***

d. ***Introduce the idea of meetings at a pleasant or neutral time, not in the heat of an argument or after a child has been reprimanded.***

e. ***Invite the family to participate; don't make the meetings seem like a mandatory event.***

3. *Guidelines for conducting a home family meeting: suggestions from the clinician.*

a. ***Everyone in the home should be invited.***

b. ***Parents should select a comfortable, quiet place*** (e.g., the living room, the dining room table).

c. ***Parents should select the most convenient time*** (e.g., after dinner [with a favorite dessert], Saturday morning, Sunday evening [with a snack]). The time should be as consistent as possible.

d. ***Ideally, meetings should be scheduled weekly because that interval provides timely feedback and reinforcement.*** A schedule should be posted on a bulletin board or on the refrigerator.

e. ***During the first meetings, the family should establish time guidelines.*** How long should the meeting last? Initially, the meeting should be 20 to 30 minutes in length. Families also need to discuss how long each member is allowed to speak and how much time should be devoted to one topic. To time these once the limits have been decided, parents can use a watch or an egg timer.

f. ***During the first meetings, the family should determine what issues to discuss.*** Chores and general discipline should not dominate meetings and should be discussed early in the meeting. Families should realize that members can share chores but that as all family members do not have equal abilities (e.g. teenage son, preschool-age daughter), chores must also be individualized. Between meetings members can write down topics for future meetings on a piece of paper that they can post on the family bulletin board or on the refrigerator. Younger children can ask parents to include their topic in the next meeting.

g. ***Keeping a record (minutes) of each meeting (with note taking or a tape recorder) allows the family to keep track of what transpired and minimizes disagreements.*** This secretary role should rotate among family members. Agendas should be made and can be posted or handed out (e.g., review minutes of the previous meeting, go over the weekly calendar of events, discuss old business [what happened last week] and new business, share fun stories, give compliments, and pass out allowances).

h. ***The leader of the family might consider not chairing the first meeting.*** The other parent or an older child might start. This demonstrates that leadership and power are shared and also allows other members to learn leadership skills.

i. ***Tasks can be assigned at the end of the meeting, and a checklist should be posted in a central location.*** Assigning tasks and redefining roles are major goals of the meeting. Expecting each member to be responsible for his or her part is a positive powerful influence on family functioning.

j. ***The meetings should always end on a positive note.*** Meetings don't always go smoothly, especially in the beginning; but a happy ending encourages the family to continue the meetings. End with a family game or activity or with acknowledging effort, giving compliments, or even viewing a favorite TV show or watching a video.

k. ***If the family wants to cancel a meeting, to shorten or extend a meeting, or to meet at an unscheduled time, parents should be flexible.*** If a meeting deteriorates (from arguments, fatigue, lack of interest), it should end—parents should not lecture or scold when family members are angry or tired. The family can discuss what happened the following week and can use the unsuccessful meeting as a lesson. If a member is uncooperative or is feeling ill, he or she should be excused.

C. **Special time.** Making time for children is one of the most important things a parent can do. Children want to spend time with their parents, yet parents often discover that finding that time to spend with their children is difficult. Parents want more (and enjoyable) time with their children. Even when parents interact with their children, they often determine the time for the interaction, the amount of time that will be spent on the interaction, and the activity—all of which may detract from the value of the interaction. Special time is one way to fill the deep, constant needs of parents and children for mutual attention and encouragement.

Special time is specifically time together for one child and one parent. The child chooses one parent at a time, and the other parent and children make other arrangements. Parents with two or more children should alternate so that each child has time alone with each parent.

Special time is a prearranged, guaranteed, and uninterrupted time that the parent spends with the child; it is a period of time in which the two interact without the parent being judgmental or directive. Each family must decide how often to have special time—daily is ideal. Special time is a time of day in which the parent is unconditionally available to the child. It communicates a commitment to the child and demonstrates by the parent's action that the child is valued and loved.

Special time is suitable for preschoolers, school-age children, and adolescents.

1. *Purposes of special time.* The clinician explains the purposes to the family, including the following.

a. ***It offers children the opportunity to have some input into how parents spend time with them and meet their needs,*** which makes them feel competent and respected. Special time defuses a power struggle between parents and children by giving children decision-making power and the self-respect that accompanies that. During special time, the parent might say, *"You're in charge. You pick the activity and I will join you."*

b. ***Special time can eliminate conflicts.*** If a child is pestering the parent to play a game, the parent can respond that he is doing something else at this time, but that *"We can play the game during special time."*

c. ***Special time allows parents to observe children up close and to focus exclusively on them.*** The parent learns much about the child and has many opportunities to praise the child, to encourage him or her, and to express affection.

d. ***Special time helps parents alleviate their guilt over not spending enough time with their children.*** Most parents are busy with work and other responsibilities that leave little time and energy for their children. Special time provides that regular time for children.

Special Time

Special time provides a form of "time in" for parents and children, an opportunity to spend time with one another, which builds a sense of love, trust, and commitment. It provides predictable, regular, and protected time for the child and parent.

CASE 2: THE FAMILY WITH CHILDREN WHO ARE "ALWAYS PESTERING US FOR ATTENTION"

The Well-Child Family Visit

During a well-child visit, the two children (Jamar, age 5, and Nakesha, age 7) ask endless questions, make repeated requests and attempts to leave the room, and constantly tease each other. The mother's usual responses are "*Stop that!*" "*I'll tell you later.*" or "*Calm down.*" She seems tired and unsure of how to respond and grows increasingly exasperated. She looks at the clinician.

Mother: *You see what's going on. Do you have any suggestions?*

Clinician (acknowledging her feelings): *You seem pretty overwhelmed. Is this what happens at home?*

Mother: *All the time. It has really stressed our family. What can we do?*

Clinician (realizing the need for a family meeting): *I'd like to meet with the family, including your husband. I need you both here* [emphasizing the need for both parents to attend]. *I can't offer any sound advice until I learn more about the problem and the family; then we can work on some suggestions.*

Mother: *If I can bring him here, it will be a miracle.*

Clinician: *I can't have the meeting without him. If it helps, I'll schedule a late afternoon meeting.*

The First Family Meeting

Engaging and Understanding the Family

The clinician greets the family. She thanks the parents for keeping the appointment and for their punctuality. The father seems a bit tense. The clinician spends a few minutes asking about his work and then explains the purpose of the meeting. The parents agree on the problem—the children are always pestering "*us*" for attention.

The clinician gives the children books and drawing materials and asks them to each draw a picture "of you doing something with your family."

Clinician: *First, I'd like to know more about your family routines. Can you describe a typical day?*

The parents both work full-time. The children are in after school programs. Evenings are busy with dinner, homework for Nakesha, baths, TV, and getting ready for bed. The father spends evenings on his computer doing job-related work, but the children "*always want me to play with them.*" Weekends are devoted to errands and family activities, but the father often does not participate because he has to "*catch up with work.*" This adds to the mother's stress, and the children miss his presence because he "*can't give them the attention they want.*"

Mother: *I try to spend time with them, but sometimes I forget; sometimes I have to break my promises because something else comes up.*

Father: *I don't participate as much; but when I do, I must admit that I get frustrated with their endless demands. Then my wife gets upset with me, and the kids get sort of forgotten for the moment.*

Clinician: *What would you like to see happen?*

Mother: *I'd like us to find a way to give the kids their time and also to have time for my husband and me. Getting everyone organized is challenging at times; sometimes the kids just don't seem to be on the same schedule.*

The clinician explores the family context. The family history is not significant. The maternal grandparents live nearby and "*love taking care of the kids.*" The parents are very involved with their church, and the mother teaches Sunday school.

The mother comes from a middle-class background. The father comes from a "working-class poor" background, and his parents divorced early in his life. His mother, who he says was loving, worked two jobs, so she was hardly ever home. The father had worked his way through college and states, "*I am very committed to giving my kids a comfortable life. I work very hard, about 60 hours a week at work and at home. I must have gotten that from my mother.*"

Clinician: *I see you both care about your kids. Does this leave any time for family life?*

Father: *Not much.*

Mother (angrily): *And not for us as husband and wife.*

Clinician (acknowledging their feelings): *It's hard having a career and being parents and spouses.*

Meanwhile, the children finish their drawings. Jamar's drawing shows his father reading a book to him. Nakesha's drawing shows the family watching TV. The clinician asks each parent to put a child on his/her lap while the meeting continues.

The clinician compliments the children (reinforcing their good behavior and demonstrating good parenting).

Working with the Family

The clinician hypothesizes that "special time" might decrease the "pestering." It would involve the father, who would spend time with each child, and would give the mother some relief. She decides to use Jamar's drawing as a starting point. (See Chapter 7, "Assessing Family Functioning: Additional Methods," pg 120, for further discussion of this technique.)

Clinician to father (encouraging one-on-one interaction with Jamar): *Would you like to ask Jamar about his picture?*

Father: *Jamar, you drew a picture of us reading a book. Do you want Daddy to do that some more?*

Jamar smiles and says yes.

Clinician to mother (encouraging mother–daughter communication): *Would you ask Nakesha about her drawing?*

Mother: *Nakesha, tell me about your drawing.*

Nakesha explains that she has a favorite TV program that she wants the family "*to watch it together.*"

Clinician (using the family meeting as an example of being "together"): *Like sitting together as you're doing now?*

Nakesha (smiling at her parents): *Yes.*

Clinician (to parents): *Kids are pretty honest, aren't they? What do you think about their wishes?*

The parents agree that the children want some regular time with a parent or doing something together at home, but they still look discouraged. The clinician introduces and explains special time to the parents. She tells them that this could be a way for them to achieve their goal.

Mother (to the father): *If you could be around in the evening or on weekends and not on your computer, we could each give each child that special time.*

Father: *I'm not sure if I can do that. I want to, but I am so consumed with work. But I'll try.*

Concluding the Meeting

The clinician summarizes the meeting by emphasizing the busy lives of the parents, the job demands, their concern for their children, and their willingness to try "special time." Again, she compliments the children for being so well behaved.

The Next Three Family Visits

Confronting Effort, Failure, and Disappointment

The family returned for three more visits over the next 3 months. They rescheduled two of the visits because of the father's work schedule, which resulted in a month-long interval between meetings. This made it difficult for the clinician and the family to work together. In the first month, the parents both carried out special time. They reported that "*the children love it.*" The pestering had diminished by about 50%. The mother felt better. Special time had served a useful purpose. When special time worked, they all felt better, which sustained the hope that they still might be happier.

But after that, the father claimed he couldn't do it. His job demands and workaholic style were too demanding. He had broken many promises about meeting the kids for special time, and the kids were very disappointed. The children's pestering increased again, and the parents still had "*no time for one another.*"

The clinician had made a directive—that the grandparents take the kids overnight and give the parents an evening together. The parents had done that once, their first date in 6 months.

But now the mother is angry. The stress has strained their marriage. The mother had even considered a trial separation, but now she is willing to "*work it out,*" meaning that the husband and wife have decided to get couples counseling from their minister. The clinician acknowledges their persistence and commitment. She likes the family and has great empathy for it but feels that she has done all she can. She lets the parents know that she will continue to be available and supportive to them as their primary care doctor and the family counselor. The parents promise to return, but 6 months later the father is transferred; and the clinician never hears from them again.

2. *Implementing special time.* The clinician explains how to introduce and begin special time.
   a. ***The parent should suggest the notion of special time at a pleasant or neutral time and should simply ask the child if he or she would be interested in spending time together on a regular basis.***
   b. ***The parent and child select a mutually convenient time of day.*** This can vary from weekday to weekend.
   c. ***The child should choose the activity as long as it is within the limits of parental time and financial resources and if it does not violate the dignity or the authority of the parent.*** Parents may offer younger children a choice of activities. Suggested activities include reading a story, playing a board game, telling bedtime stories, playing a sport, fixing a broken toy or bike, and going out for a meal. Sharing a musical or artistic activity, going to a museum or library, and cooking a meal are other types of special time. Older children and adolescents may prefer to go shopping, to practice driving the car, or to carry out an activity over several sessions (e.g., a time-consuming craft project or a chess game).
   d. ***One of the best opportunities for talking occurs when the parent and the child take car rides so that they are away from the distractions and interruptions of the home.***

e. ***Generally, interactive activities are preferable, but occasionally, a passive activity (watching TV or a video) is okay.***

f. ***The parent and child should both decide how much time to spend together based on the parent's ability to keep the commitment.*** Starting with short periods of time is better because then fatigue and boredom are avoided (e.g., 15 to 30 minutes, depending on the age of the child).

Once a schedule has been established, the parent should post it on the refrigerator or in several places (in the bedroom, bathroom, etc.). When starting special time, parents often find that it is easy to forget or to cancel.

g. ***Parents should work hard to keep their promise of special time with the child.***

h. ***If special time needs to be rescheduled, the parent and the child need to do so together in a democratic manner.***

3. *Guidelines for special time.* The clinician offers these practical tips.

a. ***Special time should be called by any name that the child chooses*** (e.g., "fun time").

b. ***Special time should be given to each child as promised, regardless of behavior or mood.*** It is unconditional.

c. ***If a child is disruptive or uncooperative during special time, the parent has the option to cancel it or to suspend it temporarily until the child settles down.*** The parent might want to put the child in "time out" for a brief period or to impose another consequence. The parent should decide if the disciplinary action is part of the allotted time or if it is separate.

d. ***Special time cannot be "saved up" and used to extend the length of the next special time.*** Each special time should be for a predetermined amount of time, but sometimes the parent and child may both agree to extend a particular session to finish an activity.

e. ***Special time should occur without interruption of any kind, unless a true emergency arises.*** The other parent or sibling (if able) can help protect special time by answering the phone or helping out with chores.

D. **Resolving parental disagreements: natural and logical consequences.** *Natural consequences* are normal or natural results of an action. When applied to the parent–child relationship, the parent allows the child to experience the natural consequences of his or her behavior and decisions. Children's behavior improves when they experience the consequences of the natural order. Natural consequences are sometimes painful (e.g., if a child plays roughly with a cat, the cat scratches; or if a child teases others, he or she is either rejected or teased back). Parents often use natural consequences intuitively (i.e., they do not intervene to prevent the consequence). Doing this reduces the likelihood of arguments and disagreements between the parent and child or between the parents. For example, if a child breaks his toy on purpose, the result is that he or she has a broken toy that is not replaced by the parents.

Sometimes parents cannot allow natural consequences to occur because they are too dangerous, but they can apply logical consequences, which provide the opportunity for parent and child to negotiate choices that fit the nature of the misbehavior.

Logical consequences are extended natural consequences that fit the family's values, time limits, and capabilities. Parents should develop their own logical consequences. They often reduce parental disagreement very effectively as in the following example. A child rides her bicycle recklessly, and the parents agree that they must impose consequences. However, they disagree on what to do. One wants to spank the child; the other wants to ignore it and let the natural consequence play out—the child might fall off her bicycle and "learn a lesson." However, the child could be seriously hurt, which is unacceptable to the parents. In this case where the parents disagree, the logical consequence (and compromise) could be taking the bicycle away for a week.

If parents do not agree on the use of natural and logical consequences, they and the clinician might use other interventions (e.g., other consequences, avoiding "high-risk" situations).

1. *Purposes of logical consequences.* The clinician must carefully explain the purposes for using them.
   a. ***They allow children to take more responsibility for their own actions, which enhances their competence and confidence.*** The responsibility to change his or her behavior or to face the logical consequence is the child's.
   b. ***They serve as an alternative to parents imposing punishment, a source of parent–child disagreement and conflict.*** The "punishment" is the logical consequence of the undesirable behavior. The child experiences the consequence of his or her chosen action.
   c. ***They emphasize actions, not words*** (e.g., threatening, explaining, and persuading). When parents talk too much, they often become frustrated and angry and overreact (e.g., screaming, saying hurtful things or imposing a punishment that is too severe or unrealistic).
   d. ***They can reduce parental disagreement, a major source of family conflict.*** When parents differ over punishments, often one parent sides with the child, which in effect forms a coalition with the child and excludes the other parent. Children recognize these patterns and often exploit them, causing considerable family disruption.

2. *Examples of logical consequences.* In the following examples, the parents explain the consequences before they implement the plan.

a. ***A child does not put her dirty clothes in the hamper but leaves them scattered around the house.*** The mother nags the child to pick them up but eventually ends up doing it herself. The mother negotiates a plan. If the child puts her clothes in the hamper, the mother will wash them; and the child will have clean clothes. If the child does not put her clothes in the hamper, the mother will not wash them; and she will not have clean clothes. Of course, the parent must be able to tolerate the child going to school in dirty clothes; and the child must want to wear clean clothes.

b. ***A teenager refuses to get up promptly in the morning, can't find his books, and often misses the bus.*** The parents argue with him and with each other and ultimately drive the boy to school so that he will not be late. They negotiate a plan. If the boy gets up on time and is organized, he catches the bus to school. If he sleeps in, he misses the bus, stays home, and has to figure out his own way to get to school. In this case, the consequence is appropriate if the boy is safe alone and wants to go to school. If he is intentionally avoiding school, the clinician and the family need to investigate the boy's mood and perceptions, the school, and social and learning situations.

c. ***A child speaks rudely to his parents, who respond with a lot of scolding and threats.*** The parents decide to use logical consequences. When another incident occurs, the parents respond, *"This is rude behavior and is not tolerated in our presence. You may speak politely or go to your room."* The child has the choice of being polite or going to his or her room (under escort, if necessary).

d. ***Siblings fight with each other all day.*** The children are given choices. If they play together, they can go to a movie in the evening; if they fight, they miss the movie and spend the evening in their own rooms.

e. ***A child argues about watching TV beyond his usual time allotment.*** The parents negotiate a logical consequence. He can watch his show and then turn off the TV himself. If he does not, TV privileges will be removed for a week.

f. ***A child refuses to eat her main course at dinner, but she clamors for dessert.*** The child can be given a choice: eat the main course first and get dessert second (the logical sequence of a meal) or refuse the main course and get no dessert. If the child has a tantrum, the family may need some guidance on handling that.

3. *Implementing logical consequences.* The clinician must explain the process for implementing logical consequences.

a. ***Parents must discuss the choices in advance, in a calm situation, at a neutral time, and not in the heat of an argument.***

b. ***Parents should provide fair choices that are logical results of the behavior and that fit the family's values and capabilities.***

c. ***Once the choices are established, the focus shifts to the behavior; and talking is minimized.*** The child makes the choice and accepts responsibility for his or her behavior.

d. ***The parents should remain firm and calm.*** Maintaining emotional equilibrium and steadfastness is essential parent behavior that strongly influences child behavior.

e. ***Parents should be flexible.*** If a parent has overreacted, become angry, broken an agreement, or imposed a consequence that is too long or harsh, he or she should apologize and renegotiate.

E. **Family rituals and traditions.** Family rituals and traditions give families stability, cohesion, strength, pleasure, and identity. They also provide a sense of connection and belonging to the extended family and the community. Some families have never developed rituals and traditions. Others forget their rituals and traditions when they are working too hard or when they are undergoing a transition (divorce, forming a blended family). The clinician should inquire about family rituals and traditions and should help these families revive or create them.

CASE 3: THE FAMILY WITH "NO FAMILY LIFE"

The Phone Call

The father of a 12-year-old boy calls because his son Fred seems "withdrawn from the family." The clinician schedules a family meeting.

The First Family Meeting

Understanding the Family

The clinician briefly socializes with the family and then explains what the family meeting is and how it will work.

Clinician: *I'd like to hear about your concerns.*

Father: *I am concerned about Fred. He seems withdrawn.*

Mother: *He spends lots of time at his friends' homes; but when he is home, he's watching TV and on the computer. He's doing well in school, though.*

Clinician (noting that Fred seems somewhat hesitant): *Fred, you might be feeling a little nervous now, and that's normal. But I'd really like to hear from you.*

Fred: *I don't know why we're here.*

The clinician realizes that Fred does not understand the purpose of the meeting. He explains it carefully again. Then he begins to explore the family context.

About a year ago, the father had transferred from California, which removed the family from its life-long home and the extended family members.

Father: *We miss them a lot.*

Clinician (acknowledging the impact on the whole family): *It must be hard on everyone.*

Fred: *We have no family life.*

Clinician (encouraging Fred to talk): *No family life?*

Fred: *Home is boring.*

Clinician (helping the family elaborate): *Can you tell me more?*

Mother: *I think I have an idea. We've never had much of an organized family life. Even before we moved here, we worked all the time, but our relatives were a big part of our lives . . . holidays, family reunions, occasional picnics.*

Father: *Now we do even less as a family. It's like having three separate lives under one roof, each of us coming and going. We seldom sit down together for meals, and even those are fast.*

After a few minutes of listening to descriptions of the family's lifestyle, the clinician turns to Fred and inquires about his strengths as a way to determine if Fred has some satisfying peer relationships.

Clinician: *Mom said you're doing well in school and have friends.*

Fred: *I really like spending time with my friends.*

Clinician: *What do you do with your friends?*

Fred: *Just hang out with them at their homes. We have fun. More fun than at home.*

Clinician: *Can you explain that a bit more?*

Fred: *We play word games, like hangman or Boggle, sometimes with their parents.*

Clinician: *Do you want that at home?*

Fred: *Yeah.*

Clinician: *Would you consider that your goal—more family life?*

The family clarified family life: regular meal times, family routines, and establishment of some traditions.

Concluding the First Meeting

The clinician summarizes the situation by pointing out the difficulties with the loss of family supports and activities and by reminding the family of its strengths (the members are coping, are attending family meetings, and Fred is doing well in school and has made friends). They will explore some strategies for achieving their goal at the next meeting.

The Second Family Meeting

Working with the Family

Clinician: *I have a few ideas in mind, but first what do you think would help?*

Father: *That's why we're here. But our last meeting did help just because we sat and talked together.*

Mother: *We like coming to these meetings, but we know they are only temporary. In a way, they are a routine.*

Clinician (encouraging the members to develop their own solutions): *What could you do to have more family life?*

Father: *Maybe leave my work at the office.*

Clinician: *How could that help?*

Mother: *We could have a regular dinner time.*

Fred: *With enough time to play Boggle.*

The clinician helps them identify who will be in charge of the two tasks: dinner and Boggle. They each describe what they will do. The mother appears to be the family leader as she leads the talk. The mother will plan three meals during the week. The father will get home by 6 P.M. on those days. He will help his wife fix dinner. The mother and Fred will buy a Boggle game, which Fred will be in charge of arranging after dinner. All the family members participate in the planning during the meeting.

The Third Family Meeting

The family returns 3 weeks later. Most of the meeting is devoted to discussing what has happened. They have averaged two dinners per week. The father just can't do it more. Fred was bitterly disappointed the first time that his father did not come home on time. He cried, retreated to his room, and refused to play Boggle that night. The mother was also upset. The family decided to set the goal for two dinners, but Fred had a hard time accepting the change and kept pestering his father. Finally, the mother told Fred that even though it wasn't what he wanted, it was better than before. Maybe later they could try to have three dinners a week together.

Clinician: *Do you want to try anything else?*

Mother: *Sunday is the best day for family time.*

Father: *How about church?*

Mother: *We could try it. Fred would see his friends there.*

Clinician: *It's a nice way to get involved with the community. Who's going to be in charge of getting to church?*

Father: *It's my idea.*

Clinician: *Fred, we haven't heard from you.*

Fred: *I want to call my cousins in California.*

The parents agree that calling the relatives every other week would be okay. Fred will be in charge of that task.

The Fourth Family Visit

Three weeks later the family returns. They have attended church weekly. The parents met the parents of Fred's best friend, and they all went out to dinner. Fred had called the relatives in California. The twice weekly family dinners are going well, and Boggle is enjoyed by all. It has been a smooth and pleasant period.

The parents still express some regret that "life isn't what we'd like" (they want more dinners at home together), but they are doing okay. The clinician ended the sessions by reminding them of all that they had done. They had established four family routines (dinners, Boggle, bi-weekly phone call to the relatives, and attending church). They had also met the parents of Fred's friend and feel that they are more a part of the community.

1. *Family rituals and traditions include the following:*
   a. ***Family activities.*** Family rituals and traditions create the structure for bringing the family together and leave lasting positive memories. Examples include:
      (1) **A regular dinner time.**
      (2) **A video or board game on Sunday evening.**
      (3) **Regular (home) family meetings.**
      (4) **A regular weekly activity (e.g., going to the library or a museum, doing errands, working around the house, taking a walk, viewing a favorite weekly TV show, or playing sports).**
      (5) **A special breakfast on Saturday or Sunday morning (e.g., pancakes at home or going to a restaurant).**
      (6) **Calling, writing, or e-mailing relatives on a regular basis.**
   b. ***Other rituals and traditions.***
      (1) **Celebrating holidays and special family events.** Holidays (Thanksgiving, Halloween, the Fourth of July, summer vacations, school holidays) provide an opportunity for the family to come together, to enjoy family togetherness, to rest, and to celebrate. Celebrating holidays also promotes a sense of family tradition and a feeling of cultural or national identity. It provides a chance to join with other family members and/or friends.
      (2) **Celebrating special family events** (weddings, graduations, birthdays, bar mitzvahs) serves many of the same purposes as celebrating holidays but is more personal and more family-centered. These celebrations connect family members in a common cause and provide a chance to express affection and support.
      (3) **Participating in spiritual–religious activities.** These traditions and rituals provide families with spiritual and religious strength, a sense of identity, and a connection to the community. Examples include attending weekly services at a religious institution (church, temple, mosque), celebrating religious holidays (Christmas, Hanukkah, Easter, Passover, Ramadan), or practicing a religious or spiritual activity at home (the Friday Sabbath, prayer, meditation).
      (4) **Visiting extended family.** Connecting to the extended family provides a sense of belonging, security, and origin. Examples include visiting or inviting relatives for holidays, birthdays, weddings, and births and taking vacations together.
      (5) **Exploring family history.** Learning about one's family history creates a sense of family identity, history, and pride. Examples include gathering oral family histories from relatives, creating a family time-

line, collecting photos and documents for a family album, arranging and/or attending family gatherings, and even visiting family burial sites.

(6) **Participating in community activities.** Activities in the community offer a connection to the world outside and provide a sense of belonging to something larger, something more than the family. Examples include participating in a school, community, or religious institution activity (bake sales, fund-raising drive, volunteer activities, neighborhood cleanups, visiting residents in a nursing home) or participating in local sports and recreational activities (e.g., those offered through the local YMCA or parks and recreation department).

F. **Writing assignments and the compliment box.**

1. *Writing assignments.* A writing assignment promotes the expression of feelings and thoughts by family members who prefer this kind of expression or who wish to use it from time to time. Many people find that expressing feelings and describing experiences through writing are very therapeutic. Some family members feel more comfortable expressing themselves through writings and drawings than they do vocally. Writing allows the individual to read his or her own mind, to trust the inner feelings, and to improve personal self-image and self-esteem.

Writing assignments can help family members communicate about any topic, especially about feelings, which some members can find difficult to articulate.

Children might write about their parents' divorce, the loss of a friend or relative, a conflict with a friend, the death of a pet, or disappointment over a lost opportunity. They also may want to write about pleasant events, like a family outing, a birthday party, or a personal achievement. Parents might suggest that they write a letter to a family member or friend or that they keep a private journal or diary. Some children prefer writing stories. No matter what form they take, these writing assignments can be private, or they can be shared with an individual or with the whole family.

Clinicians might suggest this activity if they or the parents note that a child is very shy or has difficulty using expressive language (speaking). This also is an excellent technique for children who love to draw.

Parents can introduce the idea of writing assignments in a private conversation with a child or at a family meeting. Parents can also share their own writings as a way to introduce writing assignments.

Children might want to include drawings and photographs with their writing. They should be encouraged to write without worrying about spelling, grammar, or neatness. They can choose any media they want to record their "writings," including by hand, on the computer, or even as a dictation into a tape recorder.

2. *The compliment box.* The purpose of the compliment box is to encourage the expression of compliments and feelings to one another. Clinicians might suggest this if parents and/or children have difficulty with praising each other or with expressing sadness, anger, or happiness. This can also be another way to boost the self-esteem of a child. Family members should write compliments and then deposit them in the box. Each member should write a compliment about another member. The compliments are then shared at dinner, a family meeting, or any other time the family deems appropriate. A member may write a compliment anytime. The idea of a compliment box can be introduced in a family meeting. Compliments reduce blame, negative attitudes, and anger and instill feelings of competence, recognition, appreciation, and love.

Compliments, a form of positive feedback, are a way to acknowledge and recognize another's efforts and achievements. They promote communication. Compliments express affection and increase motivation to do something well and to repeat behaviors that earn praise.

Compliments work for the whole family. Giving compliments is good parenting. They encourage parents to look for what is right and what is working instead of what is wrong. Children should not be the only ones to get compliments. Children should learn to compliment their parents and siblings. Parents can compliment each other as another way of expressing their appreciation for one another.

Compliments can be verbal (words), nonverbal (smiles, hugs, kisses), and written (notes, letters). Writing assignments and the compliment box are usually short-term solutions to improve family communication and relationships. When they cease to be useful, they are discontinued. If necessary, they can be revived again later.

III. Summary

Enhancing family functioning includes clinician directives, such as recommending readings, offering advice, prescribing medication, and suggesting specific strategies. Suggestions (and directives) are useful if the family wants them and is ready and able to try them. Finally, to be successful, these strategies or interventions must "fit" the problem. Six strategies have been described in this chapter: giving and receiving feedback; conducting home family meetings; implementing special time; resolving parental disagreements using natural and logical consequences; developing family rituals and traditions; and using writing assignments and the compliment box.

ADDITIONAL READING

Center for Journal Therapy. Ph: 888-421-2298. On the web at: www.journaltherapy.com.

Cohen R, Cohler BJ, Weissman SH. *Parenthood: a psychodynamic perspective.* New York: Guilford Press, 1984.
DeSalvo L. *Writing as a way of healing.* San Francisco: Harper, 1999.
Dialogue House Associates. Ph: 800-221-5844. On the web at: www.intensivejournal.org.
Doherty WJ. *Take back your kids.* Notre Dame, IN: Sorin Books, 2000.
Doherty WJ. *The intentional family: simple rituals to strengthen family ties.* New York: Avon Books, 1997.
Dreikurs R. *Children: the challenge.* New York: Hawthorn-Dutton, 1964.
Ehrensaft D. *Spoiling childhood: how well-meaning parents are giving children too much but not what they need.* New York: Guilford Press, 1997.
Hewlett SA, West C. *The war against parents.* New York: Houghton-Mifflin, 1998.
Howard BJ. Discipline in early childhood. *Pediatr Clin N Am* 1991;38(6):1351–1369.
Kurcinka MS. *Kids, parents, and power struggles.* New York: Harper Collins, 2000.
Main F. *Perfect parenting and other myths.* Minneapolis: CompCare Publications, 1986.
Neumann JK, Chi DS. Perceived maternal religious value similarity and church attendance: their potential stress response and psychological effects. *Stress Medicine* 1998;14:169–173.
Pipher M. *The shelter of each other: rebuilding our families.* New York: Grossett/Putnam, 1996.
Pryon K. *Don't shoot the dog: the new art of teaching and training.* New York: Bantam, 1985.
Schor EL. *Caring for your school-age child.* New York: Bantam Books, 1995.
Turecki S. *The emotional problems of normal children.* New York: Bantam Books, 1994.
Vance T. *Letters home.* New York: Pantheon, 1998.
Wallace JMJ, Forman TA. Religion's role in promoting health and reducing risk among American youth. *Health Education & Behavior* 1998;25:721–741.

13 Dealing with Disappointment and Failure: Avoiding Pitfalls and Working with Difficult Families

I. **Purpose**

Family meetings do not always go as planned. Clinicians and families will experience disappointments, frustrations, and failure. Families often are already discouraged and worn down. Clinicians often fall into the trap of offering advice too quickly, or they miss "clues" that signal family problems. Beginning clinicians must carefully select their families and problems.

When clinicians encounter a family with which they do not feel qualified to work, they should refer the family to another source as soon as possible. See Chapter 14, "Making a Mental Health Referral," for more details.

This chapter describes how the clinician can avoid common pitfalls in family meetings, can work with difficult families, and can select families and problems that fit his or her skills and experience.

II. **Avoiding Pitfalls**

Pitfalls are "breakdowns" in the clinician's interviewing. These problems are naturally part of the learning process, so the clinician should consider them as opportunities for growth. If the clinician does not encounter occasional problems, he or she is missing something and is not monitoring the quality of the interview, as reflected in the family's behavior, his or her own behavior, and family–clinician interactions.

As a general rule, the clinician should always:

- Ask the family for feedback about the meeting.
- Evaluate the meeting and his or her behavior in the post-interview phase.
- Measure the family's progress and use that to gauge his or her effectiveness. This can only be accomplished with follow-up visits.
- Seek advice or supervision from a colleague if a second opinion is needed. (See Chapter 9, "After the Interview: The Post-Interview Phase, Follow-Up, and Choosing a Termination Point for the Meetings," for further discussion.)

This section briefly describes nine common pitfalls and solutions (Table 13.1).

A. **Too much information.** Families can give and/or clinicians can request too much information. For example, the family might recount numerous, detailed examples of the problem behavior when one or two examples sufficiently reveal the problem. Too much data overwhelm the clinician, distract the family, consume valuable time, exhaust everyone, and prevent deeper exploration of the family context. The clinician therefore must limit the content and must focus more on the process.

Table 13.1. Nine pitfalls to avoid in interviewing

Too much information
The slow pace
The fast pace
The clinician judges and takes sides
The family that is reluctant to change
The clinician has a "rescue fantasy"
The clinician becomes part of a dysfunctional system
The clinician does not search for strengths
The clinician does not protect his or her personal life

B. **The slow pace.** The clinician paces the interview too slowly and/or is reluctant to explore the family context and assess family functioning so that the interview does not move beyond the friendly chatting of the first step ("Engaging the Family"). To remedy this, the clinician must actively monitor the pace and must proceed to the second step ("Understanding the Family") as soon as he or she has greeted the family, explained the purpose of the meeting, and started the "joining" process.

C. **The fast pace.** At times, the clinician paces the interview too quickly and fails to "join" the family (form a therapeutic alliance) at an adequate level and to explain the purpose of the meeting. As a result, the quality of the meeting diminishes. Rushing the interview (and not scheduling enough interview sessions) can be perceived by the family as a lack of empathy, respect, and/or professionalism. The clinician should monitor and adjust the pace to fit the allotted time; schedule more time for the interview; and schedule more meetings, if necessary.

D. **The clinician judges and takes sides.** The clinician can develop affinities or sympathies for a particular family member and can side with that member against another, a phenomenon that is not uncommon. For instance, a clinician can side with a parent(s) against a child or with a child against a parent(s). However, the clinician must maintain an impartial family systems perspective, so he or she should review his or her performance in the post-interview phase and should ask the family for feedback. *("Does everyone feel they were treated equally or given equal time?"* and *"Does anyone feel blamed or picked on?")*

E. **The family that is reluctant to change.**

1. *Families who feel that the clinician is pushing them too fast are reluctant to change.*
2. *Families also appear "reluctant" if the clinician does not observe their interactions, ignores "clues" and "messages," and hence misses opportunities to move the family forward and create change.*

3. *Some families have compelling, powerful secrets and forces within the family system that prevent change* (e.g., families who maintain the symptom to preserve the family balance and to sustain their relationships).

When families are or appear reluctant, the clinician must consider these possible causes. If a family is maintaining the symptom, the clinician must decide whether to acknowledge or confront its need to maintain the symptom. If he or she does not, he or she must then determine whether to make smaller changes in the system, terminate the meetings, and/or make a referral.

F. **The clinician has a "rescue fantasy."** The clinician is moved and/or motivated by the family's problems and pain. The clinician promises to try to help the family more than he or she can or more than the family desires because the clinician feels compelled to "save" the family. The situation can be described with the sentiment "*Let me help you. It helps me so much.*" Families become disappointed when the clinician can't keep promises to help them, so they become "resistant" to further efforts or end the relationship.

Disappointment and resistance from the family are signals to the clinician. When the clinician detects these signals, he or she needs to assess whether or not he or she is trying to meet some personal needs at the expense of the family. If this is the case, the professional relationship may have to end if the clinician cannot adjust.

G. **The clinician becomes part of a dysfunctional system.** The clinician is drawn into acting as certain family members do in the conflict. The clinician develops the same feelings of helplessness or anger or the same behaviors that are part of the problem in the family system. The clinician may join in family arguments as if he or she were one of the members. As a result, the clinician ceases to be an effective force in the family system treatment plan.

H. **The clinician does not search for strengths.** At times, the clinician fails to explore the family's resources and the strengths it brings with it to the meeting (e.g., past successes, supports, commitment, resilience, and love for one another). Families need to hear "good news" and to be reminded of their strengths because they have often forgotten them or have discounted them. Families feel even more discouraged and unmotivated if the clinician dwells only on their problems.

I. **The clinician does not protect his or her personal life.** In this scenario, the clinician encourages families to call at any time of the day or night, schedules appointments during nonclinic hours, and responds to every crisis. Because of this, the clinician becomes overwhelmed and consumed. Seeing too many families exceeds the clinician's "available" time, resources, and patience. When this happens, both the clinician and the family lose. Clinicians must "protect" themselves by specifying when they are available and how the family should contact them and by limiting the number of families in their practice.

III. **Working with Difficult Families**

Clinicians often encounter "difficult" families, which consequently cause them to feel worn down and discouraged. These families, which may be chaotic, distrustful, angry, or depressed, frustrate and challenge the clinician. In these situations, the clinician must exert strong leadership, provide more structure to the meeting, and give the family extra support, if possible. The clinician may also consider a referral or transferring a family's care to a trusted colleague.

This section describes six types of difficult families and offers suggestions for working with them (Table 13.2).

A. **The chaotic family**. Some families are chaotic. They can be loud, overactive, and disorganized. They interrupt, talk over others, and have difficulty complying with requests and tasks in the meeting. These families can be good-natured, irritable, confused, or worried. The clinician establishes control by structuring the meeting and by setting rules to make it orderly. A few suggestions to accomplish this are listed below.

1. *Before the meeting begins, the clinician states a few rules.*

Clinician: *I'd like to explain a few rules that will make the session more comfortable and productive for you:*

- *Please let each person speak without interruption.*
- *Only one person may speak at a time.*
- *Please don't interrupt or talk over someone.*
- *Speak for yourself, not for someone else.*
- *Speak to the person you wish to communicate with instead of to me.*

2. *Structuring also makes the session feel safe*. Every member needs reassurance that the family meeting is a safe place to express thoughts and feelings without fear of blame, threats, punishment, criticism, or loss of the family's love and approval. The clinician introduces this below.

Clinician: *The family meeting is a safe place where everyone can speak honestly without fear of being criticized. No one will be blamed or punished. Everyone's thoughts and feelings are important.*

Table 13.2. Six types of difficult families

The chaotic family
The discouraged family
The family that is stuck on the problems or has unrealistic goals
The family with a parent who "refuses" to attend the meeting
The family that has difficulty adhering to the time limits of the visit
The angry, aggressive family

If one member yells, calls another member names, or accuses another, the clinician must quickly and firmly intervene.

Clinician: *I know you feel very strongly about this, but I must ask you not to yell or call anyone names. Please tell us what you think or feel in a calm voice. You can do this without blaming anyone.*

3. *The clinician must help the family members cooperate by remaining neutral and not taking sides.* Active listening and allowing each member approximately equal time to communicate convey interest and neutrality. Sometimes however, the clinician needs to be more direct.

Clinician: *I want to say that I am not taking sides in this meeting. My role is to help you all work together and to provide any help in order for you to achieve your goal.*

4. *The clinician can structure the meeting if he or she keeps the family on its stated topic or points out its difficulty staying focused, as in the following situation.*

Clinician: *Let's go back to the topic that you agreed on as the one you wanted to discuss. We can talk about the other issue you raised at another time.* **Or** *Can you see how the family jumps around from topic to topic? It appears that it is hard to stay on one topic.* **Or** *Everyone seems to have a different agenda. Maybe this is one of the problems.*

5. *If the children run around and act disruptively, the clinician should let the parents respond first.* If they do not respond or if they respond ineffectively, the clinician should ask them what they would like to do. Sometimes parents hesitate to respond firmly or angrily in the office, or they are waiting for "permission" from the clinician.

Clinician: *Is this what happens at home? What would you like to do when Johnny runs around and interrupts?*

a. ***The clinician can distract and calm children by offering them toys, books, or drawing materials to use in the room or in the hallway just outside the room.***
b. ***Older children can play in the office playroom if one is available.***
c. ***The clinician can determine if the child is hungry or if he or she needs a diaper change or to use the bathroom.***
d. ***Some children calm down when sitting on their parents' laps or when addressed with a firm word.***

e. ***The clinician should remind parents to bring snacks, toys, and books as necessary.***
f. ***Sometimes leaving infants and children at home, if they are not actively involved in the meeting, works best.***

What hurting families need to know

When families are in pain, they need to know how much the clinician cares much more than they care about how much the clinician knows.

B. **The discouraged family.** Families seek help when they have experienced failure and disappointment so they feel discouraged and hopeless. The interpersonal relationships have often been strained, and they have negative perceptions of others and themselves. When working with a discouraged family, the clinician should always acknowledge its feelings. A short discussion and/or ventilation of feelings often proves helpful. Then the clinician can initiate a search for individual and family strengths; the search for positives improves the family's perceptions by reminding it of its individual and family strengths and successes. This realization reduces the sense of hopelessness and the intensity of the negative feelings by shifting the focus from problems to solutions. The family's thoughts now might be that "Yes, we may have some problems, but we also have strengths. We are doing something right."

1. *The clinician helps the family find its strengths by making a "request."* The request is an indirect compliment to the family because it implies that the clinician believes the family has past successes and forgotten strengths. The requests may be about the following:
   a. ***About themselves***. For example, the clinician may say, *"Julie, tell us something about yourself that you are proud of, that you recently did, or that makes you feel good."*
   b. ***About one member's perceptions of another***. The clinician may ask a parent something, such as, *"Ms. Cohen, tell us something about Julie that you are proud of or that makes you happy."*
   c. ***About relationships***. The clinician searches by saying, *"Julie, tell us about something enjoyable that you and your mom do together or did recently."* or *"Ms. Cohen, tell us about some activity, errand, or chore that you and Julie have recently done together."*
2. *The solution-oriented questions.* The clinician begins the interview with selected questions that emphasize strengths, possibilities, and solutions. Problem-oriented questions, which can perpetuate discouragement, should be

asked later in the interview. The three solution-oriented questions described below include goal, exception, and scaling questions. The clinician should choose the one that best seems to fit the family.

a. ***Goal question***. The clinician, in exploring goals, says, *"Let me begin with a different kind of question. If you could wish to make things better, what would you wish for?"* or *"What would you like to see happen by coming to this meeting?"* The clinician might use the magic wand with the child to facilitate these questions. See Chapter 7, "Assessing Family Functioning: Additional Methods," for more details.

b. ***Exception question***. To introduce this question, the clinician begins by saying, *"Let's begin with a new kind of question. Suppose things were better, what would be different?"* or *"Tell me about a time when things were better, when the problem wasn't happening as much."*

c. ***Scaling questions***. The clinician uses the following process to ask these questions. He or she says, *"I'm going to begin our meeting with a different kind of question. On a scale of 1 to 10, 1 represents the worst things have been and 10 is the best things could be. Where are you right now?"* The clinician always uses the answer to initiate a search for strengths. *"So you are at 4. That's pretty good. Almost halfway there. You must be doing something right. Tell me what you are doing to be there."*

Everyone should participate so that a sense of cooperation, competence, and support is built. For more details, see Chapter 8, "Three Models of Brief Family Interviews," The Solution-Oriented Interview, page 165.

C. **The family that is stuck on the problems or has unrealistic goals.** Sometimes families get stuck on problems or have unrealistic goals. A session or two may be needed to get them "unstuck." The family needs a new "map," which will create new directions and movement, to shift it off the problem and on to realistic goals. Table 13.3 offers a few suggestions for dealing with this type of family.

D. **The family with a parent who "refuses" to attend the meeting.** Clinicians often encounter families in which one parent refuses to attend the family meeting. The parent who is present at the meeting (or on the phone) speaks for the absent parent, reporting that the absent parent "refuses" to attend.

The clinician should consider the following possibilities and responses:

1. *The parent present in the meeting (or on the phone) is deliberately excluding the other parent for many reasons, including possibly because they disagree about parenting, because the parents are experiencing marital conflict, or because the absent parent has a personal problem (e.g., alcoholism, depression).* The parent in the meeting may offer

Table 13.3. Getting the family off the problem and on to realistic goals

Family	Clinician
1. Perseverates on problem	Emphasizes and rephrases goals and exception questions
2. Discusses many problems; can't prioritize or agree	*Helps family focus*: "What is the most important issue *now*?" *Guides family*: "I think communicating better with each other is more important than taking out the garbage. What do you think?"
3. States vague goals ("To get along better")	*Helps family specify goal behaviors*: "What would you each be doing when you two are getting along better?"
4. States grand, goals ("To always be a happy family")	*Helps family construct realistic goals*: "What would be the first hint that you were beginning to be a happy family? Let's work on that first."
5. Talks of negative behaviors as a goal (less of or the absence of a problem: "Not to mess up in school")	*Asks exception questions to state goal as a positive behavior*: "When you are not messing up in school, what are you doing instead?" "When did you last do well in school? What did you do differently? How would your teacher know?"
6. Relies on someone else changing ("If only my son would obey")	*Elicits description of parent's own behavior in the relationship and how parent behavior influences the child*: "So suppose your son were obeying, what would you be doing differently?" "How does your behavior help him obey?"

excuses, such as "He's not really involved" or "Her work schedule is too demanding."

2. *This situation often represents the parents' inability to cooperate at home and thus represents part of the problem* (e.g., "We can't agree on how to raise our child."). The clinician should share his or her concern in one of the following ways: *"I sense that you might not want your spouse to attend the meeting"* or *"I sense that the inability for both of you to be here and work together is another form of your disagreement. I need you both to attend the meeting if I am to help you."*

3. *The absent parent deliberately chooses to not attend the meeting because he or she feels or thinks one of the following things:*

a. ***He or she doesn't understand the purpose of the family meeting.***
b. ***He or she doesn't think a family meeting is necessary.***
c. ***The individual has had a "bad" experience in the past with mental health professionals.***
d. ***The parent thinks a family meeting is "family therapy," which he or she doesn't want.***
e. ***He or she feels that his or her authority is being challenged.***
f. ***He or she worries about being blamed.***

The clinician should ask the parent who is present about these issues and should suggest that the meeting be postponed until both parents agree to attend. He or she should explain the purpose of the family meeting and should emphasize the importance of participation from both parents.

If the absent parent still refuses to attend, the clinician should schedule a partial family meeting with the other members. Although this solution is not ideal, it may exert a positive influence on the whole family, like the "ripple effect" of a pebble dropped into a pond. Eventually, the absent parent may attend another meeting. This is preferable to the option of abandoning the family altogether or to making a referral that it is unlikely to accept. The clinician should never just give up on a family.

E. **The family that has difficulty adhering to the time limits of the visit.** Family meetings often do not proceed as efficiently or as predictably as routine medical visits. The clinician may be responsible for this as is described in "Avoiding Pitfalls" earlier in this chapter. However, more often the family simply needs time to "warm up"; once it does, it wants to talk quite a bit.

The clinician should take the following steps:

1. *Remind the family early in the visit of the time limits of the visit and that other appointments will be scheduled for it.* This takes pressure off the clinician (to complete the entire interview now) and the family (to offer all the explanations now) and creates an appropriate expectation for each visit.

Clinician: *We have 30 minutes* (or *We have until 2:30*). *Let's spend this visit talking about your concerns. In the next visit, we'll talk about suggestions, what to do. We will schedule more visits after that.*

See Chapter 6, "The Four Steps of a Family Interview," Engaging the Family, page 96, for further discussion.

2. *Keep the focus on the purpose of this particular visit* (e.g., to discuss the problem and the goal that the family defined in the first part of the meeting). The clinician might

say, *"Let's stick with the curfew problem and your goal of negotiating a compromise. We can talk about your other concerns at another meeting."*

3. *Place two clocks in the office; one should be easily visible to the family and the other to the clinician.* This allows all participants to watch the time and to pace the visit and reduces the likelihood of the meeting ending abruptly, which is dissatisfying to everyone. Close to the end of the visit, the clinician should glance at or point to the clock and say, *"As you can see, it's almost time to end. I'd like to take the last few minutes to summarize our visit and answer your questions."* The readily visible clocks eliminate the need for the clinician to make furtive glances at a wristwatch, which can convey a sense of disinterest and haste.

4. *Signal the end by deliberately placing notes on the desk, shifting position, and stating,* "It's been a good meeting. Let's end at this point."

5. *Stand up, if the family does not respond to these signals to end the meeting, and announce,* "I am sorry, but we need to conclude the meeting."

6. *Arrange for the nurse to knock on the door or for the receptionist to call on the phone at a designated time to announce that the next patient is waiting.*

7. *Refuse to explore new topics or to answer questions about new topics (e.g., the family history or medications) at the end of a visit.* These areas can be addressed at the next meeting. See Chapter 3, "Getting Ready for a Family Meeting," The Well-Child Visit/Doorknob Question, page 29, for further discussion.

F. **The angry, aggressive parent.** Sometimes in the office or clinic, a parent will yell or swear at the child and/or yank, hit, or slap the child. A parent who acts angrily and aggressively with the child in the clinic may actually be signaling for help. The behavior is usually symptomatic of several issues: a situational, acute stress; inadequate parenting skills; or a chronic personal or family social-emotional problem. The clinician should never ignore this behavior. Instead, the clinician can do the following:

1. *Always Acknowledge Affect (AAA).* The clinician might say, *"It is very challenging being a mother sometimes"* or *"It looks like you've had a hard day."*

2. *Briefly explore the immediate context of the behavior.* For example, was the parent waiting a long time in the waiting room or exam room? Is the clinician running late? Did the parent have a difficult time at the registration desk? Is the child being especially difficult? Is the child hungry and tired? Was the parent treated rudely by the receptionist, nurse, or clinician and therefore is taking his or her anger out on the child? If something occurred in the clinic, the clinician should apologize and should try to fix it later.

3. *Ask if this (angry) behavior happens at home and if so, how often.* The clinician can ask, *"Does this happen at home or just when you are here?"* or *"How often does this happen at home?"*

4. *Ask if other stresses exist at home or work.* The clinician can say, *"Are there things going on at home or at work that are stressful?"*

5. *Explore other ways for the parent to respond to the child.* The clinician can respond with *"I know it is difficult being in this small room with Johnny. Let me see if I can help out when he's demanding."*

6. *Explore a parenting technique for a similar situation at home.* The clinician can do this in the following ways: *"When this happens at home, are there times that you respond calmly and more effectively?"* or *"Let me suggest a strategy that might work."*

7. *Remain nonjudgmental and supportive.* The parent is very stressed, so the clinician should not lecture, moralize, embarrass, or challenge the parent.

8. *Ask about how the other parent or partner disciplines the child.* For example, the clinician might say, *"How does your husband (wife, partner) handle things or respond to Johnny?"*

9. *Ask if the parent has a support system.* The clinician can explore this with *"When things are tough or you feel overwhelmed, do you have someone you can call for help and support? Who is this person?"*

10. *Intervene in a positive, yet authoritative manner.* The parent needs guidance. The clinician can calmly take the child, sit the child on his or her lap, and engage the child in play. If possible, the clinician could let the child go to the playroom while the parent calms down. Not only does this response give the parent a break and a chance to talk to the clinician alone, but it also demonstrates or models a positive parenting technique. In effect, the clinician is saying, *"Kids can be frustrating sometimes. Let me show you another way to deal with this behavior."*

11. *The parent's angry behavior is often a call for help and provides an opportunity to offer more ongoing assessment and intervention.* The clinician's response communicates that empathy by saying, *"It's hard to be patient with a young child. It takes an extra effort and that's not easy. Let's schedule a meeting to help make things easier."*

IV. The Clinician Just Beginning to Use a Family-Oriented Approach

The clinician just beginning to use a family-oriented approach should try to select families and problems that match his or her skills and experience. However, as a word of caution, remember that nothing guarantees that "what you see is what you get." An apparently simple, "straightforward" complaint (e.g., "tantrums" in a 3-year-old) may be the symptom of a deeper, more severe, complex problem (e.g., domestic violence). The clinician can only rely on the parent's presenting complaint and on his or her initial judgment when making a decision to work with a family. With this in mind, the clinician should consider the following recommendations.

A. **Tips for success and survival.** Clinicians should do the following:

1. *Work with families that are known to them and with whom they have a good relationship.*
2. *Work with families that appear caring, competent, and capable of effective problem solving and communication.*
3. *Select apparently easy, simple problems*. Clinicians just beginning this phase of their practice should start with level 1 problems and should then explore the family context. With more experience, they can work with level 2 problems.
4. *Stay focused on the presenting complaint—do not try to reconstitute the family.*
5. *Seek out a mentor and supervisor, who can observe them working with a family or who at least is available for consultation and help.*
6. *Make a referral when they first realize that the problem exceeds their skills, time limits, and energy.*
7. *Remain confident that their early work (such as forming a therapeutic alliance and generally assessing the problem) has paved the way for a successful referral.*
8. *Seek more formal training if they wish to further develop their skills in the family-oriented approach to behavioral and interactional problems.*

B. **Other issues.**

Other psychosocial issues and situations may require a family-oriented approach. Describing them is beyond the scope of this book, but some examples are listed in Table 13.3.

V. **Summary**

Working with families is not always smooth, easy, or successful for the clinician or the family. Sometimes the clinician will experience disappointment and failure. These setbacks are part of the learning process for the clinician. Two sources of difficulties are pitfalls and difficult families. Pitfalls are clinician "errors" in commission or of omission in the interviewing process (e.g., a "rescue fantasy" or failing to observe and respond to a clue in family interactions). Difficult families include those who are discouraged, angry, tired, or chaotic. Therefore, those beginning to use the family-oriented approach need to select their families and problems carefully. Several strategies for doing so are described.

ADDITIONAL READING

Allmond B Tanner JL. *The family is the patient.* Baltimore: Williams & Wilkins, 1998.

Dodson LS. *Family counseling, a systems approach.* Muncie, IN: Accelerated Development, Inc., 1977.

Doherty WJ, Baird MA. *Family therapy and family medicine.* New York: Guilford Press, 1983.

Finney JW, Brophy CJ, Friman PC, et al. Promoting parent–provider interaction during young children's health supervision visits. *J Appl Behav Analyses* 1990;23:207–213.

Green M. Coping with the "helpless" parent. *Contemp Pediatr* 1997; 14(11):75–88.

Groves JE. Taking care of the hateful patient. *New Engl J Med* 1978; 298:883–887.

Johnson SB. Guidelines for short term counseling. In: Gable S, ed. *Behavioral problems in childhood: a primary care approach*. New York: Grune and Stratton, 1981.

Lewis M, Haviland JM. *Handbook of emotions.* New York: Guilford Press, 1993.

McDaniel S, Campbell TL, Seaburn DS. *Family-oriented medical care: a manual for medical providers.* New York: Springer-Verlag, 1990.

Quill TE. Barriers to effective communication. In: Lipkin M, Putnam S, Lazare A, eds. *The medical interview*. New York: Springer-Verlag, 1995.

Stuart MR, Lieberman JA. *The fifteen-minute hour: applied psychotherapy for the primary care physician*, 2nd ed. Westport CT: Praeger, 1993.

14 Making a Mental Health Referral

I. Purpose

Clinicians frequently encounter problems that exceed their capabilities and therefore require a referral to an agency or another professional (hereafter called mental health professionals). Making a mental health referral, an important part of family counseling, requires skill and sensitivity. This chapter describes the elements of the referral process, including gaining the family's trust, learning about benefits of mental health insurance plans, giving descriptions of various mental health professionals, working with mental health professionals, and conducting follow-up visits.

II. Elements of the Referral Process

The clinician often encounters psychosocial problems that require referral to a mental health professional. The referral might be for the child (e.g., depression), a parent (e.g., alcoholism), the parents (e.g., marital conflict), and/or the entire family (e.g., relationship/communication problems).

The referral process is a multi-element process, the components of which are listed in Table 14.1.

CASE STUDY: THE FAMILY WITH A CHILD WITH ATTENTION-DEFICIT/HYPERACTIVITY DISORDER AND PARENTS WHO ARE EXPERIENCING MARITAL CONFLICT

The First Child Visit

The mother of Joey, a 10-year-old boy who was diagnosed with attention-deficit/hyperactivity disorder (ADHD) 2 years before, makes an appointment because the "ADHD is coming back." Joey had been doing well in school and had been relating well to his peers. Initially he responded well to medication, but about 4 months ago he became "irritable and hyperactive." The clinician reviews the situation, but neither the teacher nor Joey and his mother identify any recent stresses. The clinician increases Joey's daily medication dose.

The Next Three Child Visits

During three more visits over a 2-month period, Joey's symptoms do not improve. The clinician focuses on Joey and his symptoms and prescribes different medications and combinations of various medications. Each attempt fails to alleviate the symptoms. The mother becomes increasingly frustrated ("the medicine isn't working"). Joey appears to have little insight into his difficulties as he responds to most questions with "I don't know." At the fourth visit, the father joins the mother and Joey because he says that he is very worried because Joey's "ADHD is really stressing our family life." The father reports that Joey has been sent to the principal's office two times for "defiant behavior." The father appears defeated ("I don't know what to do"), and Joey refuses to talk about it.

Table 14.1. Elements of the referral process

Gain the family's trust
Know when to refer
Know which problems to refer
Discuss the referral with the family
Mental health benefits of the health plan and description of various professionals: what the family needs to know
When the clinician chooses the mental health professional: what the clinician needs to know
The clinician and the mental health professional: working together
Follow-up visits: what happens to the child and family after the referral
When a referral fails
Locate mental health professionals

Clinician (seeking to understand the impact on the family): *How are you responding?*

Mother: *I'm upset with everyone.*

Clinician (clarifying): *Everyone?*

Mother (not answering the question): *There's just a lot of strain.*

Her eyes well up with tears.

Clinician (acknowledging her feelings and exploring the family's coping ability): *Sometimes when a child has a problem, the family has a hard time coping, which makes things even more difficult.*

Father: *We're having a hard time.*

At this point, the father and Joey exchange glances.

The clinician is confused and realizes that he needs to know more about the family (e.g., family history, recent changes, and the parents' relationship).

Clinician: *It's very apparent that it's been hard, and I appreciate your openness. Our time is almost up, but I'd like to make our next meeting a family meeting.*

He explains the purpose of the meeting.

The parents exchange glances. Joey looks back and forth from parent to parent.

Mother (expressing doubt about a family meeting): *I'm not sure if that would be helpful.*

Clinician (gently confronting and clarifying): *Can I ask what you mean?*

The father answers for her. He states that they will think about it. He then asks if they would have some time alone with the clinician. The clinician answers affirmatively.

A. **Gaining the family's trust.** When the family trusts the clinician, they are more likely to reveal important information and to accept a referral. The clinician gains the family's trust, which is the basis of a good clinician–family relationship, by respecting the family's stated concerns, joining with all the members, and working with them in a professional and supportive manner. Two potential clinician–family relationship problems hinder the referral process. If the relationship is one of "disengagement" (distant, remote), the family might interpret the clinician's referral as a sign of disinterest or of disdain for the family. The clinician can prevent this by taking time to get to know the family, supporting the parents and the child, and acknowledging every member's feelings. If the clinician–family relationship is one of "enmeshment" (overly involved, very attached), the family may interpret the referral as a sign of rejection, disappointment, and loss. Clinicians can prevent this by maintaining a family systems perspective, by monitoring their own behavior, and by examining feelings that the family evokes in them. See Chapter 13, "Dealing with Disappointment and Failure: Avoiding Pitfalls and Working with Difficult Families," for further discussion.

B. **Knowing when to refer.** Clinicians often make a referral under the following circumstances:

- When the clinician and family agree about the urgency of a situation (e.g., an acute crisis).
- When the presenting problem falls outside of the clinician's abilities (e.g., alcoholism).
- When the family requests a referral.
- When the real problem or the "hidden agenda" is revealed after several visits, and it exceeds the clinician's skills (e.g., domestic violence).
- When the clinician has worked at length with the family, but the numerous interventions have failed. The clinician is confused, and the family is frustrated.

C. **Knowing which problems to refer.** Determining which problems to refer can be difficult if the family has a "hidden agenda" or a family secret or if the clinician focuses too exclusively on the symptom and/or fails to explore the family context.

1. *Nature of the problem.* The clinician must first decide if the nature of the problem falls within his or her own interest or expertise, even if it is a level 2 problem. Some clinicians have interests and skills in a broad range of problems (e.g., communication problems, mood disorders in children, parental disagreements, and sibling rivalry). Others have a narrow range of skills and interests (e.g., ADHD in children). Some clinicians prefer to work with toddlers and families; others prefer to work with adolescents and families.

Clinicians working at level 3 of family involvement should refer level 3 problems (family psychosocial problems) or level 2 problems (relationship/communication problems) that have not responded to their efforts. See Chapter 2, "Determining Which Problems Are Suitable for Family Counseling," for more discussion.

2. *Severity of the problem.* The clinician should assess or estimate the level of severity of a problem when considering a referral. Factors that influence the clinician's perception of the problem or that indicate severity include the following: disproportionate parental worry; the affected domains of function of both the child and the family; and a preponderance of risk factors.

a. ***Parental worry can influence the clinician's perception of the problem.*** Some parents may be too worried about a problem; this worry stems from their anxiety, overprotectiveness, or their unrealistic expectations for themselves and the child. They may exaggerate, or even exacerbate, the symptoms and insist on unnecessary tests or treatments. The parent's anxiety affects the clinician, causing him or her to overestimate the severity so that he or she feels compelled to make a referral. On the other hand, some parents do not worry enough about a problem. They may be in denial, unaware of the implications of the problem, or distracted by other life issues. Their attitude may lull the clinician into agreeing with their perception of the problem; as a result, the clinician underestimates the severity of the child's problem. The clinician must determine the appropriateness of the parents' worry and help them adjust their level of concern to "fit" the problem. Once the parents' level of concern is appropriate for the problem, they are more likely to accept the clinician's diagnosis and to work with him or her.

b. ***Affected domains of function are those areas of the child's and family's functioning that are influenced by the problems.*** The child's depression may be severe enough to affect his or her school learning and peer interactions. The family hierarchy may break down so that boundaries become diffuse. A sibling may be ignored, or the marriage may be strained. The pervasiveness (number of affected domains or sites) and the functional impairment (severity of the impact) help the clinician determine the severity of the problem and the level of help needed.

c. ***Assessing both the risk and protective factors helps the clinician consider the overall level of severity.*** Risk factors exert a destabilizing or negative influence on the child and/or family; protective factors exert a stabilizing or positive influence. Assessing these factors helps the clinician determine the level of severity. The clinician might treat a child with depression (instead of referring him or her) and suggest a referral for the child's father to Alcoholics Anonymous for his drinking problem. The clinician might refer a child with bipolar illness in a multi-problem family to a child psychiatrist and a social worker. Protective factors should be recognized and nurtured (e.g., a family should be encouraged to reach out to its extended family for support; a family's willingness to meet and talk should be nurtured through office visits).

Child risk factors can include medical or emotional illness, difficult temperament, and learning problems. Family risk factors include teenage parents, divorced/single parent, unemployment, poverty, lack of transportation, inadequate housing, homelessness, marital conflict, parental depression, and alcoholism or drug abuse.

Protective child–family factors incorporate the child's good medical health, success in school, an intact family, financial security, and/or being involved with the local church, temple, or mosque. Community protective factors include access to medical and mental health resources, affordable housing, a crime-free neighborhood, the presence of friends, and recreational facilities. Protective factors provide a buffer for the child and family and reduce the impact of risk factors.

D. **Discussing the referral with the family.** After the clinician decides to refer, he or she needs to consider the following issues: when to discuss the referral in the meeting; how to help the family understand the problem and need for a referral; the family's past experiences with mental health services, if any; and how to explain the referral to the family.

1. *When to discuss the referral in the meeting.* The idea of referral should be voiced early enough in the family meeting so that sufficient time remains to review past interventions, explain the reasons, describe the referral process, and answer questions. If too little time is left, the clinician should schedule another meeting. Sometimes, the idea of a referral arises during a parent–child visit for a behavioral problem that initially seems simple and mild. The clinician must decide whether to discuss a referral then or to schedule a family meeting instead. The family meeting is preferable for these reasons:

a. ***It provides additional information that helps the clinician select the most appropriate mental health professional.***

b. ***The family should discuss it (and usually wants to) and should decide as a family with the clinician present.***

c. ***The family leader must approve the referral.***

CASE STUDY (CONTINUED)

The Family Meeting

During the pre-interview phase before the family meeting, the clinician considers the following: Joey has been doing well until 4 months ago. No obvious stresses have been identified, and medication trials have failed to improve the symptoms of his ADHD. Joey is doing worse, and at the last visit, the parents seemed discouraged. When the mother mentioned the family strain, she was especially sad. The clinician senses that the problem exceeds his capabilities. He thinks a referral might be needed, but he is not sure what kind of referral is necessary. He needs more information to help him understand the problem within a family context. During the family meeting, his plan is to:

1. Review Joey's situation, focusing first on Joey (still the identified patient), and then allow the family to respond.
2. Explore family relationships, and let the family respond.
3. Suggest an appropriate referral.

Clinician (after greeting the family): *We're meeting because you want to see Joey doing better. Meeting as a family helps everyone understand the problem better and find appropriate solutions. Let me briefly review the situation.* [After he reviews it] *Let me hear from you. What are your thoughts and reactions?*

The parents state that they are mystified and that they hope that the clinician can help. They have spoken with Joey's teacher, who is supportive but who is also confused.

Clinician (getting Joey involved): *Joey, what would you like to say? We need to hear from you, too.*

Joey: *I want things to be good again.*

Clinician (acknowledging Joey's feelings): *Joey, I know this has been hard on you and I appreciate you being here.*

Joey looks down and is silent.

Clinician (seeking clarification and more information): *What do you mean by "be good again?"*

Joey continues to look down and does not respond.

Clinician (exploring the parents' perceptions): *This must be hard on you, too. What do you think Joey means?*

Parents: *We think he wants to end his ADHD problems.*

Clinician (exploring the parents' coping abilities): *How do you respond to Joey's problems?*

The parents do not punish him for the problems at school, and they both give him extra attention at home.

Clinician (using the mother's comment in the previous visit about "strain" to expand the inquiry): *At our last meeting you mentioned "lots of strain" and seemed very sad.*

The clinician purposefully states this in an open-ended manner without asking a specific question. He pauses and waits.

The mother starts to say something, but she looks at Joey and hesitates.

Clinician (deciding that he needs to speak with the parents only and remembering the father's request for "time alone"): *I'd like to excuse Joey for a few minutes so we can talk. Joey, you can wait in the playroom.*

When they are alone, the clinician sits silently to let the parents compose their thoughts and speak first. They sit silently for 15 to 20 seconds, staring at the floor and exchanging glances. Neither seems willing to talk. The clinician decides to begin by using an indirect opening—focusing on Joey—not on the parents or their relationship, as they seem hesitant and uncertain.

Clinician: *Have there been any stresses or strains that might be influencing Joey?*

The parents explain that they have been experiencing "marital tension" for almost a year. Several months ago, it escalated to heated arguments. Although they waited until Joey had gone to bed, they were sure that he heard them yelling and crying; but they did not know how to tell him or even if they should. They have not told anyone (teacher, relatives, friends) about their marital problems.

Clinician (probing the parents' perception of a possible link between their problems and Joey's problems): *Do you think that the marital tension affects Joey and that his problem is not just ADHD?*

Mother: *It must.*

Father: *Maybe.*

2. *The family's experience with referrals.* The clinician should inquire about the family's past experience with referrals (if it has had any and if those referrals were successful) and about preconceived fears or beliefs about mental health professionals. Thus informed, the clinician can avoid making the same referral or making it in a way that has failed or has been rejected by the family in the past. The clinician tailors the referral to produce the best match with the family's needs and beliefs. Below are several questions the clinician can use to make the appropriate determination:

- "In the past have you or any family member been referred to a counselor or mental health professional? If yes, what was the problem?"
- "Who made the referral?"
- "Did you understand the reason for the referral?"
- "Did you keep the appointment? If not, what happened?"
- "Who (what type of counselor) did you see?"
- "What happened? What was the counselor's approach?"
- "Was it helpful? If yes, why? If no, why not?"

CASE STUDY (CONTINUED)

When actually suggesting a referral, the clinician frames it as something that other people experience as well.

Clinician (introducing the idea of a referral): *Every couple experiences problems in their marriage. Sometimes they get to a point where they need some professional help. This is especially true when the marital problems affect the children.*

The clinician pauses to give Joey's parents a chance to respond. They nod slightly and look at each other.

Clinician (after about 15 seconds of silence): *Have you ever seen anyone or considered getting help?*

The father (revealing an experience that influenced his attitude) replies that friends of theirs had gone to a marriage counselor but that the husband felt he was being blamed for everything, so after two visits, he stopped going. His friends' experience makes him doubt the usefulness of marital counseling.

The mother (revealing another influence) replies that her mother tells her to "just hang in there," which she has tried, but it isn't working.

3. *How to explain the referral.* If the clinician has not done so yet, he or she should now briefly review the problem and any attempted interventions and outcomes. The family is more likely to accept a referral if the clinician takes the following actions:
   a. ***Makes sure that family members understand the problem and its impact on family functioning.***
   b. ***Helps them understand that a referral is necessary.***
   c. ***Clearly explains the potential benefits of a referral to the parents and the child.***
   d. ***Has personal or specific information about the mental health professional.***
   e. ***Does not imply that he or she is trying to "get rid of" the family.***
   f. ***Provides follow-up visits with the family.***

CASE STUDY (CONTINUED)

The clinician summarizes the situation and reviews the apparent relationship between the marital problems and Joey's feelings/ behavior.

Clinician: *You have shared that you've had marriage problems for a year, but you've hesitated to seek help. You agree that the marriage problems are affecting Joey; his problems began occurring about the same time your problems were intensifying. He is probably feeling sad and anxious that you might separate or divorce. Sometimes, children blame themselves for their parents' problems, which only adds to their worry. At other times they are angry with their parents. Joey's behaviors and moods at school may be an expression of all these feelings.*

When Parents and the Clinician Disagree

Parents may disagree that "their problem" is affecting "the child's problem." The clinician should not force his or her viewpoint on the parents. They will become defensive. Instead, the clinician should propose that a combination of child factors (temperament, neurodevelopmental status) and family–social factors may explain the "child's problem." Parents sometimes need time to think about the referral or to speak with friends or relatives.

Father: *I hadn't realized how worried Joey was about us. I just thought he was worried about his ADHD and his school behavior.*

Mother: *I feel so bad that we have waited so long.*

Clinician (emphasizing the need to attend to the marital problem): *It sounds to me like you both agree that resolving the marital problem is important.*

They nod.

Clinician (mentioning the referral very openly and directly): *Would you like me to suggest a counselor, or do you want to look around and see who is on your health plan?*

The parents decide to find a counselor who is on their health plan.

The clinician should suggest the referral in a confident, supportive, and directive manner.

Clinician: *I know you feel hesitant about seeing a marriage counselor, but I also feel very strongly that it would be helpful.*

The parents nod.

Clinician (anticipating a common occurrence and planning an alternative strategy): *If that counselor is not the right "fit" for you, I can help you find another.*

The parents nod silently.

Clinician (letting the family know that he wants to follow it during/after the referral process): *We will continue the family meetings until Joey is doing better.*

Making a Referral

The clinician should give the family names and phone numbers of mental health professionals whom he or she can recommend with confidence.

Some families do better if the clinician calls to make the appointment while the family is in the office.

E. **Mental health benefits of the health plan and descriptions of various professionals: what the family needs to know.** The clinician can recommend/choose a mental health professional for the child/family, or the family can choose its own; sometimes the family's choices are limited to those endorsed by its health plan. Regardless of who chooses the mental health professional, the family needs to know the mental health benefits of its health plan. The clinician might have this information available so that he or she can share it with the family, or the family can obtain it from its health plan (Table 14.2).

When families inquire about their mental health benefits, they are sometimes given a list of professionals by their health plans. Sometimes families are unclear about the differences (e.g., training or the field of expertise) among various professionals. Below are descriptions of various professionals who can provide mental health services/counseling.

Table 14.2. Mental health benefits of the health plan: what the family needs to know

1. What mental health services are covered by the family's insurance policies, health maintenance organization (HMO), or preferred provider organization (PPO)?
2. Is the recommended professional approved as a provider by the family's insurance company or organization?
3. What percentage of the professional's fees is covered by the policy?
4. Is there a limit on the number of visits per year? Over the life of the policy?
5. Does the policy cover psychological tests and evaluations?
6. Does the policy cover psychotherapy (talk therapy) and/or medications?
7. Does the family need to get a referral first from its primary care provider?
8. What happens if the entire family or certain members do not like the recommended professional?
9. What happens if the family wishes to use a professional from outside the network of approved providers?

1. *Psychiatrist (M.D. or D.O.)*. This individual has formal training in adult psychiatry. A child and adolescent psychiatrist has extra training (usually a 2-year fellowship working with children or adolescents). Some psychiatrists practice individual, marital, and family therapy. Others may specialize in other areas (e.g., substance abuse). Psychiatrists can prescribe medications.

2. *Behavioral–developmental pediatrician (M.D. or D.O.).* This individual has 3 years of general pediatric training and extra training (a 2- to 3-year fellowship) in behavioral pediatrics and/or child development. Fellowships vary greatly in their emphasis—some focus on infants and young children with developmental disabilities and others focus on all ages and a broad range of problems. Pediatricians can prescribe medications.

3. *Family physician (M.D. or D.O.).* This practitioner has 3 years of general family medicine training and, possibly, extra training in family counseling/therapy. Family physicians can prescribe medications.

4. *Clinical psychologist (a counselor with a master's degree [M.A.] or doctoral degree in psychology [Psy.D. or Ph.D.] or education [Ed.D.]).* These individuals can provide clinical services that include both diagnosis/assessment (e.g., mental health, cognitive ability, academic achievement) and therapy (e.g., individual, group, marital, or family). Those with a doctoral degree have completed graduate school with the accompanying practicum, a dissertation, and a clinical internship. The psychologist should be listed in the National Register of Health Services Providers and

licensed by the state. Psychologists cannot prescribe medications.

5. *Social worker (a counselor with a bachelor's degree [B.S.W.], master's degree [M.S.W.], or doctoral degree [D.S.W. or Ph.D.]).* Social workers are accredited by the Academy of Certified Social Workers (ACSW) if they have a master's degree from an accredited school of social work, have completed 2 years of supervised work, and have passed a written examination. Social workers have a wide range of skills and interests (e.g., assessing the family–social environment) and providing counseling (e.g., individual, family). The National Association of Social Workers (NASW) keeps a national register of clinical social workers.

6. *Psychiatric nurse (registered nurse [R.N.]).* This individual has completed a 4-year nursing program and an 18- to 24-month master's program (academic and clinical work with supervision) in psychiatric training focused on children, adolescents, and families. After passing a national examination, psychiatric nurses are certified by the American Nurses Association. They cannot prescribe medications.

7. *Marital and family therapist (master's degree [M.A.] or doctoral [Ph.D. or M.D.]).* In addition to the advanced degree, these individuals have completed many hours of supervised training in marital and family therapy.

F. **When the clinician chooses the mental health professional: what the clinician needs to know***

If the clinician recommends a specific mental health professional, knowing something about this individual (style and approach) to provide a good "fit" between the counselor and the client/patient is helpful. The clinician can learn about local mental health professionals in several ways: talking to them on the phone; meeting them for lunch; and inviting them to give talks at grand rounds, office practice meetings, and state medical society meetings. Reading their reports and soliciting feedback from those who have worked with these specialists (colleagues, families, and school counselors) can give additional insight. Local and state mental health associations provide some background information. Below are some helpful questions the clinician should consider.

- What are the modalities of treatment (e.g., medication, behavior modification, individual and/or family therapy)?
- How available is the specialist to the family (e.g., does he/she return phone calls)?
- Does the specialist accept low-income families?

* To clarify the titles and roles in this particular chapter, a "clinician" is the professional working at level 2 or 3 of family involvement with level 1 or 2 problems. A "mental health professional" or "specialist" works at level 4 or 5 of family involvement with level 2 or 3 problems. See Chapter 2, "Determining Which Problems Are Suitable for Family Counseling," for further discussion.

Referrals and the Health Plan

In the era of managed care, the clinician has less control over who the child, parent(s), or family may see on a referral basis; but the clinician can learn about the approved mental health professionals and may be able to direct the family to a particular individual.

- How long will the family have to wait to get an appointment?
- Are appointment times flexible and convenient for the family?
- Where is the specialist's office located? How convenient is it for the family?

G. **The clinician and the mental health professional: working together.**

The clinician and the mental health professional often collaborate in several ways, as listed below:

1. *The mental health professional provides specialized services* (e.g., marital therapy), *and the clinician provides primary care for the family* (e.g., counseling and individual interventions for the child).
2. *The mental health professional treats the child/family for a specified number of visits, and then the clinician continues the treatment.*
3. *The mental health professional serves as an occasional consultant to the clinician, and the clinician provides all of the treatment.*

The clinician and the mental health professional should develop a working relationship that provides the best care for the child and family. Elements of a good working relationship between the clinician and the mental health professional are listed in Table 14.3.

The Clinician–Specialist Relationship

Some families may not want the clinician to know everything they share with the mental health professional. Some specialists prefer not to share information with the clinician even though the clinician and family want to share it. When these issues arise, the clinician, the family, and the mental health professional should resolve them expeditiously.

Table 14.3. Elements of a good working relationship between the clinician and mental health professional

1. **Communicating the specific purpose of the referral to the mental health professional**
   When making the referral, the clinician should clearly communicate the purpose of the referral (e.g., refer Joey to a child psychologist or psychiatrist to evaluate Joey's situational sadness/anxiety and recommend treatment [medication, individual therapy with a mental health professional, or continued family counseling with the clinician]).
2. **Defining the responsibilities of the clinician and mental health professional**
   When the mental health professional and the clinician are both physicians, they must decide who is prescribing the medication. If a child psychiatrist is seeing a child with severe psychiatric illness, the psychiatrist should prescribe the medication; and the clinician should provide family counseling and well-child care. The family should be informed so they know who to call for help or advice for a particular problem.
   When the mental health professional is not a physician providing individual child therapy and the clinician is prescribing medication, they need to define their roles and respect each other's expertise. If the parents have a question about medication, they should consult the clinician. If they have a question about therapy, they should first consult the mental health professional.
3. **Exchanging information between the clinician and the mental health professional**
   The clinician and the mental health professional need to decide what information to exchange with each other. This information might include detailed background information at the time of referral, their hypotheses, detailed or general summaries of each visit, a summary every few months or only at the end of treatment, and/or notification if the family has not kept its appointments. The clinician and the mental health professional can decide on the best way to communicate (e.g., office and home phone, e-mail, or dictated notes).

III. Follow-up Visits: What Happens to the Child/Family After the Referral?

A. **Follow-up visits.** Follow-up visits are an integral part of ongoing child and family care. A referral does not mean that the clinician is abandoning the family or is relinquishing his or her role as a care provider or advocate for the family.

After the referral, the clinician should schedule a follow-up visit to assess the family's progress and its satisfaction with the mental health professional. Knowing the clinician is still interested, still involved, and available comforts the family. Follow-up visits enable the clinician to reevaluate the child and the family, to interpret new information, and to incorporate these data into the profile of the family (e.g., adding information to the genogram). See Chapter 7, "Assessing Family Functioning: Additional Methods," The Child and Family Evaluation (CAFÉ), page 134, for additional information.

Follow-up With the Specialist

The clinician should ask the mental health professional to notify him or her if the family does not keep the initial appointment.

B. **When a referral fails.**

The clinician may learn of an unsuccessful referral with a communication from the mental health professional, through a follow-up visit, or by a phone call to the family.

When a referral fails, the clinician can take the following action:

1. *Phone the family or schedule a meeting to discuss why the family members think the referral did not work with the mental health professional if they feel comfortable doing so.* A misunderstanding between the family and the mental health professional might be cleared up, and the family might resume treatment.
2. *Remind the family that sometimes one or two visits with the mental health professional are needed to clarify expectations and to establish a comfortable relationship.*
3. *Obtain information from the mental health professional if the family consents (signs a consent form).* The clinician might share the information with the family.
4. *Help the family find another mental health professional if it is still motivated.*
5. *Address other specific problems* (e.g., helping the family find an affordable mental health professional).
6. *Reassess the family's problems in light of new information, and/or continue to explore the family context to make a more appropriate referral if it is still interested.*
7. *Maintain contact with the family if it refuses a second referral; if and when the problem worsens, it may be more likely accept the referral.*
8. *Continue to see the family, and help it (within the clinician's capabilities).* The family may or may not opt to try another referral.

Family Refusal of the Referral

When a family refuses a referral, the clinician should continue to see the family, understand its reason for the refusal, and help it appreciate the benefits of the referral. The clinician can also consult the mental health professional for advice on how to continue to support the family while attempting to convince it to accept another referral.

IV. Locating Mental Health Professionals

The clinician can locate mental health professionals in the community and state in several of the following ways:

- Ask colleagues.
- Contact state and local mental health associations.
- Call universities (e.g., School of Social Work, Department of Psychology).
- Call academic medical centers (e.g., Departments of Psychiatry, Pediatrics, Family Medicine, and Nursing).
- Contact private mental health professionals.
- The clinician can also obtain names and addresses of local or state mental health professionals through lists of national organizations.

A. Professional organizations

American Academy of Child and Adolescent Psychiatry
3615 Wisconsin Avenue NW
Washington, DC 20016-3007
Phone: 202-966-7300
Website: http://www.aacap.org

American Association for Marriage and Family Therapy
1133 15h Street NW
Washington, DC 20005-2710
Phone: 202-452-0109
Website: http://www.aamft.org

American Psychiatric Association
1400 K Street NW
Washington, DC 20005
Phone: 888-357-7924
Website: http://www.psych.org

American Psychological Association
750 First Street NE
Washington, DC 20002-4242
Phone: 202-336-5500
Website: http://www.apa.org

National Association of Social Workers
750 First Street NE, Suite 700
Washington, DC 20002-4241
Phone: 800-638-8799 or 202-408-8600
Website: http://www.naswdc.org

B. **General organizations**

Knowledge Exchange Network
Center for Mental Health Services
5600 Fishers Lane, Room 17-99
Rockville, MD 20857
Phone: 800-789-2647
Website: http://www.mentalhealth.org

National Alliance for the Mentally Ill
Colonial Place Three
2107 Wilson Blvd., Suite 300
Arlington, VA 22201-3042
Phone: 800-950-6264 or 703-524-7600
Website: http://www.nami.org

National Mental Health Association
1021 Prince Street
Alexandria, VA 22314-2971
Phone: 800-969-6642 or 703-684-7722
Website: http://www.nmha.org

V. **Summary**

Making a mental health referral is one of the clinician's most important jobs. The clinician is more likely to make a successful referral if it is done in an organized, sensitive, and supportive manner. The referral process includes several aspects:

- gaining the family's trust;
- knowing when and what problems to refer;
- discussing the referral with the family;
- helping parents know the mental health benefits of their health plans;
- knowing and locating the mental health professionals in the community;
- collaborating with the specialist; and
- helping the family deal with unsuccessful referrals.

ADDITIONAL READING

Bailey D, Garrada ME. Referral to child psychiatry: parent and doctor motives and expectations. *J Child Psychol Psychiatr* 1989; 30:449–458, 1989.

Cartland JD, Yudkowsky BK. Barriers to pediatric referral in managed care systems. *Pediatrics* 1992;89(2):183–192.

Cummings EM, Davies P. *Children and marital conflict: the impact of family dispute and resolution.* New York: Guilford Press, 1994.

Doherty WJ, Baird MA. *Family therapy and family medicine*. New York: Guilford Press, 1983.

Hansen J, Bobula J, Meyer D, et al. Treat or refer? Patient's interest in family clinician involvement in their psychosocial problems. *J Fam Prac* 1987;24:499–503.

Howard BJ. The referral role of pediatricians. *Pediatr Clin N Am* 1995;42:103–118.

Igelhart JK. Physicians and the growth of managed care. *New Engl J Med* 1994; 331:1167.

Joost JC, Chessare JB, Schaeufele J, et al. Compliance with a prescription for psychotherapeutic counseling in childhood. *J Dev Behav Pediatr* 1989;10:98–102.

Kahn RS, Wise PH, Finkelstein JA, et al. The scope of unmet maternal health needs in pediatric settings. *Pediatrics* 1999;103: 576–581.

Krugman SD, Wissow LS. Helping children with troubled parents. *Pediatr Annal* 1998;27(1):23–29.

Pangburn DA: Referral processes. In: Levine MD, Carey WB, Crocker AC, eds. *Developmental–behavioral pediatrics*, 3rd ed. Philadelphia: WB Saunders, 1999.

Plunkett JW. Parents' treatment expectations and attrition from a child psychiatric service. *J Clin Psychol* 1984;40:372–377.

Verhulst FC, Ende J. Factors associated with child mental health service use in the community. *J Am Acad Child Adolesc Psychiatr* 1997;36(7): 773–776.

15 Getting More Training and Knowledge in Family-Focused Pediatrics

For the clinician who wishes to pursue more training and to obtain more knowledge in family-focused behavioral pediatrics, many options and sources exist. This chapter describes on-site training, professional societies, academic centers, family therapy training centers, and on-line sources of information.

ON-SITE TRAINING

Clinicians can contact colleagues in their academic centers, health plans, or communities who practice family counseling and can ask them if they provide supervision or advice. These colleagues might allow the clinician to work with them as a co-therapist with selected families. They might also agree to observe the clinician working with a family and to offer feedback or might serve as informal consultants who offer advice and feedback by phone or e-mail about the clinician's skills and cases.

PROFESSIONAL SOCIETIES

Societies and associations that promote family-oriented care for children and who sponsor national continuing educational courses include:

- The Society for Developmental and Behavioral Pediatrics
- The Ambulatory Pediatric Association
- The American Academy of Pediatrics
- The Society for Behavioral Medicine
- The Society for Teachers of Family Medicine
- The American Association for Marriage and Family Therapy
- The American Orthopsychiatric Association
- The American Academy of Family Physicians
- The American Psychological Society
- The American Academy of Child and Adolescent Psychiatry
- The National Association of Social Workers
- The American College of Nurse Practitioners
- The American Academy of Nurse Practitioners.

The clinician should contact colleagues in these organizations to find out more about their services and training programs and to obtain appropriate contact information.

ACADEMIC CENTERS

The clinician can contact various academic centers (universities, medical centers) for information about and sources for advanced course work. Some of these sources include departments of psychiatry, psychology, pediatrics, and family medicine, as well as schools of nursing and social work.

FAMILY THERAPY TRAINING CENTERS

Family therapy training centers are established facilities that teach clinical family therapy. They are broad-based and are diverse enough to fit the style of the clinician and his or her practice needs. These programs provide different levels of training to suit all skill and knowledge levels from novice to expert. All offer short-term and long-term courses, seminars, and workshops on a variety of specific family therapy topics, as well as ongoing clinical supervision at their center, usually for a period of one-half to 2 days per week over 1 to 3 years.

The clinician can contact the family therapy training centers listed below for more information.

The Ackerman Institute for the Family

Founded in 1960, the Ackerman Institute is the oldest educational center devoted to teaching family therapy. It historically has had a focus on the family as a core component of the treatment of medical disorders. For information, contact: Marcia Sheinberg, M.S.W., Director of Training, 149 East 78th Street, New York, NY 10021; (212) 879-4900; http://www.ackerman.org.

The Philadelphia Child Guidance Clinic

Physically connected to Children's Hospital of Philadelphia (CHOP), the Philadelphia Child Guidance Clinic (PCGC) is affiliated with the Departments of Psychiatry and Pediatrics at CHOP. This clinic is one of the largest training programs in the United States and welcomes trainees from a range of disciplines. It is the home of the "structural family therapy" school begun by Salvador Minuchin and others. Contact: Training Administrator, Family Therapy Training Center, 34th Street and Civic Center Boulevard, Philadelphia, PA 19104; (215) 243-2777.

University of Rochester Postgraduate Family Therapy Training Program

Many members of the faculty of this program at the University of Rochester also teach family practitioners in the Department of Family Medicine. The current offerings include a 1-week "Medical Family Therapy Institute" for health care providers. For information, contact: Susan McDaniel, Ph.D., Director, Family Therapy Training Program, Division of Family Programs, Department of Psychiatry, 300 Crittenden Boulevard, Rochester, NY 14642; (716) 275-2532.

The Georgetown Family Center

The Georgetown Family Center, affiliated with Georgetown University Medical School, provides a strong theoretical foundation for understanding family systems theory from the work of the late Murray Bowen who founded the Center. Physicians are frequent trainees in this program. Contact: Director of Training, 4400 MacArthur Blvd. NW, Suite 102, Washington, DC 20007; (202) 965-0730.

The following programs are also prominent training centers in family therapy in the United States. In each case they are outgrowths of the pioneering work of their directors, who are also noted.

The Family Therapy Institute of Washington, DC

The Family Therapy Institute offers training centers on the strategic family therapy approaches developed by Jay Haley and Cloe Madanes, the Institute's directors. Contact: Cloe Madanes, Director of Training, 103 South Adams Street, Rockville, MD 20850; (301) 424-9522.

The Minuchin Center for the Family

Salvador Minuchin is the founder of the Minuchin Center for the Family. In addition to his major impact on the field of family therapy, Minuchin has considerable experience in working with the families of children with psychosomatic and chronic illness. Contact: David Greenan, Director, 114 E. 32nd Street, Suite 406, New York, NY 10016; (212) 481-3144; http://www.ourworld.cs.com/minuchincenter.

The Institute for Contextual Growth, Inc.

The founder of the Institute for Contextual Growth is Ivan Boszormenyi-Nagy, originator of the "contextual therapy" school that has especially focused on intergenerational issues in families. Contact: 126 South Bethlehem Pike, Ambler, PA 19002; (215) 542-1775.

The Brief Family Therapy Center

The particular emphasis at the Brief Family Therapy Center is based on a brief therapy model elaborated and championed by the Center's co-directors, Steve de Shazer and Insoo Kim Berg. Contact: Brief Family Therapy Center, 1907 Wanwatosa Avenue, P.O. Box 13736, Milwaukee, WI 53213; (414) 302-0650; http://www.brief-therapy.org.

The Mental Research Institute

Original home of family therapy pioneers, such as Virginia Satir, Don Jackson, Gregory Bateson, and John Weakland, the Mental Research Institute (MRI) continues to provide training to a broad spectrum of professionals in the San Francisco Bay region. Contact: Phyllis Erwin, Administrator, MRI, 555 Middlefield Road, Palo Alto, CA 94301; (650) 321-3055; http://www.mri.org.

Other training centers to consider include:

The Family Institute of Cambridge

Director: Tim Nichols
Contact: William Madsen, Training Director
51 Kondazian Street
Watertown, MA 02472
Phone: 617-924-2617
Website: http://www.familyinstitutecamb.org

The Family Institute of Westchester

Director: Dr. Elliott Rosen
Contact: Lillian Fine, Administrator

7-11 South Broadway, Suite 400
White Plains, NY 10601
Phone: 914-684-1313

The Family Therapy Practice Center

Director: Marianne Walters
2153 Newport Place NW
Washington, DC 20037
Phone: 202-861-0541

Chicago Center for Family Health

Directors: John Rolland and Froma Walsh
35 E. Wacker, Suite 2700
Chicago, IL 60601
Phone: 312-321-6040

The Family Institute

Affiliated with Northwestern University Medical School
Contact: Angela Heisler, Training Director
618 Library Place
Evanston, IL 60201
Phone: 312-609-5404
http://www.family-institute.org

JOURNALS

Journals that are concerned with and focused on family-oriented care include the following:

- *Family Systems Medicine*
- *The Journal of Behavioral and Developmental Pediatrics*
- *Family Process*
- *American Journal of Orthopsychiatry*
- *Journal of Behavioral Medicine*
- *Journal of the American Academy of Child and Adolescent Psychiatry*
- *Journal of Clinical Psychology*
- *Journal of Family Practice*
- *Social Work: Journal of the National Association of Social Workers*
- *The Nurse Practitioner*
- *American Journal of Primary Health Care*
- *Clinical Nurse Specialist: The Journal for Advanced Practice Nursing*
- *The Journal of Child and Family Nursing*

OPPORTUNITIES FOR PEDIATRICIANS

For the pediatrician who wants more training in family counseling, several possibilities exist for receiving that preparation.

Fellowships

Pediatricians may obtain family counseling training in fellowship programs in behavioral and developmental pediatrics, although the amount of training varies among fellowships. A listing of such fellowships can be found each year in the January issue of the *Journal of Pediatrics* and in the May issue of the *Journal for Developmental and Behavioral Pediatrics.*

Collaborative Office Rounds

The federal office of the Maternal and Child Health Bureau sponsors the Collaborative Office Rounds (COR), a series of monthly consultative seminars for practicing pediatricians led by both a behavioral and developmental pediatrician and a child psychiatrist. Case discussions are the focus of training. Practitioners present their challenging cases and receive advice and feedback from the two leaders and their fellow practitioners. Seminars can be conducted in the morning at an office or in the evening at someone's home. The leaders receive a stipend of $5,000 to $10,000.

COR programs can be found within Departments of Pediatrics at Yale University in New Haven, Connecticut; Dartmouth University in Hanover, New Hampshire; Children's Hospital of Philadelphia (CHOP); Children's Hospital in Cincinnati; Case Western Reserve University in Cleveland, Ohio; University of Indiana in Indianapolis; University of Michigan in Ann Arbor; Vanderbilt University in Nashville, Tennessee; University of California at San Francisco; and other centers. For more information, contact: Ms. Nanette Pepper, Maternal and Child Health Bureau, 5600 Fishers Lane, Room 18A-55, Parklawn Building, Rockville, MD 20857; (301) 443-0757.

Online Sources

Many web sites on the internet provide useful information for both parents and clinicians. Examples of on-line resources include the following:

www.beansprout.net	A privately-held company that networks parents, pediatricians, and child-care services.
www.cfah.org	The Center for the Advancement of Health conducts meta-analysis to establish intervention effectiveness, with some initial work in maternal and child health interventions.
www.childrensinstitute.org	This Los Angeles based organization models and supports comprehensive care for at-risk children and their families and publishes a very good newsletter.
www.childtrauma.org	An interdisciplinary educational site with resources on a range of trauma and domestic violence issues.

www.familycenteredcare.org	The Institute for Family Centered Care clearinghouse and advocacy website.
www.familyeducation.com	A parent community dedicated to children's learning that includes health and psychosocial concerns.
www.familyreunion.org	Includes information from former Vice-President Al Gore's 1998 Families and Health Conference with an emphasis on family-centered care.
www.familyvoices.org	A sophisticated grassroots organization of parents and advocates for children with disabilities and special healthcare needs.
www.mediconsult.com	Health and medical information for parents, including a pediatric site.
www.nnfr.org	The National Network for Family Resiliency focuses on resources for parent education.
www.parentingproject.org	Multidisciplinary professionals and advocates organized this nonprofit organization aimed at bringing parent education to all America's schools. Curriculum and advocacy resources.
www.rtc.pdx.edu	National Institute on Disability and Rehabilitation Research (NIDDR) Research and Training Center on Family Support and Children's Mental Health summarizes programmatic research and provides a resource clearinghouse.
www.strengtheningfamilies.org	This site of the Office of Juvenile Justice and Delinquency Prevention emphasizes family approaches to addressing juvenile crime and substance abuse.
www.unt.edu/cpe	The Center for Parent Education at the University of North Texas chronicles research and resources for parent involvement and parent education.

SUMMARY

For clinicians who want to gain more knowledge and to pursue more training in family counseling, many options and sources representing all the disciplines (e.g., pediatrics and social work) can be found. These resources and options include professional societies and continuing education courses, professional journals, universities and academic medical centers, on-site training in the community, established family therapy training centers, and various online resources.

ACKNOWLEDGMENT

The author would like to thank Dr. Lane Tanner, Department of Pediatrics, University of California, San Francisco, for compiling the list of family therapy training centers and Dr. Donald Wertlieb of Tufts University Center for Children in Boston, Massachusetts for compiling the list of on-line resources.

ADDITIONAL READINGS

Tanner JL. Training for family-oriented pediatric care. In: WL Coleman and EM Taylor, eds. Family-focused pediatrics: issues, challenges and clinical methods. *Pediatr Clin N Am* 1995;42(1): 93–209.

Glossary

The clinician often encounters new words and terms in the family counseling/therapy literature. Below are definitions of some common words and terms.

Accommodation: The adjustment required by a family or subsystems to coordinate and maintain optimal functioning

Adaptation: The ability of the family to adapt to alternative interaction patterns in the face of internal or external stress and change. Poor adaptability is a common source of family dysfunction.

Alliance: A healthy, positive relationship between any two members of a family (e.g., the parents working together or two siblings forming a good relationship).

Blended families or stepfamilies: Separate families joined by marriage.

Boundaries: The rules that govern who participates in a subsystem and how they participate. Boundaries protect the integrity and identity of the subsystems. For example, the marital subsystem (husband–wife unit) normally is distinguished from a parent–child subsystem by a boundary (set of rules). Subsystems must be clear and strong enough to prevent a breakdown but flexible enough to provide contact and communication. Assessing boundary clarity and integrity is an essential part of working with families.

Coalition: A relationship among at least three persons in which two collude or join against a third (e.g., a parent and child taking sides against the other parent or a clinician joining with the patient [child] against another family member).

Concurrent therapy: Individual treatment of two or more persons usually by different therapists. The physician might see the family, and a marital therapist might see the parents.

Conflict avoidance: When family members do not openly disagree, but allow silent tension and unexpressed needs (covert disagreement) to impact the family negatively. Members may avoid conflict by working harder, by spending more time at their careers or jobs, by interacting less with other members, or by invoking unspoken family "rules." See Chapter 10, "Family Communication Problems," pg. 205, for examples.

Conjoint therapy: Treatment of two or more persons together in a session.

Cross-generational coalition: An inappropriate or harmful coalition between a parent and a child against a third member of the family. For example, a mother and child may form a coalition against the father.

Cohesion: The amount of closeness (or lack of closeness) in the family relationships.

Contingency contracting: A behavioral therapy technique in which family members agree to exchange rewards for desired behaviors.

Disengagement: Psychological isolation. This term implies that the boundary is too rigid between a subsystem and an individual or between two individuals. Members are emotionally distant and unresponsive to each other. For example, if the parent dyad is distant and disengaged with the children, children receive little protection, affection, or support.

Enmeshment: Loss of autonomy due to a blurring of the boundaries. The term implies that the boundary is poorly defined. The family has few or no interpersonal boundaries and little individual autonomy. For example, the marital subsystem has no intimacy/privacy from the children, or a parent may answer questions for a teenager. If little differentiation exists between the parent subsystem and the children, the parental authority is diminished. Enmeshment can also cause family members to be overly involved in each other's feelings and activities; therefore, parents overreact to stress experienced by a child, or a child can overreact to stress experienced by a parent.

Extended families: All the descendants of a set of grandparents.

Family homeostasis: The tendency of families to resist change in order to maintain their steady state or balance; a balanced steady state of equilibrium and family functioning.

Family life cycle: The predictable stages of family life, including leaving home, marriage, birth of children, raising children, growing older, retirement, and death. See Chapter 7, "Assessing Family Functioning: Additional Methods," Child and Family Evaluation (CAFÉ), page 134, for examples.

Family structure: The functional organization of families that determines members' relationships and how they interact.

Family hierarchy: Family functioning based on a power structure where parents maintain control and authority.

Family interaction patterns: The rules and behaviors that families develop to maintain their stability and structure. These repeating interaction patterns are often passed from generation to generation.

Homeostasis: See Family Homeostasis, above.

Identified patient: The symptom bearer or the symptomatic patient of a disturbed family system. The presenting patient as identified by the family (e.g., the child who presents with depression in a family with domestic violence).

Joining: The act of the clinician accepting and accommodating to families in order to gain their trust and to circumvent resistance. Part of forming the therapeutic alliance with a family.

Modeling: Observational learning. The parent demonstrates a desirable behavior as a way to teach the child. The clinician may also model desirable behavior as a way to teach the parents.

Nuclear family: The parents and their children.

Overprotectiveness: This occurs when family members are not allowed to deal with their own problems or when parents are too fearful of the possibility that their child might experience an unpleasant event. For example, a mother may refuse to let her child play with other children for fear that he will get hurt.

Parentified child: A child who has been given parent-like power and responsibility to care for a sibling. This phenomenon is adaptive when done deliberately in a large family or single-parent home. It is maladaptive when it stems from unplanned abdication of parent responsibility or when the child "parents" the parent. For example, a depressed single parent may depend on the child to cook the meals, clean the house, and provide comfort to the parent.

Process/content: *Process:* How family members interact and communicate. *Content:* What members communicate about.

Reframing: Relabeling a family's description or perception of a behavior to make the family more accepting of a different explanation or amenable to change (e.g., describing a child's temperament/behavior as "strong willed" instead of "oppositional").

Reinforcement: An event, action, or object that increases the recurrence of a particular response. A positive reinforcer is an event or object whose contingent presentation increases the rate of responding. A negative reinforcer is an event or object whose contingent withdrawal increases the rate of responding, whereas a negative consequence is a contingent presentation that decreases the rate of responding.

Rigidity: Family interaction patterns are repeated inflexibly; change is discouraged and resisted.

Subsystems: Smaller units in families determined by generation, gender, or function (e.g., the parental [mother–father] unit, the spousal [husband–wife] unit, the parent–child unit , the siblings, or an individual in the family). Subsystems help families carry out their various roles of mutual support, regulation, and socialization. For example, the parent subsystem nurtures and socializes the children; the spousal subsystem provides adult mutual support.

Transference/countertransference: *Transference:* The patient's distorted emotional reaction to a present relationship (including with the physician) that stems from early family relationships. *Countertransference:* The physician's emotional (often unconscious) reaction to the patient or a family member.

Triangulation: A relationship in which a third person is drawn into a two- person system to diffuse worry or to avoid conflict about personal issues (e.g., intimacy) between the two persons. For example, a mother and father focus on and argue about their son's behavior instead of confronting their own marital tensions.

Appendix Family Apgar Questionnaire

The Family Questionnaire*

The following questions have been designed to help us better understand you and your family. You should feel free to ask questions about any item in the questionnaire.

The space for comments should be used when you wish to give additional information or if you wish to discuss the way the question is applied to your family. Please try to answer all questions.

Family is defined as the individual(s) with whom you usually live. If you live alone, your "family" consists of persons with whom you now have the strongest emotional ties. For each question, check only one answer

	Almost always	Some of the time	Hardly ever
I am satisfied that I can turn to my family for help when something is troubling me.	☐	☐	☐

Comments: ______________________________

____

	Almost always	Some of the time	Hardly ever
I am satisfied with the way my family talks over things with me and shares problems with me.	☐	☐	☐

Comments: ______________________________

____

	Almost always	Some of the time	Hardly ever
I am satisfied that my family accepts and supports my wishes to take on new activities or directions.	☐	☐	☐

Comments: ______________________________

____

I am satisfied with the way my family expresses affection and responds to my emotions, such as anger, sorrow, and love. ☐ ☐ ☐

Comments: ____________________

____

I am satisfied with the way my family and I share time together. ☐ ☐ ☐

Comments: ____________________

____

*See Chapter 7, "Assessing Family Functioning: Additional Methods," pg. 143, for additional information.

Subject Index

Note: Page numbers followed by *f* indicate figures; those followed by *t* indicate tables.

Q

S